ASSESSMENT, EVALUATION, AND ACCOUNTABILITY IN ADULT EDUCATION

ASSESSMENT, EVALUATION, AND ACCOUNTABILITY IN ADULT EDUCATION

Edited by Lilian H. Hill

Foreword by Amy D. Rose

STERLING, VIRGINIA

COPYRIGHT © 2020 BY STYLUS PUBLISHING, LLC.

Published by Stylus Publishing, LLC.
22883 Quicksilver Drive
Sterling, Virginia 20166-2019

Library of Congress Cataloging-in-Publication Data

Names: Hill, Lilian H. (Lilian Helen), 1957- editor.
Title: Assessment, evaluation, and accountability in adult education /
    Edited by Lilian H. Hill ; Foreword by Amy D. Rose.
Description: First edition. | Sterling, Virginia : Stylus Publishing,
    LLC, 2020. | Includes bibliographical references and index.
Identifiers: LCCN 2020013811 | ISBN 9781620368510 (paperback) |
    ISBN 9781620368503 (hardback) | ISBN 9781620368527 (pdf) |
    ISBN 9781620368534 (ebook)
Subjects: LCSH: Adult education. | Educational evaluation. |
    Educational accountability.
Classification: LCC LC5215 .A87 2020 | DDC 374--dc23
    LC record available at https://lccn.loc.gov/2020013811

13-digit ISBN: 978-1-62036-850-3 (cloth)
13-digit ISBN: 978-1-62036-851-0 (paperback)
13-digit ISBN: 978-1-62036-852-7 (library networkable e-edition)
13-digit ISBN: 978-1-62036-853-4 (consumer e-edition)

Printed in the United States of America

All first editions printed on acid-free paper
that meets the American National Standards Institute
Z39-48 Standard.

Bulk Purchases

Quantity discounts are available for use in workshops and
for staff development.

Call 1-800-232-0223

First Edition, 2020

*To Alan, my husband; Christopher, my
son; and Lucian, my grandson*

CONTENTS

FOREWORD

Assessment and evaluation have always been important issues in education, but over the last 20 years they have become imperatives, driving constant calls for the reform and improvement of education at all levels. On one level, evaluation is seen as key to determining the real impact of educational programs and whether the programs are worth the investment. However, on a deeper level, these calls for improvement and the concomitant efforts to evaluate and assess have shifted the focus to measurable outcomes at the expense of an understanding of the processes involved in the teaching/learning dynamic. In a similar vein, as programmers grapple with making the case for adult education amid myriad other claims for funds and investment, discussions of return on investment (ROI) have taken place in almost all adult education settings. *Assessment, Evaluation, and Accountability in Adult Education* is welcome because it returns the discussion of assessment and evaluation to a primary place in adult education while analyzing some of the more complex issues that arise when policy is based on evaluations. This book is for both the new administrator and the seasoned professional. It will help everyone understand the dynamics of assessment and evaluation and to see them from a fuller perspective.

Lilian H. Hill has provided a service to the field in pulling together these diverse essays. The chapters offer a window into the strengths and problems associated with incorporating evaluation and assessment into all aspects of adult education program planning. Most important, the contributors discuss the difficulties associated with narrowly defining purpose, thereby limiting our understanding of the changes that can take place during the educational process.

None of this is new, but it is a strength of this provocative book that it examines the issue from multiple perspectives. To provide some perspective, it may be helpful to think about adult education as both the incubator and the stepchild of most U.S. educational reform movements. For example, Ralph Tyler proposed reinventing the entire American education system by focusing on what is learned rather than on the process of learning. From his time at the Progressive Education Association to his work on the development of GED™ tests, he has advocated for an education that would move away from *seat time* to assessment of actual learning. In fact, one could argue that the present-day structure of the adult basic education system in the United States owes its existence to Tyler and his ideas about assessment (Bloom, 1986; Rose, 1991).

Additionally, the evaluation of social and educational programs became widespread after it was a condition of funding for the War on Poverty programs of the 1960s. Yet, it was unclear what model of evaluation should be used. Stufflebeam (1966) noted that this caused a crisis in the field of evaluation. Indeed, Stufflebeam also noted that the federal legislation requiring evaluation needed to be followed with support for evaluation research since the field was so weak at that time. The problems that Stufflebeam found in education were exponentially greater when evaluators turned to social service programs. Carol Weiss (2002) and others have written about the problems inherent in assessing social and educational programs. One of the primary pitfalls was how to assign causation when random assignment was not possible. Gueron (2002) laid out the ways that the Manpower Demonstration Research Corporation (MDRC) approached the evaluation of workforce training programs for the poor, discussing at length the ways that social experiments can be constructed using randomized samples in social situations. Gueron cautioned that outcomes are easier to measure than impacts and are often more favorable. She preferred to approach evaluation impact through comparisons of innovative interventions. Additionally, she narrowed program properties into smaller, measurable components. However, Gueron admitted that this approached placed particular burdens on programs and evaluators. The first burden or challenge was to make sure that the evaluation addressed the most important or pressing questions. The second challenge was to question whether it would even be possible to design an experiment that addresses this issue. She cautioned, "The answer may be 'no'" (p. 20). The central concern was impossibility of a control group, as well as the ethical problems involved in non-laboratory situations. Ethical practice demands that individuals may not be denied a service. Despite these problems, policy developers still consider randomized studies to be "most reliable approach to determining the net impact of employment and training initiatives" (p. 24), to name just one example. Weiss (2002), in contrast, cautioned that randomization was very difficult, if not impossible, when the goal was to change communities, rather than individuals. She added that "the 'empowerment' of residents is often viewed as a goal in itself, as well as an instrument for making community services more responsive to local needs" (p. 199). Yet, this goal is almost impossible to quantify.

The chapters in this book expand on this initial research. Questions about how to assess and evaluate programs for adults draw from the education and social science literature. They deal with ROI and ask what is important to know as well as how to design a study to know it. Also asked is how we consider outcomes and impacts in light of a whole program, rather than merely a single innovative approach. The answers are quite complex, and it is fascinating to read how the individual contributors in this book work through the answer from a multitude of perspectives. Indeed, the chapters in this book discuss these inherent dilemmas while also magnifying the fact that evaluation and assessment are complex and multidimensional. Although there are many ways to approach the topic, the division into varied educational settings is both appropriate and interesting. Through this lens we see the complexity of adult education and the different ways that evaluation and assessment may be approached. We can also view commonalities and areas of mutual concern. We are invited to think about how assessment and evaluation can be accomplished and, more importantly, how it can be used to strengthen adult education. Essentially, adult educators need to make the case for their programs while concomitantly recognizing that evaluation and assessment are limited. Since they cannot capture the learning and change that occurs outside of the classroom, evaluation and assessment efforts will always portray only part of the story. Even with these limitations, however, the topic is one of vital interest to adult educators and this book brings the issue back to basic arguments about the purpose and future of adult education. It is a vital contribution and one that I hope will serve to broaden discussion of assessment and evaluation.

Amy D. Rose
Professor Emerita
Northern Illinois University

References

Bloom, B. (1986). Ralph Tyler's impact on evaluation theory and practice. *Journal of Thought, 21*(1), 36–46.

Gueron, J. M. (2002). The politics of random assignment: Implementing studies and affecting policy. In F. Mosteller & R. F. Boruch, (Eds.), *Evidence matters: Randomized trials in education research* (pp. 15-49). Washington DC: Brookings Institution Press.

Rose, A. D. (1991). *Ends or means: An overview of the history of the Adult Education Act.* Washington DC: Office of Educational Research and Improvement.

Stufflebeam, D. L. (1966). A depth study of the evaluation requirement. *Theory Into Practice, 5*(3), 121–133.

Weiss, C. H. (2002). What to do until the random assigner comes. In F. Mosteller & R. F. Boruch, (Eds.), *Evidence matters: Randomized trials in education research* (pp. 198–224). Washington DC: Brookings Institution Press.

ACKNOWLEDGMENTS

A book of this nature does not come about because of one person's efforts. I am indebted to the chapter contributors and awed by the company I have been keeping. Given the diversity of the adult education field, this book would not have come together without their knowledge, experience, and contributions. I am grateful to David Brightman, of Stylus Publishing, who understood the vision, created the opportunity, and was unfailingly encouraging and helpful. Two friends and colleagues, R. Eric Platt of the University of Memphis and Simone Conceição of the University of Wisconsin–Milwaukee, motivated, supported, and sometimes pushed me in working on this book. Graduate assistants David Taylor and Andrea Blake contributed practical assistance. Finally, my husband, Alan, has been my sounding board and confidante and has been wonderfully patient while I was preoccupied with writing and work.

PART ONE

INTRODUCTION

WHAT AND WHY OF ASSESSMENT, EVALUATION, AND ACCOUNTABILITY IN ADULT EDUCATION

Lilian H. Hill

P eople make decisions all the time but often do not pay attention to the mental processes used to make them. We stand in the grocery aisle pondering whether to purchase one brand of peanut butter or another, quinoa or farro, kale or Swiss chard, whole wheat or multigrain bread, or to ditch the healthy stuff and go for chocolate. We may select a product based on habit, nutrition labels, or our newest diet restrictions. In our precious free time, we decide whether we would enjoy going out to a movie or staying home to garden or read a novel. Usually, we make this kind of selection quickly without much deliberation. Some decisions are of greater significance, such as whether to enroll in an education program, accept a job offer or seek another opportunity, or move to another city. When we make these choices, we are more conscious about the criteria used for decision-making.

Despite the ubiquity of making judgments in daily life, some adult educators are reluctant to approach learning about assessment, evaluation, and accountability. In fact, the topic has been neglected in the United States, whereas considerable attention is being paid to these issues in Europe, Australia, and New Zealand. Although other fields have assessment texts, no books have been published in the past decade in the United States that focus on student assessment or program evaluation in adult education. The need for a text that addresses assessment, evaluation, and accountability in adult education is urgent. Stakeholders in adult education are demanding accountability through the use of direct measures, meaning those that involve asking students to demonstrate what they have learned through course assignments (e.g., homework assignments, examinations and quizzes, research papers, presentations, role playing, artistic expression) designed to measure students' achievement of course objectives rather than self-reported or indirect measures, such as student course evaluations, time activity logs, and unsolicited feedback in the form of cards or e-mails. Dwindling funding for some forms of adult education, especially literacy education, coupled with current accountability standards in which programs must show their worth in quantifiable and financial terms, such as return on investment, mean that adult educators must develop their skills to advocate for valuable programs with language that is most likely to be heard. Decreases in funding compared to the need is particularly visible in areas that attract government funding such as literacy education, General Educational Development (GED™) preparation, and remedial education for adults in community colleges. However, lack of funding and demands for accountability are also pervasive in other forms of adult education in which programs must demonstrate their worth in quantifiable metrics.

Existing texts on assessment, evaluation, and accountability that are specific to adult education are dated. For example, three texts that address assessment of adult learning were published in the late 1990s (Moran, 1997; Rose & Leahy, 1997; Vella, Berardinelli, & Burrow, 1998). Books that address assessment and evaluation in specific areas of adult education practice include adult literacy (U.S. Office of Educational Research and Improvement, 2002), continuing education (Knox, 2002; Queeney, 1995), informal learning (Mejiuni, Cranton, & Táiwó, 2015), and adult basic education (Bingman, Ebert, & Bell, 2000; Campbell, 2007; Grotelueschen, Gooler, & Knox, 1976; Merrifield, 1998). Although books have been published that address assessment, evaluation, or accountability in other disciplines, including higher education, student affairs, online learning, counseling, psychology, and special education, there are few accessible texts that address student and program assessment in adult education. No existing books tackle assessment, evaluation, or accountability from a critical perspective that examines how control of adult education is asserted through government policy and agency funding.

Many educators in adult and higher education have had to learn assessment, evaluation, and accountability skills in the course of conducting their work. These skills include fostering student learning, employing data to document student and program success, using validated scales for diagnostic purposes, employing formative and summative assessments to evaluate student and program success, discerning when assessment procedures are constructive, and using assessment and evaluation data for program improvement.

We may need to defend a program's continued existence or write reports for regulatory or funding agencies and other stakeholders. Not all graduate programs in adult education directly address these learning needs, and there are few resources available specific to adult education's diversity that support learning how to conduct effective student and program assessment and evaluation.

Purpose

Assessment and evaluation are critical educational responsibilities. They focus on producing information to guide changes that foster student learning (Kuh et al., 2015). This activity has been in place for K–12 education for many years, which has in turn influenced higher education practices, and assessment and accountability demands are now permeating all forms of education including adult education (Banta & Palomba, 2015; Cumming & Miller, 2017; Hill, 2017; Kuh et al., 2015). This book is meant to be a resource for people working in adult education with responsibilities for assessment and evaluation, particularly those who are new to such responsibilities. It also provides guidance for more experienced practitioners to remain current with trends influencing the need for and format of assessment, evaluation, and accountability processes. It could be used as a textbook in adult education courses. Adult educators who have been asked to serve on assessment committees, produce detailed reports for funding and accreditors, create a culture of assessment in their program and organization, and develop reports for accountability purposes should find it helpful. Overall, this book is intended to help adult educators become better informed about assessment, evaluation, and accountability as these have become critical functions of teaching adults as well as administering adult education programs.

Definitions

Assessment and evaluation can be employed to contribute to student learning and foster program viability. The terms *assessment* and *evaluation* tend to be used interchangeably. For the purposes of this book, *assessment* refers to the measurement of individual student learning that may be used for screening, diagnosis, providing feedback, monitoring progress, and designing educational interventions. *Evaluation* involves the application of learning assessments to make judgements for program improvement and providing information to stakeholders, regional and professional accrediting bodies, and accountability systems (Galbraith & Jones, 2010). Accountability systems are designed to produce evidence that education was conducted appropriately; progress was made; and resources, particularly taxpayer monies, were used efficiently (Tusting, 2012).

Assessment in Adult Education

Although higher education has provided essential leadership in developing many assessment practices (e.g., Banta & Palomba, 2015; Barkley & Major, 2016; Cumming & Miller, 2017; Kuh et al., 2015; Massa & Kasimatis, 2017; Suskie, 2018), these practices are more aligned with the educational participation and characteristics of younger learners. Adult students participate in learning opportunities in a more fluid way than traditional students and move back and forth among home, work, and adult education opportunities. Many of our busy, overcommitted students are involved in all three at once. Adults require learning environments that value their experiences, foster active engagement in learning, and promote meaning-making (Addae, 2016). Addae advocates for teaching to be a dialogical process in which teachers and learners alike are involved in decision-making about activities that will help learners achieve course learning objectives and construct their own meaning.

Assessment has instructional and diagnostic purposes. It enables adult educators to discern learners' understanding of the subject matter and adjust their instruction to the learners' needs. Addae (2016) states that adults' interest in immediacy of application renders diagnostic assessment (i.e., identifying where students are having difficulty) critical because, through regular assessment, the instructor is able to "gather enough information about learners' difficulties with the content of the course and as such be in a better position to address them" (p. 190). Addae promotes several principles for planning assessments: (a) educators are responsible for designing assessments, but learners should be involved in their planning; (b) assessment must take place alongside instruction so the instructor can make immediate adjustments to instruction when needed; (c) questioning to promote students' ability to reflect on learning should be an essential part of teaching; (d) instructors should be attentive to students' ability to articulate their learning; and (e) formal assessments should entail application projects in which learners work together to solve a problem. Assessment allows learners to reflect on their learning and make their own adjustments in their efforts to learn.

Based in key principles of adult learning, Table 1.1 shows Kasworm and Marienau's (1997) five principles to guide adult-oriented assessment of learning that remain pertinent.

TABLE 1.1
Assessment Strategies to Guide Adult-Oriented Assessment of Learning

Key Premises of Adult Learning	Key Principles of Adult-Oriented Assessment Practice
Learning is derived from multiple sources.	Recognizes multiple sources of knowing; that is, learning that occurs from interaction with a wide variety of informal and formal knowledge sources
Learning engages the whole person and contributes to that person's development.	Recognizes and reinforces the cognitive, conative, and affective domains of learning
Learning and the capacity for self-direction are promoted by feedback.	Focuses on adults' active involvement in learning and assessment processes, including active engagement in self-assessment
Learning occurs in context; its significance relates in part to its impact on those contexts.	Embraces adult learners' involvement in and impact on the broader world of work, family, and community
Learning from experiences is a unique meaning-making event that creates diversity among adult learners.	Accommodates adult learners' increasing differentiation from one another given varied life experiences and education

Note. From Kasworm and Marienau (1997). Reprinted with permission.

Assessment methods compatible with Addae's (2016) and Kasworm and Marienau's (1997) principles include dynamic assessment and sustainable assessment. Dynamic assessment is a system of theories that consider learning and cognition to be modifiable during interactions with other people in a sociocultural context (Robinson-Zañartu, 2013). It examines the difference between an individual's current performance level in comparison with their capabilities (Malmeer & Zoghi, 2014). Because performance assessment is congruent with the goals and contextual experiences of adult learners, learners are able to demonstrate their learning by responding to a realistic scenario or task (National Research Council, 2002). By providing immediate feedback, this interactionist and holistic form of assessment is meant to be developmental with the purpose of improving student performance. Instead of static measurement of current ability, dynamic assessment provides learning support tailored to students' learning needs during ongoing social interactions between learners and instructors.

Sustainable assessment (Nguyen & Walker, 2016) was designed to provide assessment for learning and relies on formative assessment with an emphasis on developing skills for future learning. The provision of sustainable feedback involves teachers in providing detailed and effective feedback; students' active participation in the feedback process; engagement of students in dialogue with teachers about the feedback; and fostering students' lifelong learning abilities for "self-regulation, self-evaluation, and the use of feedback from multiple sources to improve their learning over time" (Nguyen & Walker, 2016, p. 98). Boud and Soler's (2016) framework emphasized encouraging learners to become reflexive and more accurate judges of their learning and promoting students' ability to take a more active role in the feedback process. This approach aligns learning assessment with lifelong learning.

Assessments should move beyond measuring only the cognitive aspects of knowledge acquisition (knowing something) to include examining individuals' growth in competence (knowing how) in the face of continuous change (Su, 2015). Assessment of competence, the "capacity to perform or act in particular contexts, . . . highlights the learner's problem solving and completion of tasks in context, . . . required to ensure effective adaptation to contextual changes in life" (p. 78). Su further notes that assessment of learners' competence is insufficient without assessment of learners' commitment to continue learning, meaning "the learner's dedication to learning and development based on his or her feeling of meaningfulness when facing the changing future to address life's challenges" (p. 80). Assessment of competence is pragmatic, whereas assessment of commitment is existential.

Program Evaluation in Adult Education

Program evaluation entails systematically collecting and analyzing data to make informed judgments about whether a program met its objectives, how to improve its effectiveness, and how to plan for future programming (Cervero & Wilson, 2006; Fitzpatrick, Christie, & Mark, 2009). Evaluation processes may describe whether the program (a) fulfills compelling personal and societal needs, (b) merits changes in its delivery and management, (c) is responsive to the sociopolitical context, (d) is justified in its costs and use of resources, and (e) prepares students to apply their learning to their personal and work needs (Caffarella & Daffron, 2013). Depending on the purposes of evaluation, multiple methods may be used, including observations, interviews, surveys, pre- and post-tests, portfolios, focus groups, cost-benefit analyses, self-assessments, and even storytelling. Multiple methods may be appropriate depending on the evaluation goals. Each of these qualitative and quantitative methods have strengths and weaknesses, so evaluators must make careful decisions about the types of evaluation data they will collect and analyze.

When planning programs, some people fail to plan for program evaluation in advance and resort to devising a so-called happy sheet that measures participants' satisfaction with the facilities, refreshments, handouts, content, and delivery of the program and addresses only minimally whether participants' learning goals were met. The program evaluation may have been devised without much forethought and consideration of the sociopolitical context in a "wait, wait, better hurry" approach to program evaluation that produces poor or irrelevant results. Failure to conduct rigorous program evaluations may conceal the very successes being realized in adult education programs (Vella et al., 1998).

Difficulties with conducting program evaluations can occur because of lack of knowledge and skills, resources, or even motivation (Cervero & Wilson, 2006). According to Moore (2018), "Effective program evaluation entails a dynamic, long-term evaluation process that tracks multiple contributing factors and outcomes measurements" (p. 57). For program evaluation to be meaningful and useful, program planners must carefully consider what goals they are trying to meet, what criteria will be used to measure success, the data they wish to collect, and who will be involved in making these evaluations (Fitzpatrick et al., 2009). Evaluators must be cognizant that adult learners, teachers, and program sponsors are making their own informal judgements and will consider their own perceptions alongside the conclusions of a formal evaluation (Caffarella & Daffron, 2013; Cervero & Wilson, 2006). Unfortunately, program planners may find they are being held accountable to a measure that was not anticipated. Therefore, careful planning, flexibility, and political astuteness are needed to conducting successful program evaluations.

Cervero and Wilson (2006) and Cervero, Wilson, and Associates (2001) addressed the need to acknowledge various stakeholders in program planning and evaluation. Program planners must routinely negotiate social and political outcomes so the needs of adult learners, organizational hosts, sponsoring funders, accreditation bodies, and the public are reconciled and met. Producing the evidence that will satisfy each of these audiences is a tall order. Therefore, it is important to focus on the primary purpose of evaluation: making judgements about the value of a program. Program evaluators should base their work on the "educational, management, and political objectives" (Cervero et al., 2001, p. 224) articulated at the outset of the program, "manage the politics of evidence and criteria" (p. 224), and "anticipate how power relations frame program evaluation" (p. 230).

Accountability in Adult Education

An emphasis on market solutions to public problems has resulted in privatization and reduced funding for public services, accompanied by criticisms of education for not preparing students for a competitive workforce (Spencer & Kelly, 2013). As education becomes increasingly commodified, accountability practices such as checking credentials and measuring results have become mandatory and narrowly defined (Tusting, 2012). Government policy in many countries equates schooling as preparation for work and adult education with occupational training and retraining (Spencer & Kelly, 2013). Adult education is subject to demands from regulatory agencies; funders; sponsors; policy frameworks; and, in some instances, accreditation agencies that require documentation of student achievement of learning outcomes (Fenwick, 2010). Torrance (2017) and Milana (2017) commented that governments use policy as a means of controlling education's purposes and desired outcomes and employ adult education as a means of addressing social problems in Western societies, particularly through compensatory and remedial education. National and state governments work with each other as well as with nongovernmental agencies in setting career and technical training standards or conducting national and international literacy assessments (Milana, 2017). Funding is often dependent on meeting outcomes imposed by external sources that are not fully relevant to learners in the program. Fenwick (2010) states, "In the lean streets of (post) recessionary budget cuts, adult education programs must fight to maintain what little funding is still allotted to them" (para. 2).

Brookfield and Holst (2011) argued that adult education has become estranged from its historical purpose of education for citizenship and democracy. The political economy of globalization has led to a growing dispossessed population that lacks access to the means of production and even meaningful employment. Holst and Brookfield defined the term *meaningful* in the sense that the work has meaning for the individual and pays a living wage. With the ascension of compartmentalized labor, robotics, and the export of manufacturing overseas, all designed to reduce production costs, human labor is becoming irrelevant to the fabrication of goods and services. The ascension of the knowledge economy has driven the need for a highly educated and flexible workforce (Torrance, 2017). In a neoliberal era, education is viewed as too expensive for governments to invest in, but at the same time, these governments seek to maintain control of education through policies and public messages designed to shape adults' desires and responsibilities for themselves and their communities (Spencer & Kelly, 2013; Torrance, 2017). Calls for preparation of a trained workforce in a globalized knowledge economy have rendered adults responsible for gaining employment skills and paying for their own education and training rather than education being provided to citizens as a right (Milana, 2017; Spencer & Kelly, 2013). As a result, increasing numbers of people are consigned to underemployment, serial employment, or an underground economy to meet basic survival needs.

Like many sectors of society, adult education is subject to increased calls for assessment, evaluation, and accountability based on standardized metrics, competition, reduced resources, and questioning of the value of education in light of its costs (Spencer & Kelly, 2013). Some educational practices are now considered unsustainable because of their financial, time, and labor costs (Boud & Soler, 2016). The pursuit of limitless economic growth, wealth, and materiality characteristic of the global economy has resulted in commodification of many aspects of our life, including education, with a resulting need to count and account for everything in relation to its market value. Although assessment and evaluation are important to effective program and curricular improvement, Owczarzak, Broaddus, and Pinkerton (2016) argued that best practices often refer to a "collection of impartial, evidence-based, and objective information in the form of quantifiable measurements in order to satisfy accountability requirements" (p. 327) to the exclusion of other forms of obtaining valuable information. "Testing is politically attractive" (Spencer & Kelly, 2013, p. 68) because of its supposed objectivity; however, "it is far easier to cite test results, uncluttered by any considerations of social equality . . . than to deal with the complex nature of standards and equity" (p. 67). Program success is then reduced to meeting quantifiable goals; documenting goal attainment; and sharing results with funders, management, and ultimately the public (Owczarzak et al., 2016).

Apple (2005) described the intrusion of an audit culture as a response to the erosion of public trust in education and the expansion of market logic and business ideologies into multiple social enterprises. Owczarzak et al. (2016) defined *audit culture* as "norms and practices of assessment through which accountability and 'good practices' are demonstrated" (p. 326). In principle this may sound like responsible educational practice; however, it is important to be aware of the unintended consequences of the audit culture. According to Milana (2017), government policy links adult education to primary and secondary education for children and university education for adults, and "at the same time, it tends toward flattening the distinctive approaches of diverse adult education providers, while underplaying their capacity for reaching out to different populations" (p. 182). Accountability can insert distance between students and adult educators, restricting educational programming and practices to those that are most easily measurable. Time-consuming preparation and completion of required documentation of student outcomes may take precedence over educators forming genuine connections with students. The coercive devices of the audit culture (Ocean & Skourdoumbis, 2015) alter relationships and practices in adult education. Meaningful program evaluation practices may be replaced with time-consuming documentation requirements that are quite possibly irrelevant to educators' and students' goals. Relying on quantitative measurements may obscure or diminish students' capacity for empowerment, critical thinking, and social change (Owczarzak et al., 2016).

Whether you refer to it as *audit culture* (Apple, 2013), *monitoring culture* (Milana, 2017), or the *evaluator state* (English, & Mayo, 2012), it is clear that "increasing levels of 'accountability' have been introduced in a range of settings, particularly in publicly funded arenas such as education and health care" (Tusting, 2012, p. 121). Quantification has taken on the guise of "truth," which policy and practice are based on, and serves as a foundation for control and imposed conformity (Ocean & Skourdoumbis, 2015, p. 443). Like other forms of education, adult education is no longer considered a public good but has become a consumer good in which accountability systems are devised that ensure that work is being done and public monies are being used wisely (Tusting, 2012). To contest the neoliberal values of the global economy of materialism and the pursuit of limitless economic growth influencing education, educators in adult education must fuse knowledge of assessment, evaluation, and accountability with critical viewpoints to strengthen our skills to advocate for adult education programs, the centrality of adult learners, and social justice as a central value.

Organization of the Book

This book addresses contemporary perspectives on assessment, evaluation, and accountability in adult education. The contributors were challenged to address the purposes of assessment and evaluation and describe assessment and evaluation practices, skills practitioners need to develop and strengthen, sources of assistance, and how best to advocate for program viability. They were asked to explain how programs can demonstrate that adult learners have learned what was intended and document that programs are effective in regard to regulatory, accrediting, and funding agencies. Finally, they were asked to take a critical perspective and explain how best to advocate for program viability in a time of dwindling resources.

Part One begins with this introductory chapter, which defines the purposes, terms, and organization of the book. Chapter 2 by Lilian H. Hill focuses on learning assessment, and chapter 3 by Larry G. Martin and Kevin Roessger is similarly structured to describe program evaluation. Following these introductory chapters, Part Two, Part Three, and Part Four describe assessment and evaluation practices in different arenas of adult education practice. Each of these chapters is self-contained and may be read independently. Read together, they demonstrate the diversity and complexity of assessment and evaluation practices in adult education.

Although not comprehensive, the chapters in Part Two represent adult education's diversity by describing assessment and evaluation practices in different areas of adult education. In chapter 4, Alisa Belzer and Daphne Greenberg describe assessment and evaluation practices in adult literacy and basic education. They note that a wide range of existing practices are used, but requirements for assessment are trending toward the implementation of more quantitative assessments. In chapter 5, Royce Ann Collins, COL Ryan Welch, and James B. Martin describe assessment and evaluation practices in professional military education. They indicate that performance demands of military personnel mean that assessment and evaluation practices are embedded in a culture of evidence and quality. Paul E. Mazmanian, Meagan W. Rawls, and J.K. Stringer begin their discussion of assessment and evaluation practices in continuing professional education in chapter 6 by describing the growth of licensed professions, such as law, engineering, nursing, medicine, and others, and continuing professional education. They state that assessment practices have deepened beyond simple attendance counts to examine practitioners' growth in skill performance and the ability to apply new learning to their work. Evaluation practices are similarly evolving toward an examination of practitioners' ability to apply what they have learned to practice settings.

Chapter 7 by Lilian H. Hill, Sharon E. Rouse, and Cyndi H. Gaudet addresses assessment and evaluation practices used in human resource development and the training, career, and organizational development functions in nonprofits, businesses, and other organizations. They begin by stating that assessment in human resource development mainly refers to needs assessment to identify gaps in performance and applies training and other processes to foster organizational success, whereas performance assessment practices are closer to the way learning assessment is described throughout the book. Hill, Rouse, and Gaudet continue by discussing the importance of learning transfer and program evaluation. Elizabeth A. Roumell, Corina Todoran, and Nima Khodakarami's chapter 8 presents a conceptual framework for assessment practices applicable to building community capacity for implementing evidence-based initiatives in response to government legislation and funding agencies' policies that demand better evidence of effectiveness and cooperation among adult education and other public service agencies, including public health and social services.

Part Three examines assessment and evaluation practices for adult learners in higher education. In chapter 9, Wendy M. Green indicates that health professionals are influenced by dominant worldviews of positivism and constructivism. She describes assessment practice relevant to behavioral and constructivist perspectives on education and recommends the adoption of a transformative perspective in planning, implementation, and evaluation practices that takes into account social justice, patient needs, and community perspectives.

In chapter 10, Simone C.O. Conceição provides information about practical tools available to support assessment and evaluation practices in adult distance education and notes that technology applications provide a variety of choices that support learning. In chapter 11, Jovita M. Ross-Gordon and Royce Ann Collins describe the use of assessment of prior learning, portfolio-based assessments, and competency-based education for adult students in higher education settings. They challenge educators who administer post-secondary and degree programs designed to accommodate adult learners to develop an assessment culture based on examining evidence of learning using stringent assessment and program evaluation metrics. Chapter 12 by Mary V. Alfred and Patrice B. French addresses assessment and accountability of graduate education programs with an emphasis on graduate adult education. They note that because graduate education programs are held to the same assessment standards as undergraduate programs, they can be constricted to producing assessment information that is not fully relevant to what they are trying to accomplish. Similarly, in chapter 13, Natalie Bolton and E. Paulette Isaac-Savage indicate that faculty working in higher education settings need support in their implementation of assessment and evaluation practices. They document and provide links to helpful resources. Using a case study, they illustrate the types of support most appreciated by faculty. In Part Four, Lilian H. Hill wraps up the book in chapter 14 by addressing the question of whether there are assessment and evaluation practices that are unique to adult education. She contends that although they are not unique, it is critical for us to seek to influence and advocate for assessment and evaluation practices that integrate knowledge about adult learning, recognize learners' needs, and honor adult education's distinctive value systems.

Conclusion

Declining funding coupled with governmental and accrediting bodies' demands for outcomes data have made the need for assessment, evaluation, and accountability in adult education urgent in an era when those in all sectors of education need to be able to advocate for their discipline's value. Reduction in funding is most acute in government-funded adult basic education. Most adult education is outside this purview and is even further marginalized, but it may be less often affected by calls for accountability. For adult learning to continue as a meaningful experience, rather than a solely measurable experience, educators need to strengthen their knowledge of student and program assessment and evaluation to advocate for the needs of adult learners and program viability. Educators in adult education need to strengthen their skills in student and program assessment and evaluation and collaborate with skilled program evaluators, statisticians, and psychometricians when necessary. It is essential for adult educators to combine their knowledge of assessment, evaluation, and accountability with critical viewpoints to form the skills and strength of purpose to discern what learning needs to be assessed and evaluated, for what purposes, and to advocate for the value of adult education programs and the needs of adult learners.

References

Addae, D. (2016). Promoting effective teaching and learning in adult education: A model-based approach. *Turkish Journal of Education, 5*(4), 184–192.

Apple, M. W. (2005). Audit cultures, commodification, and class and race strategies in education. *Policy Futures in Education, 3*(4), 379–399.

Apple, M. W. (2013). Audit cultures, labour, and conservative movements in the global university. *Journal of Educational Administration and History, 45*(4), 385–394.

Banta, T. W., & Palomba, C. A. (2015). *Assessment essentials: Planning, implementing, and improving assessment in higher education* (2nd ed.). San Francisco, CA: Jossey Bass.

Barkley, E. T., & Major, C. H. (2016). *Learning assessment techniques: A handbook for college faculty.* San Francisco, CA: Jossey-Bass.

Bingman, M. B., Ebert, O., & Bell, B. (2000). *Outcomes of participation in adult basic education: The importance of learners' perspectives.* Washington, DC: National Center for the Study of Adult Learning and Literacy.

Boud, D., & Soler, R. (2016). Sustainable assessment revisited. *Assessment and Evaluation in Higher Education, 41*(3), 400–413.

Brookfield, S. D., & Holst, J. D. (2011). *Radicalizing learning: Adult education for a just world.* San Francisco, CA: Jossey Bass.

Caffarella, R. S., & Daffron, S. R. (2013). *Planning programs for adult learners: A practical guide* (3rd ed.). San Francisco, CA: Jossey Bass.

Campbell, P. (2007). *Measures of success: Assessment and accountability in adult basic education* (3rd ed.). Edmonton, Alberta, Canada: Grass Roots Press.

Cervero, R. M., & Wilson, A. L. (2006). *Working the planning table: Negotiating democratically for adult, continuing, and workplace education.* San Francisco, CA: Jossey-Bass.

Cervero, R. M., & Wilson, A. L, & Associates. (2001). *Power in practice: Adult education and the struggle for knowledge and power in society.* San Francisco, CA: Jossey-Bass.

Cumming, T., & Miller, M. D. (2017). *Enhancing assessment in higher education: Putting psychometrics to work.* Sterling, VA: Stylus.

English,L. M., & Mayo, P. (2012). *Learning with adults: A critical pedagogical introduction.* Rotterdam, The Netherlands: Sense.

Fenwick, T. (2010). Accountability practices in adult education: Insights from actor-network theory. *Studies in the Education of Adults, 42*(2), 170–185.

Fitzpatrick, J., Christie, C., & Mark, M. M. (2009). *Evaluation in action: Interviews with expert evaluators.* Thousand Oaks, CA: Sage.

Galbraith, M. W., & Jones, M. S. (2010). Assessment and evaluation. In C. E. Kasworm, A. D. Rose, & J. M. Ross-Gordon (Eds.), *Handbook of adult and continuing education* (pp. 167–175). Thousand Oaks, CA: Sage.

Grotelueschen, A. D., Gooler, D. D., & Knox, A. B. (1976). *Evaluation in adult basic education: How and why.* Urbana, IL: University of Illinois at Urbana-Champaign.

Hill, L. H. (2017). Adult education in an age of assessment and accountability. In A. Knox, S. C. O. Conceição, & L. G. Martin (Eds.), *Mapping the field of adult and continuing education: An international compendium* (pp. 265–268). Sterling, VA: Stylus.

Kasworm, C. E., & Marienau, C. A. (1997). Principles for assessment of adult learning. *New Directions for Adult and Continuing Education, 1997*(75), 5–16.

Knox, A. B. (2002). *Evaluation for continuing education: A comprehensive guide to success.* San Francisco, CA: Jossey-Bass.

Kuh, G. D., Ikenberry, S. O., Jankowski, N. A., Reese Cain, T., Ewell, P. T., Hutchings, P., & Kinzie, J. (2015). *Using evidence of student learning to improve higher education.* San Francisco, CA: Jossey-Bass.

Malmeer, E., & Zoghi, M. (2014). Dynamic assessment of grammar with different age groups. *Theory & Practice in Language Studies, 4*(8), 1707–1713.

Massa, L. J., & Kasimatis, M. (2017). *Meaningful and manageable program assessment: A how-to guide for higher education faculty.* Sterling, VA: Stylus.

Mejiuni, O., Cranton, P., & Táiwó, O. (Eds.). (2015). *Measuring and analyzing informal learning in the digital age.* Hershey, PA: Information Age.

Merrifield, J. (1998). *Contested ground: Performance accountability in adult basic education.* Washington, DC: National Center for the Study of Adult Learning and Literacy.

Milana, M. (2017). *Global networks, local actions: Rethinking adult education policy in the 21st century.* New York, NY: Routledge.

Moore, D. E. (2018). Assessment of learning and program evaluation in health professions education programs. *New Directions for Adult and Continuing Education, 2018*(157), 51–64.

Moran, J. J. (1997). *Assessing adult learning: A guide for practitioners.* Malabar, FL: Krieger.

National Research Council. (2002). *Performance assessments for adult education: Exploring the measurement issues: Report of a workshop.* Washington, DC: National Academies Press.

Nguyen, T. T. H., & Walker, M. (2016). Sustainable assessment for lifelong learning. *Assessment and Evaluation in Higher Education, 41*(1), 97–111.

Ocean, J., & Skourdoumbis, A. (2015). Who's counting? Legitimating measurement in the audit culture. *Discourse: Studies in the Cultural Politics of Education, 37,* 442–456.

Owczarzak, J., Broaddus, M., & Pinkerton, S. (2016). Audit culture. *American Journal of Evaluation, 37*(3), 326–343.

Queeney, D. S. (1995). *Assessing needs in continuing education: An essential tool for quality improvement.* San Francisco, CA: Jossey-Bass.

Robinson-Zañartu, C. (2013). Dynamic assessment: An intervention-based approach. In B. J. Irby, G. Brown, R. Lara-Alecio, & S. Jackson (Eds.), *The handbook of educational theories* (pp. 793–799). Charlotte, NC: Information Age.

Rose, A. D., & Leahy, M. A. (1997). *Assessing adult learning in diverse settings: Current issues and approaches.* San Francisco, CA: Jossey-Bass.

Spencer, B., & Kelly, J. (2013). *Work and learning: An introduction.* Toronto, Ontario, Canada: Thompson Educational.

Su, Y. (2015). Targeting assessment for developing adult lifelong learners: Assessing the ability to commit. *Australian Journal of Adult Learning, 55*(1), 75–93.

Suskie, L. (2018). *Assessing student learning: A common sense guide* (3rd ed.). San Francisco, CA: Jossey-Bass.

Torrance, H. (2017). Blaming the victim: Assessment, examinations, and the responsibilisation of students and teachers in neo-liberal governance. *Discourse: Studies in the Cultural Politics of Education, 83*(1), 38–96.

Tusting, K. (2012). Learning accountability literacies in educational workplaces: Situated learning and processes of commodification. *Language and Education, 26*(2), 121–138.

U.S. Office of Educational Research and Improvement. (2002). *Testing and accountability in adult literacy education: Focus on workplace literacy resources for program design, assessment, testing, and evaluation.* Washington, DC: Author.

Vella, J., Berardinelli, P., & Burrow, J. (1998). *How do they know they know? Evaluating adult learning.* San Francisco, CA: Jossey-Bass.

2

ASSESSMENT OF LEARNING
IN ADULT EDUCATION

Lilian H. Hill

Assessment is integral to teaching and learning. The purpose of assessment is to improve learning. According to Galbraith and Jones (2010), "Assessment, without a purpose, is a wasted effort" (p. 170). For example, an adult literacy tutor may measure students' progress in acquiring new vocabulary or grammar to provide them with feedback, a self-directed learner may measure progress toward their own learning goals to adjust learning strategies, or an organizational developer may determine how well new work-flow processes are being integrated into daily work practices to learn if adjustments are needed. The diversity of adult education practice means that adult educators must discern which assessment practices are best suited for their purposes and master varied assessment skills to serve their students. In all settings, assessment is not an empty exercise but instead provides valuable information about what adult learners know, what they are learning, and what needs to happen next to facilitate continued learning.

Assessment in adult education shares many similarities with other forms of education; however, there are some significant differences. Addae (2016) indicates that the relationship between educator and adult learner should be dialogic, meaning students and teachers are equally involved in the teaching and learning process as well in as in planning and conducting the assessment process. Because adult learners are more independent, self-directed, and have a rich source of experiential knowledge, education programs should be tailored to their interests and foster immediate application of learning. Therefore, learning assessments should measure the degree to which students can apply new knowledge to their desired settings. Learning transfer becomes a critical issue in assessment.

Learning transfer, sometimes known as knowledge or training transfer, involves an adult's ability to transfer knowledge, behavior, and skills learned in one setting to another. Learning should be structured so that adult learners are able to apply knowledge and skills gained from learning activities to activities in their home, community, social interactions, and workplace. The more relevant and authentic a learning activity, the more it contributes to learning transfer (Foley & Kaiser, 2013; Kaminski, Foley, & Kaiser, 2013). It is important for adult educators to plan for transfer by structuring learning activities with realistic case scenarios, role modelling, opportunities to practice skills with appropriate guidance in internships or practicum, training in self-assessment, and provision of a plan for how to transfer learning from one setting to another (Caffarella & Daffron, 2013). The more dissimilar the settings are, the more difficult it may be to transfer knowledge. Assessment for learning, as opposed to assessment of learning, should be future oriented and prepare students for monitoring their own lifelong learning. Boud (2000) indicates that adult learners need to learn assessment methods they can take with them for use as lifelong learners.

This chapter describes the purposes of assessment, principles for effective assessment practice, perspectives on assessment that can be employed when assessment processes are planned and implemented, and methods of assessment. The chapter concludes with a few cautions.

Purposes

Those of us in adult education have benefited and learned from the energy higher education institutions have invested in assessment and the books, journals, and articles that energy has produced. However, adult education values and perspectives on learning must guide the assessment work that we do. Assessment choices can be based on whether we are helping students identify their own learning goals and needs and helping them meet those needs.

As a meaningful aspect of teaching and learning, assessment practices should be used to improve instructional practices and student learning. Massa and Kasimatis (2017) defined *assessment* as "the systematic process for understanding and improving learning" (p. 6). They elaborated on their definition to indicate that a systematic process implies that assessment is a carefully planned and regular activity. They use the term *understanding* to indicate that instructors want to learn what students know at the outset and what they have learned as a result of instruction, the term *improving* means that assessment information is used to improve student learning, and they end the definition with student learning because that is the central purpose for conducting assessment. Assessment may take place at the level of individual students, courses, or programs. Massa and Kasimatis describe assessment as a fluid, cyclical pattern that incorporates the following steps: "articulate mission and goals"; "identify specific outcomes"; "determine practice used to achieve outcomes"; "gather evidence, review and interpret results"; and "recommend actions" (pp. 7–10). Ideally, assessment practices are informed by instructors' beliefs about adult learning and contribute to improving students' learning opportunities. It matters whether learning is viewed as knowledge acquisition; as changes in behavior, attitudes, skills, and reasoning abilities; or as a social, developmental, or transformative process. When assessments are conducted poorly, treated as an afterthought, or imposed by external stakeholders, assessment practices have the potential to undermine adult learning (Nguyen & Walker, 2016).

Assessment processes should be meaningful to and driven by adult educators organizing programs and teaching students because they are responsible for articulating learning outcomes, selecting assessment activities, evaluating results, and undertaking actions based on assessment results. Assessment can be a collaborative activity among students, faculty, and administrators, but all participants should be able to see that their contributions are meaningful and valued. Given the fact that many adult education programs operate with limited budgets, assessment processes should be efficient and technically feasible so they won't detract from the teaching-learning process. Once initiated, assessment goals and processes are not meant to become automatic and taken for granted; therefore, assessment results should be used for improvement of teaching and learning; transparent (i.e., made public); and reflective, meaning they are reviewed periodically to ensure the assessment goals and methods remain appropriate (Bresciania-Ludvik, 2019).

Assessment can begin with helping adult learners recognize what they already know and determine appropriate learning goals that contribute to their growth. Assessment may provide students with meaningful and detailed feedback so they can adjust their learning practices and at the same time provide information to instructors so they can adjust their teaching strategies. Assessment processes may be conducted for screening or diagnostic processes for admissions and program placement purposes. Assessment results can be used to construct course grades, ensure that students are ready to progress in a sequenced course series, or produce outcome results relevant to program evaluation.

Principles of Effective Assessment Practice

Assessment may be viewed as a type of action research to inform instruction and student learning (Barkley & Major, 2016). Effective assessment consists of the following components:

1. Identifying and communicating learning goals and outcomes;
2. Helping students achieve these goals through activities that promote active; engaged learning; and
3. Analyzing, reporting, and reflecting on results in ways that lead to continued improvement. (Barkley & Major, 2016, p. 3)

Likewise, the American Association of Higher Education's following nine principles of good practice in assessment were written by Hutchings, Ewell, and Banta (2012), who are well recognized for their work in higher education assessment:

1. The assessment of student learning begins with educational values.
2. Assessment is most effective when it reflects an understanding of learning as multidimensional, integrated, and revealed in performance over time.
3. Assessment works best when the programs it seeks to improve have clear, explicitly stated purposes.
4. Assessment requires attention to outcomes but also and equally to the experiences that lead to those outcomes.
5. Assessment works best when it is ongoing not episodic.
6. Assessment fosters wider improvement when representatives from across the educational community are involved.
7. Assessment makes a difference when it begins with issues of use and illuminates questions people really care about.
8. Assessment is most likely to lead to improvement when it is part of a larger set of conditions that promote change.
9. Through assessment, educators meet responsibilities to students and to the public. (pp. 3–5)

Assessment measures can be selected depending on the goals of instruction or the adult education interaction. Instructors analyze student work to inform instruction, curriculum, advising, and student support. Standardized tests or objective measures are not required but may be used when appropriate. Direct measures measure student learning, whereas indirect measures involve soliciting information from students, alumni, or employers about how well they learned or their ability to perform.

Perspectives on Assessment

Multiple perspectives about assessment have been discussed in the literature. This chapter notes only a few that seem most relevant to adult mative and summative assessment, authentic assessment, ...ve assessment, self-regulated learning and metacognition, and dynamic assessment.

Formative and Summative Assessment

Practice and feedback are essential to student learning (Ambrose, Bridges, DiPietro, Lovett, & Norman, 2010). Feedback can be used to help students achieve a desired level of performance relevant to target criteria and is considered effective when it prompts learners' thinking and continued effort. To be useful, feedback must be timely, detailed, individualized, meaningful, and purposeful in communicating to adult learners what they need to understand better, how to adjust their performance to meet an articulated standard, or ways to redirect their energies to improve learning and performance. Feedback can improve student learning when it is (a) focused on the key knowledge and skills students are to learn, (b) timed when students are most likely to benefit, and (c) linked to opportunities for further practice. Effective feedback should be dialogical and employ information from multiple forms of assessment.

Formative assessment, sometimes known as assessment for learning (Box, 2018), is conducted during the learning process and provides students with information about their performance, whereas summative assessment involves judgments at the end of a course of learning often communicated through course grades or certificates of completion based on identified criteria. Formative assessment often uses qualitative research processes, and summative assessment is more likely to employ quantitative methods and measures student performance with an articulated standard aligned with course goals and objectives. Several authors suggest putting more emphasis on formative assessment that is supportive of lifelong learning and that there should be more interconnection between summative and formative assessment processes (Boud & Soler, 2016; Nguyen & Walker, 2016; Su, 2015). Su (2015) contends that formative and summative assessment lay a foundation for lifelong learning when they relate to goals the learner values, foster self-assessment, and provide information the learner will use in future learning.

Authentic Assessment

Authentic assessment is "a form of assessment in which students are asked to perform real-world tasks that demonstrate meaningful application of essential knowledge and skills" (Strachan, Pickard, & Laing, 2010, para. 7).

Students are asked to apply what they know to meaningful tasks analogous to what could realistically be expected of adult citizens, consumers, or practicing professionals in their daily life. Rather than isolating and testing individual skills, performance of authentic tasks requires the application of acquired knowledge and integration of multiple skills. To complete these authentic tasks, students can be engaged in progressive assessments that determine they know what to do and how to do it, perform component tasks, and then demonstrate that they can accomplish the task in its entirety (Moore, 2018). Use of authentic assessment can be motivating to students by engaging them in tasks relevant to their interests and providing instructors with useful information regarding students' capabilities (Ambrose et al., 2010). Varied assessment tasks can be employed including community service, internships, demonstrations, written work, presentations, and portfolios. However, Hathcoat, Penn, Barnes, and Comer (2016) question the validity of authentic assessment when scores are limited to written assessments without using other information sources.

Sustainable Assessment

Ultimately, education is judged on long-term results in terms of equipping adult learners to face complex challenges and perform effectively in a complex global world (Boud & Soler, 2016). Sustainable assessment involves practices that work in the present and foster students' abilities to meet their future learning needs. From this viewpoint, assessment is a sociocultural process that is mutually constructed among instructors and learners. It requires fostering students' skills in judging their own capabilities and attainment in learning performance. What makes it sustainable is its future orientation, assistance to students in meeting life challenges and planning for persistence of educational benefits beyond an immediate application, evidence of student knowledge and practice of articulated standards, and preparation for learning after completion of the course or program.

Sustainable assessment can foster students' "independence, intellectual maturity, and creativity" (Boud & Soler, 2016, p. 403). Five key elements of students becoming informed judges about their own learning are "(1) identifying oneself as an active learner, (2) identifying one's own level of knowledge and the gaps in this, (3) practising testing and judging, (4) developing these skills over time, and (5) embodying reflexivity and commitment" (p. 402). To improve their learning, students need to become informed about the criteria or standards used for judgement in the relevant learning domain. Instructors should integrate instruction about learning skills in the curriculum and pedagogy to build students' abilities in taking responsibility for learning, self-assessment, self-monitoring, reflection, and peer review.

Self-Regulated Learning and Metacognition

To take more responsibility for their own learning, learners need to increase their understanding of their current performance in relation to what they aim to do, and in some cases, their understanding about the accepted standards for performance in a desired domain. Reflective self-assessment allows learners to shape their own future performance based on an understanding of their current cognitive processes. Research on metacognition indicates that it involves self-regulation of learning that includes skills in planning, information management, comprehension monitoring, self-assessment, and evaluation (Sitzmann & Ely, 2011). Metacognitively aware people are able to use a greater variety of learning strategies and perform better than their less aware peers. Knowledge of cognition and its regulation are required for metacognition to occur: "Goal level, persistence, effort, and self-efficacy were the self-regulation constructs with the strongest effects on learning" (Sitzmann & Ely, 2011, p. 421). The control, or regulation, of cognition requires the learner to plan, sequence, and monitor their learning in a way that improves performance. Accuracy in self-assessment of skill performance is essential to effective learning.

Dynamic Assessment

According to Fenwick (2001), "Dynamic assessment seeks to capture what unfolds in social environments where meanings and perceptions are complex" (p. 79). It is grounded in three principles. First, learning is dynamic and constantly evolving, meaning that taking a snapshot of students' progress at a single point in time is inadequate. Second, learning develops in interaction with others, so an individual learner's progress should not be measured in isolation. Instead, the influence of systems of language, cultural context, and social interactions on learning are examined critically. Third, the focus of assessment should encompass more than what a person is learning and include how they are developing new meanings and refining the accuracy of their perceptions. Reflective inquiry is an important part of the process, as is dialogue among learners, instructors, and assessors so that learners have a clear but fluid benchmark to work toward.

Four dimensions are characteristic of a dynamic assessment approach. First, self-assessment enables learners to examine their own beliefs and values, clarify their values, and judge their own performance. Second, by engaging in this process, learners may become more independent of external approval and chart their own course for what and how to learn. Third, assessment needs to be continuous and ongoing throughout and after the learning process. To adjust their learning processes, adult learners need ongoing feedback that is based in clear criteria that are meaningful to them. Fourth, dynamic assessment is holistic and authentic. It recognizes the complexities of human relationships, communities, and influences on knowledge. In accepting these complexities, "assessment must be understood as partial, contestable, and fallible" (Fenwick, 2001, p. 90).

Methods of Assessment

Assessment means little in the absence of establishing goals for learning. Instructors should begin by thoughtfully determining and articulating what they want their students to accomplish. They may work in collaboration with other instructors, with external stakeholders, or with the adult learners who will be involved. If students believe they are capable of achieving the learning goals, and the learning goals are motivating to adult students, they are more likely to invest their time and effort in learning (Ambrose et al., 2010).

Assessment methods and approaches may be classified as selected responses or constructed responses (Cumming & Miller, 2017). Selected responses can include multiple choice, true or false, matching, listing, fill in the blanks, or guided essay; they are commonly used in tests. Constructed responses mean that adult learners are asked to produce a product in response to an assignment. Examples may include essays, journals, oral presentations, demonstrations, panel discussions, artwork, graphic organizers, or research papers. Assessment processes can be used to appraise prior knowledge and understanding, analysis and synthesis, critical thinking, creative thinking, values and self-awareness, and learner attitudes toward instruction. The following information describing varied assessment methods is intended as a brief guide. Entire books and articles devoted to each of these assessment methods are available.

Needs Assessment

Needs assessment is discussed in this chapter because it is important to determine what student learning needs are before instruction is devised. Needs assessment tasks may start before an individual participates in an adult education program or process and may involve seeking information regarding (a) what students hope to gain by participating in adult education, (b) baseline data about what students already know, and (c) the knowledge and skills they already have relevant to the course goals and objectives. Assessment processes can also be used to identify any gaps or weaknesses in their knowledge that a course or program can address; however, care must be taken to avoid treating adult learners as deficient. A variety of techniques is available including questionnaires, observations, interviews, focus groups, pre-tests, job and task analyses, performance reviews, and informal interactions depending on the purposes of the needs assessment, staff capabilities to conduct the techniques and use resulting information, the difficulty and expense of data gathering, characteristics of the audience, and the depth of information desired (Caffarella & Daffron, 2013).

Learning Objectives

Needs assessment can lead to the development or modification of course and program objectives. One method of communicating learning goals is to create course and module objectives that specify the knowledge, skills, or attitudes to be learned. The very idea of writing learning objectives may prompt automatic resistance to focusing on behavioral manifestations of learning and the need to devise ways to capture measurable behavior change; however, when assessment is thought of as communication with students and provision of learning support, these feelings can be overcome. Learning objectives should provide clear information about what results students can expect to gain by participating in learning activities. Objectives should be specific and feasible given the resources available (Caffarella & Daffron, 2013). Learning objectives lack relevance when they are not tailored to adult learners' needs.

Many learning objectives are written in behavioral terms; for example, students will be able to perform x skill to y standard when z conditions are provided. The ABCDs of learning objectives include the audience (who will be learning), the behavior (what the learner will become able to do), the conditions in which learners are expected to demonstrate their new capabilities, and the degree or standard they must meet in their performance (Mager, R., 1997). Objectives can be written for cognitive, psychomotor, or affective learning. Bloom's (1956) taxonomy provides useful categories of cognitive learning beginning with knowledge or recall, comprehension, application, analysis, synthesis, and evaluation, with convenient verb lists associated with each level (Anderson, Krathwohl, & Bloom, 2000). Expanded taxonomies are available for psychomotor and affective learning. Although the taxonomies have been critiqued as being too linear to capture the fluid nature of adult learning, they may be used as a "framework upon which students can attach their own experiences and ideas thereby making the content more personally relevant and meaningful" (Williams, 2017, p. 5).

Informal Assessment of Student Learning

Employing methods for informally assessing student preparation and learning can provide information about what students already know, what they are learning, and what they are retaining. Informal assessment methods are typically inexpensive and can help with understanding whether students are prepared for learning, are motivated to learn, and are experiencing difficulty in understanding material. Examples include asking students to write one-minute reaction papers on directed topics, write definitions or applications, list key concepts or ideas they heard, or even develop exam questions. Student response systems can be used to conduct instant polls of knowledge or opinions. Applications, or apps, for this purpose exist and are free for use on a smartphone (Gross, 2009). More examples of informal assessment that can be implemented in online courses are described in chapter 10.

Rubrics

Rubrics, or matrices, are a useful method of communicating performance expectations related to activities or assignments to adult learners. Typically, a rubric consists of a table organized with rows detailing competencies students are expected to develop and columns containing the performance levels students are expected to reach (e.g., unsatisfactory, poor, good, and excellent). Alternatively, the columns may detail the competencies, and rows may show the performance levels. Articulation of the expected (or targeted) performance of each competency helps students understand what knowledge and skills they are expected to attain and also helps instructors in their aim to be consistent in providing feedback (Ambrose et al., 2010; Barkley & Major, 2016). Adult learners may need coaching in how to use a rubric for guidance about their own learning performance. When multiple collaborators write rubrics to measure the performance of professional competencies, vocabulary should be consistent across performance levels with agreed-on meanings for terminology for each performance level. This can lead to lively discussions about the relative meanings of evaluative descriptors such as consistent, often, sometimes, and occasionally (Hill, Delafuente, Sicat, & Kirkwood, 2006). Rubrics have also been used in research about adult learning. For example, Rapchak, Lewis, Motyka, and Balmert's (2015) study used rubrics to assess students' information literacy skills.

Tests

Tests are commonly used in classroom settings and may be created by the instructor or an outside agency. Tests can be used to measure knowledge, skills, or performance and may be devised for diagnostic purposes, pre-test and post-test comparison, or summative assessment of student achievement. Tests can take many forms and include different types of items ranging from multiple choice, matching, rating, true or false, short- and long-answer questions, and essays. Care must be taken with developing open-ended questions because grading them requires a detailed answer key, which can be time consuming to create. Testing may also include performance of real-world skills in a classroom or practical setting. No matter the format, tests are intended to measure students' progress in learning. Instructors who write their own tests must learn skills to create accurate items and to engage students in analysis and critical thinking in responding to test items rather than emphasizing simple recall. Although testing is not used in adult education settings as often as it is in K–12 education settings, tests do have their place in adult education.

It is important to differentiate between criterion and norm-referenced testing. The former type of testing measures student performance in relation to a specified criterion, learning goals, or standards, whereas the latter measures student performance with a comparison, or standard, group of students (Cumming & Miller, 2017). Criterion-referenced tests are used to measure how much a student has learned and are therefore closely matched to previously articulated learning outcomes or objectives. Test results may be used to determine how well students are learning or for the assessment of the curriculum and teacher performance. Norm-referenced tests are primarily used to classify students, and their effectiveness is determined by how well a test can discriminate among different student achievement levels. In standardized testing, the norm is established by administering the test items to a large group of students before the items are published or integrated into existing tests.

Standardized Tests

Adult educators may be called on to design or, more often, interpret standardized test results that are used for literacy assessment, testing vocational aptitude, college or university placement and admissions processes, and professional licensure. A standardized test means that the "administration, format, and scoring of a test are the same for all examinees—which is an essential requirement to producing interpretable data" (Warne, Yoon, & Price, 2014, p. 570). Although the format of standardized tests varies, frequently these are multiple-choice tests administered by computer or by using a bubble sheet, a paper-and-pencil format in which students fill in a circle that corresponds to the answer they choose. Funding for adult basic education and literacy is often dependent on formal placement and outcomes assessment using the Comprehensive Adult Student Assessment System and Test of Adult Basic Education (discussed in chapter 4). Community college placement is often accomplished using the College Placement Test. College and university admissions processes may require scores on the ACT, Scholastic Achievement Test, Graduate Record Exam, or the Graduate Management Admissions Test. These are proprietary commercial tests that are developed using sophisticated psychometric analysis by the Educational Testing Service and other agencies. Use of standardized testing for graduate admissions is discussed in chapter 12.

An advantage of using standardized tests is that students are measured against a national standard; however, a disadvantage is that the test may not measure what students desire to learn or what instructors are actually teaching. It may cause instructors to change what they are teaching to help students pass the test, thereby consuming much instructional time and energy. Care and healthy skepticism should be employed in interpreting test results as there are some problems with predictive validity, meaning test results may not accurately predict future performance. A single test cannot take into account all the sociocultural context concerns relevant to adult learning. Worries about test bias are pertinent in high-stakes testing situations including college and university admissions or employment testing. It is beyond the scope of this chapter to discuss test bias (when test scores have different meanings for different groups of examinees) in the detail it deserves. Warne et al. (2014) indicate there are

> five common interpretations for the phrase *test bias*: (1) mean score differences between groups, (2) differential predictive validity, (3) differential item functioning, (4) differences in item factor structure, and (5) consequences of a test that disadvantage members of some demographic groups. (p. 579)

Biased assessments can be the result of language bias, professional bias, practice bias, and instrument bias, which are generally rooted in lack of acknowledgement and understanding of diverse cultures. There is a need for the "development of culturally appropriate and culturally sensitive assessment instruments as well as the development of ethical standards and training guidelines to prepare competent professionals" (Marbley, Bonner, & Berg, 2008, p. 12).

Visualizations and Graphics

Visualizations come in multiple formats including illustrations, photographs, concept maps, flow charts, graphs, or tables. Images and visualizations are becoming an important part of the digital culture, but their potential to reach students and contribute to assessment of student learning are still being explored (Wheeldon & Ahlberg, 2012). Visualizations and graphics can be used to assess how learners' thinking is organized. For example, Figure 2.1 provides a concept map of how this chapter is organized. Concept maps may help students understand, integrate, and reflect on their learning and foster the development of higher order thinking skills and skill development. Creating a concept map engages students in active learning that emphasizes meaningful learning rather than rote memorization (Daley, 2010; Hill, 2008; Yelich Biniecki & Conceição, 2016). Having students create their own concept maps is applicable to teaching abstract concepts because students can demonstrate their individual knowledge construction and express the differing ways they understand the relationships among the concepts they are learning. Instructors can analyze the inclusion of concepts and propositional relationships to identify and help students remedy misconceptions or gaps in their knowledge (Hill, 2008). Instructors can use the information gleaned from students' concept maps to inform their teaching, and students can use the information to adjust their learning strategies. Asking students to complete repeated concept maps during a course or sequence of courses can enable students to recognize their own change and development (Ambrose et al., 2010).

Portfolios

Portfolios are defined as a collection of work organized with the purpose of demonstrating best work, growth, or skills proficiency. A portfolio may include written work and artifacts of different types (Butler & McMunn, 2006) and may be maintained in a hard-copy format or electronically. The inclusion of reflection on learning is what differentiates a portfolio from a diary or log book. Developing a portfolio can serve to document evidence of the experiential learning of adult learners (Michelson & Mandell, 2004). Documenting the multiplicity of skills acquired over time through their participation in education, work, community, social, and family settings in a portfolio process may enable adult learners to view their capabilities in a tangible way and increase their self-confidence and communication, organizational, and reflective abilities. In a book devoted to the use of electronic portfolios, Eynon and Gambino (2017) indicated that individuals engaged in

Figure 2.1. Concept map of chapter organization.

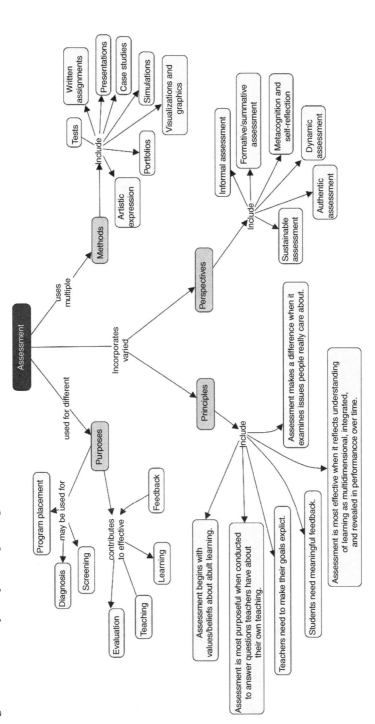

portfolio development may increase their self-knowledge, value learning garnered from their work and mentors, and appreciate the role of self-reflection: "ePortfolios make student learning visible to students themselves, to their peers and faculty, and to external evaluators" (p. 1). By writing about professional and personal experiences, adult learners further their insight about their own learning, construct a context for experiencing themselves as skilled and knowledgeable, and obtain a mechanism for establishing greater control of their own learning goals and strategies.

The purposes and goals of the portfolio determine the types of artifacts that are appropriate for inclusion. Written work, videotapes, artwork, professional certifications, and examples of best work in an arena are all possibilities. In their tips for getting started, Eynon and Gambino (2017) indicated that adult learners need preparation to understand the purposes and relevance of portfolios to their learning goals. Instructors should think about what kind of reflection students should engage in (reflection as a systematic and disciplined connection, as social pedagogy, or as an attitude toward change) and can design learning prompts to focus students' attention on key issues (Eynon & Gambino, 2017). Students can be engaged in determining the criteria for, or justification of, why selected items are included; the organization and narrative explanation of the portfolio; and the format and how portfolios are preserved for storage. To reduce frustration and improve portfolio products, it is important for students to receive regular feedback that promotes sophistication in learning and that they are informed in advance about how their portfolio will be assessed. The use of a portfolio for documenting professional growth relative to continuing professional education is described in chapter 6, and chapter 11 discusses portfolio assessment in the context of graduate programs in adult and higher education.

The use of portfolios for prior learning assessment is common in academic programs using competency-based assessment and may be related to assessing for academic credit for prior life and work experience related to an equivalence of credit hour acquisition, sometimes referred to as *seat time*. Rust and Brinthaupt (2017) indicate that current national and state policies relating to college completion are an impetus for increasing the number of adults with degrees earned through postsecondary education. A prior learning assessment of a portfolio can save students tuition money and decrease the time to degree (Olson & Klein-Collins, 2004; Rust & Brinthaupt, 2017).

Written Assignments

Students produce a great variety of written work in response to assignment requirements ranging from journals, autobiographies, self-reflective essays, research papers, and theses and dissertations. Effective writing skills are essential to classroom and workplace success, and students who can express their ideas clearly and effectively have an advantage (Gross, 2009). Assessment practices must relate to the purposes of the assignment, and adult educators can display a great deal of creativity in developing written assignments. Students will do better if educators provide them with rubrics or another form of grading criteria before they undertake the assignment. It is helpful for instructors to provide feedback to students on first drafts so that students can revise their papers before final submission for grading. Instructors should allow themselves enough time to read the papers holistically before assigning any grades, written comments should be legible or typed, negative and positive comments should be balanced, criticism can be structured as clarifying questions, sarcasm is to be avoided, feedback should be concrete and specific, and suggestions for improvement need to be provided (Gross, 2009).

Presentations

Oral presentation skills are an essential skill for the workplace and educational settings in which adult learners participate, especially given rapid changes in digital communication technologies. Unfortunately, many adults have not fully developed their public speaking and oral presentation skills, and for many, phobias about public speaking may be acute. Therefore, it is important to create conditions of safety to reduce fear. Before expecting students to make oral presentations, it is constructive to provide instruction in presentation skills. Similar to assessing written work, it is important to provide students with the assessment criteria in advance and to follow the criteria in providing assessment feedback. Commonly used criteria include clear and audible speech, organization, relevance of the topic to the audience, positive eye contact and body language, knowledge of the topic, and timing. Rubrics for assessing oral presentations are available online and may be adapted to the instructors' purposes for the assignment ("How to Use and Evaluate Student Speaking & Oral Presentations," 2006).

Case Studies

Case studies are used extensively in teaching in many fields because they illustrate realistic scenarios that teachers can use to engage students in applying key principles or practices taught in the class (Gross, 2009; Schmidt, 2010). Essentially they consist of a narrative that illustrates how key aspects of a phenomenon are interdependent and reflect the complexity of life but with controlled consequences. They provide an opportunity for students to critically analyze the aspects of the scenario and make recommendations for action. In designing case studies, instructors should begin with the course objectives, the learners, the resources available, and the context to determine how a case study exercise can support learning. Debriefing involving self-reflection and instructor feedback are important for learning to occur.

Simulations

Simulations are designed to provide students with learning experiences and can be simple or complex. They can be instructor-created classroom role-plays or games, and they can involve sophisticated computer-mediated simulations of real-world situations. For example, to provide safe opportunities for students to practice, health professions education employs robotic simulated patients that are programmed to demonstrate symptoms and react to treatment in realistic ways. The military uses simulations to provide practice opportunities that do not endanger life and consume valuable resources. How well simulations approximate real life, how reliable the assessment results are, and how feedback is provided to adult learners are critical questions. Research has demonstrated that simulations are effective in education and that repeated simulation exercises can serve to improve critical thinking and clinical decision-making (Macauley, Brudvig, Kadakia, & Bonneville, 2017). Chapter 5 discusses applications of simulations used in the army.

Artistic Expression

Artistic expression in many forms can help adults uncover hidden knowledge, understand and express their current realities, appreciate other cultures, or represent their wisdom and life experience (Lawrence, 2005). Arts used in adult education can include drama, dance, poetry, creative writing, and many forms of visual art including collage, painting, pottery, and photography. Rather than overemphasizing cognitive learning, arts education can foster diverse ways of thinking "including affective, somatic, and spiritual domains [and] participants can more fully express what they know" (Lawrence, 2005, p. 4). Very little of the literature regarding arts education addresses ways that it can be used for assessment, possibly because literature about this topic is still developing. Perhaps because teachers and adult students tend to devalue their own artistic ability, they are reluctant to assess someone else's artistic expressions. Nevertheless, adult education instructors can develop their own assessment measures in collaboration with their students.

Cautions

Several cautions must be considered when conducting assessment of student learning. In writing this chapter, I experienced discomfort with repeated use of the words *progress, measure, performance,* and *achievement* because the danger is that assessment can become a process that measures students against an external standard instead of whether they are accomplishing their own learning goals. This external measurement will inevitably produce results irrelevant to adult learners. Some adult students have been traumatized by their previous educational experiences and have lost confidence in their ability to learn. They will react badly to high-stakes assessment, meaning assessments used to make decisions about students including admissions, placement, or progression. Using assessments to make judgments instead of foster learning is risky. Producing assessment results for purposes other than improving teaching may mean that the educational process has been co-opted for purposes external to the teaching-learning transaction. Additionally, care should be invested to ensure that assessment processes do not reinforce bias and discrimination. Culture, race, gender, sexual orientation, religion, age, disability, health status, and characteristics of an individual's social interactions need to be considered in designing and administering assessments. The risk is that adult education can reproduce society's dominant values, leaving students feeling marginalized (Galbraith & Jones, 2010). Galbraith and Jones (2010) indicate that it is important for teaching and learning to be adapted to meet diverse students' needs and learning assessments should be appropriately contextualized.

Robust assessment means working with theories of learning and employing multiple methods, qualitative and qualitative. Fuzzy purposes can result in fuzzy results or "garbage in, garbage out," meaning incorrect or poor quality input will always produce faulty output. Instructors must carefully consider what they hope their students will be able to learn in an educational encounter and plan their assessments relative to those goals. Employing assessment tasks disconnected from previous assessments without giving thought to ways that learning should be organized, reinforced, or sequenced, means students do not learn for improvement or long-term purposes.

Conclusions

Conducting effective assessment will enable adult educators to meet our responsibilities to students, our institutions, and to the public (Hutchings et al., 2012). Adult learners will be able to realize their learning progress, and instructors of adults need to see that their efforts are making a difference. Assessment enables adult educators to document student success and how instruction contributed. Finally, assessment results can be used to improve instruction and contribute to program evaluation.

References

Addae, D. (2016). Promoting effective teaching and learning in adult education: A model-based approach. *Turkish Journal of Education*, 5(4), 184–192.

Ambrose, S. A., Bridges, M. W., DiPietro, M., Lovett, M. C., & Norman, M. K. (2010). *How learning works: Seven research-based principles for smart teaching.* San Francisco, CA: Jossey-Bass.

Anderson, L. W., Krathwohl, D. R., & Bloom, B. S. (2000). *A taxonomy for learning, teaching, and assessing: A revision of Bloom's taxonomy of educational objectives* (2nd ed.). New York, NY: Longman.

Barkley, E. J., & Major, C. H. (2016). *Learning assessment techniques: A handbook for college faculty.* San Francisco, CA: Jossey-Bass.

Bloom, B. S. (1956). *Taxonomy of educational objectives: The classification of educational goals by a committee of college and university examiners.* New York, NY: McKay.

Boud, D. (2000). Sustainable assessment: Rethinking assessment for the learning society. *Studies in Continuing Education*, 22(2), 151–167.

Boud, D., & Soler, R. (2016). Sustainable assessment revisited. *Assessment and Evaluation in Higher Education*, 41(3), 400–413.

Box, C. (2018, December 17). Assessment for learning: it just makes sense. *Faculty focus.* Retrieved from https://www.facultyfocus.com/articles/educational-assessment/assessment-for-learning-it-just-makes-sense

Bresciania-Ludvik, M. J. (2019). *Outcomes-based program review: Closing achievement gaps in and outside the classroom with alignment to predictive analytics and performance metrics.* Sterling, VA: Stylus.

Butler, S. M., & McMunn, N. D. (2006). *A teacher's guide to classroom assessment: Understanding and using assessment to improve student learning.* San Francisco, CA: Jossey-Bass.

Caffarella, R. S., & Daffron, S. R. (2013). *Planning programs for adult learners: A practical guide* (3rd ed.). San Francisco, CA: Jossey-Bass.

Cumming, T., & Miller, M. D. (2017). *Enhancing assessment in higher education: Putting psychometrics to work.* Sterling, VA: Stylus.

Daley, B. J. (2010). Concept maps: Practice applications in adult education and human resource development. *New Horizons in Adult Education and Human Resource Development*, 24(2–4), 31–37.

Eynon, B., & Gambino, L. M. (2017). *High-impact ePortfolio practice: A catalyst for student, faculty and institutional learning.* Sterling, VA: Stylus.

Fenwick, T. (2001). Dynamic assessment: Putting learners at the center of the evaluation. In T. Barer-Stein (Ed.), *The craft of teaching adults* (pp. 77–93). Toronto, Ontario, Canada: Irwin.

Foley, J. M., & Kaiser, L. M. R. (2013). Learning transfer and its intentionality in adult and continuing education. *New Directions for Adult and Continuing Education, 2013*(137), 5–15.

Galbraith, M. W., & Jones, M. S. (2010). Assessment and evaluation. In C. E. Kasworm, A. D. Rose, & J. M. Ross-Gordon (Eds.), *Handbook of adult and continuing education* (pp. 167–175). Thousand Oaks, CA: Sage.

Gross, B. D. (2009). *Tools for teaching* (2nd ed.). San Francisco, CA: Jossey-Bass.

Hathcoat, J. D., Penn, J. D., Barnes, L. L. B., & Comer, J. C. (2016). A second dystopia in education: Validity issues in authentic assessment practices. *Research in Higher Education, 57*(7), 892–912.

Hill, L. H., Delafuente, J. C., Sicat, B. L., & Kirkwood, C. K. (2006). Development of a competency-based assessment process for advanced pharmacy practice experiences. *American Journal of Pharmaceutical Education, 70*(1), Article 63.

Hill, L. H. (2008). Concept mapping to encourage meaningful student learning in adult education. *Adult Learning, 16*(3/4), 7–13.

How to use and evaluate student speaking & oral presentations in the classroom. (2006). Retrieved from https://www.mtholyoke.edu/sites/default/files/saw/docs/evaluating_speaking_guidelines_spring2006.pdf

Hutchings, P., Ewell, P., & Banta, T. (2012). AAHE principles of good practice: Aging nicely. Retrieved from https://www.learningoutcomesassessment.org/wp-content/uploads/2019/08/Viewpoint-Hutchings-EwellBanta.pdf

Kaminski, K., Foley, J. M., & Kaiser, L. M. R. (2013). Applying transfer in practice. *New Directions for Adult and Continuing Education, 2013*(137), 83–89.

Lawrence, R. L. (2005). Knowledge construction as contested terrain: Adult learning through artistic expression. *New Directions for Adult and Continuing Education, 2005*(107), 3–11.

Macauley, K., Brudvig, T. J., Kadakia, M., & Bonneville, M. (2017). Systematic review of assessments that evaluate clinical decision making, clinical reasoning, and critical thinking changes after simulation participation. *Journal of Physical Therapy Education, 31*(4), 64–75.

Mager, R. F. (1997). *Preparing instructional objectives* (3rd ed.). Atlanta, GA: Center for Effective Performance.

Marbley, A. F., Bonner, F., & Berg, R. (2008). Measurement and assessment: Conversations with professional people in the field of education. *Multicultural Education, 16*(1), 12–20.

Massa, L. J., & Kasimatis, M. (2017). *Meaningful and manageable program assessment: A how-to-guide for higher education faculty.* Sterling, VA: Stylus.

Michelson, E., & Mandell, A. (2004). *Portfolio development and the assessment of prior learning: Perspectives, models, and practices.* Sterling, VA: Stylus.

Moore, D. E. (2018). Assessment of learning and program evaluation in health professions education programs. *New Directions for Adult and Continuing Education, 2018*(157), 51–64.

Nguyen, T. T. H., & Walker, M. (2016). Sustainable assessment for lifelong learning. *Assessment and Evaluation in Higher Education, 41*(1), 97–111.

Olson, R., & Klein-Collins, R. (2004). *LearningCounts portfolio assessment means cost savings for students . . . and employers.* Retrieved from ERIC database (ED562015).

Rapchak, M. E., Lewis, L. A., Motyka, J. K., & Balmert, M. (2015). Information literacy and adult learners: Using authentic assessment to determine skill gaps. *Adult Learning, 26*(4), 135–142.

Rust, D. Z., & Brinthaupt, T. M. (2017). Student perceptions of and experiences with a PLA course and portfolio review. *The Journal of Continuing Higher Education, 65*(2), 115–123.

Schmidt, S. (2010). *Case studies and activities in adult education and human resource development.* Charlotte, NC: Information Age.

Sitzmann, T., & Ely, K. (2011). A meta-analysis of self-regulated learning in work-related training and educational attainment: What we know and where we need to go. *Psychological Bulletin, 137*(3), 421–442.

Strachan, R., Pickard, A., & Laing, C. (2010). Bringing technical authoring skills to life for students through an employer audience. *Innovation in Teaching and Learning in Information and Computer Sciences, 9*(2), 1–11.

Su, Y. (2015). Targeting assessment for developing adult lifelong learners: Assessing the ability to commit. *Australian Journal of Adult Learning, 55*(1), 75–93.

Warne, R. T., Yoon, M., & Price, C. J. (2014). Exploring the various interpretations of "test bias." *Cultural Diversity and Ethnic Minority Psychology, 20*(4), 570–582.

Wheeldon, J., & Ahlberg, M. K. (2012). *Visualizing social science research: Maps, methods, and meaning.* Thousand Oaks, CA: Sage.

Williams, A. A. (2017). Promoting meaningfulness by coupling Bloom's taxonomy with adult education theory: Introducing an applied and interdisciplinary student writing exercise. *Transformative Dialogues: Teaching & Learning Journal, 10*(3), 1–11.

Yelich Biniecki, S. M., & Conceição, S. C. O. (2016). Using concept maps to engage adult learners in critical analysis. *Adult Learning, 27*(2), 51–59.

3

PROGRAM EVALUATION IN ADULT EDUCATION

Larry G. Martin and Kevin Roessger

P rogram evaluation has increasingly become an important function in contemporary adult and continuing education practice. External accountability requirements are now stipulating many adult education practitioners to demonstrate evaluation skills and understand the evaluation process (McNicol, 2005). This has coincided with an emphasis on evidence-based policy (McNicol, 2005), making evidence a key concern of policymakers, funding sources, program administrators, community support groups, and current and potential program clientele. The skill sets needed to design, implement, and produce effective evaluations, however, have been overlooked in many adult education graduate programs. In this chapter, we identify these skills and discuss how adult educators may implement them in practice.

Applicability of Program Evaluation Models and Approaches

The literature on educational program evaluation describes numerous models and approaches for evaluating adult and continuing education program activities; however, many of them bifurcate evaluation into either formal or informal practices. Although informal evaluations can illuminate program successes and failures, they rely largely on casual observations, implicit goals, intuitive norms, and subjective judgments (Stake, 1967). Consequently, they often vary in quality, ranging from penetrating and insightful to superficial and distorted (Stake, 1967). Therefore, our approach focuses on formal evaluations. Additionally, evaluations may be carried out internally by an organization's evaluators, project teams, or individual service providers or externally by professionals who are either contracted or mandated by a governing body (Stufflebeam, 2003). Each will have different aims and insights into the evaluation process. Regardless of who is doing the evaluation, though, our position is that evaluators are best served by understanding historically influential evaluation models and approaches. Having knowledge of this work will serve to guide evaluators in their understanding of when and why critical evaluation skills are used.

Program Evaluation Decisions and Approaches

The practices, contexts, and requirements of adult and continuing education programs vary widely. Prominent models and approaches discussed in the literature (e.g., Kirkpatrick, 1994; Stake, 1967; Stufflebeam, 2003; and others) can provide frameworks and ideas to assist evaluators in deciding how to best approach the evaluation of a specific program. Three important decisions emerging from these works ask evaluators to consider the purpose of the evaluation, the role they should play in casting judgments, and the developmental stage of the program itself.

What Is the Purpose of the Evaluation?

An important skill of adult education evaluators is to determine the types of evaluative decisions that are appropriate to the situation and expected from stakeholders. Three decision settings that illustrate different degrees of change desired by stakeholders tend to be typical of adult education evaluations (Stufflebeam, 2003). Homeostatic decision settings employ evaluations to maintain the normal balance of an educational system, for example, using data collected routinely on program enrollments to determine course arrangements, course delivery systems, and so on. Incremental decisions involve developing activities to improve a program, such as additional courses or instructors for courses targeting the same market. Neomobilistic decisions resolve significant organizational problems that address a strategic change in the efforts of the organization, like switching to online course offerings, targeting a completely new student constituency, and so on.

What Is the Evaluator's Role?

After determining the purpose of the evaluation, evaluators should determine their role in casting judgments. Stake (1967) discussed three types of educational evaluations—descriptive, judgmental, or descriptive and judgmental—each requiring evaluators to assume a different role. When evaluators describe educational activities, they conduct decision-facilitation evaluations, meaning they clarify evaluation criteria and collect and present evidence that describes the intended and actual program accomplishments. The program's worth is then ultimately determined by its administrators and decision-makers (Stake, 1967). When conducting judgmental evaluations, evaluators not only describe the program's evaluative criteria and associated evidence but also judge the level of its success (Stake, 1967). In doing this, they may compare the program against similar programs (relative comparisons) or external standards (absolute comparisons; Stake, 1967). In some cases, evaluators will be asked to make descriptive and judgmental decisions. Evaluators should work with stakeholders and program personnel to ensure that whatever judgmental criteria they use are clearly explicated prior to evaluation.

What Is the Developmental Stage of the Program?
Prior to the evaluation, skilled evaluators must also determine the developmental stage of the adult education program or project. Scriven (1967) first used the terms *formative* and *summative* evaluation to denote different types of evaluation used for different stages of developing curriculum material. Contemporary formative program evaluations are a review of the planning decisions during program development to help stakeholders better implement the program, whereas summative evaluations are a review of the effects of the program after implementation. Their aims can be quite different, so evaluators should work with stakeholders to clarify which type of evaluation approach should be used.

When to Evaluate a Program
Evaluators must also determine when to evaluate a program (i.e., before, during, or after implementation) to best meet the aims of the program's stakeholders. In the following section, we discuss the different aims and processes associated with each.

Evaluations prior to program implementation. Often stakeholders are interested in assessing conditions that exist prior to the establishment of the program (Stake, 1967). Commonly called *context evaluations* (Stufflebeam, 2003), these queries can illuminate future planning decisions (e.g., through assessment of needs, problems, and assets), assist program administrators in establishing priorities, guide the development of goals, and inform educational objectives. Context evaluations often determine the most suitable ends for the design or improvement of an instructional program.

Prior to program implementation, evaluators can also conduct input evaluations to focus on what resources are available and how these will affect future structuring decisions (Stufflebeam, 2003). Evaluators may investigate the program's competing strategies, work plans, and budgets. They may also assist decision makers in developing structuring decisions that specify the intended means (e.g., procedures, methods, resources, and designs) for achieving its intended ends. Input evaluations provide information about how program directors may effectively and appropriately employ resources to achieve their goals and objectives, ascertain the capabilities of the educational program, and identify potential strategies for achieving the goals and objectives that emerged in the context evaluation (Stufflebeam, 2003).

Evaluations during program implementation. When evaluators investigate programs during implementation, they commonly focus on transactions occurring in and outside the program (Stake, 1967). Stufflebeam (2003) refers to this as *process evaluation*, which monitors, documents, and assesses program activities as they occur. The information gathered here can assist stakeholders in identifying defects in the program's procedural design, for example, if an instructional plan was implemented as originally conceived (Stufflebeam, 2003).

End-of-program evaluations. Evaluations occurring at the end of programs (e.g., outcome evaluations, payoff evaluations, product evaluations, etc.) are the most prominent types of evaluations used in adult and continuing education. They generally seek to determine the degree to which an educational program's objectives were achieved. Evaluators tasked with end-of-program evaluation should collect data to determine the degree to which goals and objectives are aligned and have been achieved. These data can be used to assist decision-makers in deciding whether to continue, terminate, modify, or refocus an educational program. Additionally, end-of-program evaluations may be used to gather information to improve future programs and ensure the security of the instructional unit by demonstrating how it contributes to the parent organization's objectives and goals (Kirkpatrick, 1994; Stufflebeam, 2003). Finally, goal-oriented frameworks can be supplemented with "goal-free" approaches (Scriven, 1991, p. 56).

What to Focus on in an Evaluation

Besides determining when to evaluate a program, the skilled evaluator will target program elements for evaluation that are expressly of greatest interest to stakeholders. Although comprehensive program evaluations take into account all program elements, stakeholders often seek evaluations of classroom activities, learning transfer, community impact, or adherence to external criteria.

Classroom evaluations. Kirkpatrick (1994) has argued that evaluations in the classroom should assess learners' reactions to the program as well as the extent to which they learned. Reaction evaluations, or customer satisfaction measurements, determine the extent to which learners perceived a benefit from participation and react favorably (Kirkpatrick, 1994). Positive reactions are critical because dissatisfied learners will likely not return, and enrollment-driven programs will suffer (Kirkpatrick, 1994). Learning evaluations determine the extent to which participants experienced cognitive gains (knowledge), affective changes (attitudes), skill development (physical, social, and mental), and conative changes (aspiration; Kirkpatrick, 1994). A carefully designed classroom evaluation will inform stakeholders of the types and levels of classroom changes attributed to the program.

Transference of skills evaluations. Often of greater concern to stakeholders is what learners do outside the classroom because of classroom learning. Referred to as *transference of skills*, this phenomenon is assessed through evaluations of learners' behavior (Kirkpatrick, 1994). Kirkpatrick (1994) maintains that for behavioral change to occur, learners must (a) wish to change, (b) know what to do and how to do it, (c) work in the right climate, and (d) benefit from their changes. The first two requirements are accomplished by nurturing a positive attitude toward the desired change and by teaching the necessary knowledge and skills. The third condition occurs when participants' supervisors and colleagues welcome and support their new behaviors, and the fourth is accomplished by creating reward systems in organizations to encourage learners to apply what they have learned. Evaluators focused on transference of skills must be aware of these requirements to determine if barriers beyond the program's control are limiting its effectiveness.

Community and organizational impact evaluations. Some stakeholders are largely concerned with what happens to the community or organization because of the program. When evaluators focus on such results, they seek the extent to which learners' actions affect the short, medium, and long-term health of the community they belong to. This is often measured in terms of changes to production, quality, costs, accidents, sales, turnover, and profits and return on investment (Kirkpatrick, 1994). When external accountability is required, such changes often justify the existence of educational programs.

External criteria. Program reviews are often based on judgmental models emphasizing inputs. These models are frequently employed by programs and organizations seeking accreditation or approval for long-standing institutional programs. In these evaluations, the evaluator's judgment determines the success of the educational program (Popham, 1993). The accreditation model is such an example. Accreditation evaluations are typically done by associations or regulatory organizations that target long-standing educational organizations. Representatives of the accrediting or regulatory organization visit the program and, based on previously determined evaluative criteria, judge its operation. Criteria may specify the number, quality, and characteristics of staff, students, graduates, courses, resources, and student placements.

Skill Sets for Program Evaluation

In this section, we identify and describe the specific skills needed by evaluators of adult and continuing education programs to conduct descriptive, judgmental, summative, and comprehensive evaluations of fully implemented programs. We frame our discussion in terms of skills required to (a) identify program strengths and weaknesses, (b) determine whether a program is effective, and (c) provide information to take action and improve a program.

Identify Program Strengths and Weaknesses

Our approach to program evaluation assumes the program has been implemented and begins with identifying a program's strengths and weaknesses. Therefore, as discussed earlier, one must assess the context in which the program operates (Stufflebeam, 2003). Skilled evaluators are comfortable conducting detailed environmental scans to determine trends and key factors in an organization's environment that may affect its current or future success (McDavid, Huse, & Hawthorn, 2013). Such scans provide details of an organization's size, scope, service area, course offerings, rules, standards, policies, resources, aims, and relationships to other entities.

Simultaneously, the skilled evaluator must explain the program needs to be addressed. Needs are measurable gaps between what is and what should be (Altschuld & Kumar, 2010). Needs can be conceptualized at the level of the organization, the job (or role), or the people involved with or affected by the program (Robinson & Robinson, 1989). Consider, for instance, an adult basic education program that has a 25% completion rate, whereas for comparable programs the completion rate is 45%. Teachers in this program may spend an average of 10 days on certain math lessons designed to be delivered in 7 days. Additionally, program graduates may struggle with computer

Figure 3.1. Logic model for retired adults learning program.

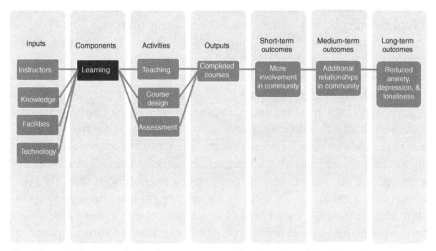

Note. The model focuses on the learning component (work unit) and its relationship to inputs, activities, outputs, short-term outcomes, medium-term outcomes, and long-term outcomes.

skills that local employers describe as requisite for employment. In each case, there is a gap between what is and what should be. When evaluators identify these gaps, they have identified program outcome weaknesses that may be targeted for improvement. In cases where evaluators find a small or no gap between what is and what should be, they have identified program strengths.

To identify factors contributing to a program's strengths and weaknesses, skilled evaluators must also illustrate the structure of a program through relationships among salient program variables. A common approach to doing this is *logic modeling*, which entails visual representations of the relationships among a program's resources, activities, and outcomes (Kellogg Foundation, 2004). More specifically, logic models contain a program's inputs (resources), components (work units), activities, outputs, short-term outcomes, medium-term outcomes, and long-term outcomes (McDavid et al., 2013). When these variables are linearly related, they depict the intended causal relationships in a program, beginning with input such as money, equipment, and people and ending with long-term impacts such as increased employment. In a single causal thread, an evaluator can name the resources that support a particular work unit, the activities performed by that unit, the countable outputs produced by those activities, and the results of those outputs. Figure 3.1 shows an evaluation of a program for promoting lifelong learning among retired adults.

Using a logic model, the evaluator notes that inputs such as instructors, knowledge, facilities, and technology are needed to support a cluster of activities called learning (component). This cluster comprises specific activities such as teaching, course design, and assessment. When these activities are completed, they lead to learners completing courses (output). When learners complete courses, they become more involved in their communities (short-term outcome); they form additional relationships in their communities (medium-term outcome); and they have lower rates of anxiety, depression, and loneliness (long-term outcome).

Although logic models allude to a program's intended results, evaluators must work with stakeholders to construct more specific, focused, and formalized statements of these intended results. These statements serve as overriding guides for logic models and help determine a program's strengths and weaknesses. Such statements, generally called *program objectives*, are often constructed simultaneously with, or in advance of, logic models. Program objectives describe the broad aims of a program, unlike instructional objectives, which refer to the learning aims of a course situated within a program. For example, McDavid et al.'s (2013) guidelines for program objectives suggest that objectives should be measurable and specify (a) the target population or domain, (b) the direction of the intended effects, (c) the magnitude of the effect, and (d) the time frame for achieving change. Using these guidelines, an evaluator may work with stakeholders to construct the following program objective: The lifelong learning program at Springfield Community Center will increase the percentage of the community's retired adults completing its courses by 10% over the next year. This specified program objective can then be related to the program's logic model to further identify potential strengths and weaknesses in its current operating structure.

Determine Whether a Program Is Effective

With a clear understanding of a program's strengths, weaknesses, salient variables, and intended aims, the skilled evaluator should work toward determining whether the program is effective. The effective means will vary by program and are largely dependent on what stakeholders see as the program's functions. Therefore, evaluators must work with stakeholders to codify program objectives before attempting to determine program effectiveness. In general, to determine a program's effectiveness, evaluators address one or more of the following questions: Are variables in the logic model causally related? Are these relationships weak or strong? Are the program's outputs correlated with its intended outcomes? And, most important, did the program cause the observed outcomes?

Skilled evaluators will narrow the scope of these general questions by constructing targeted questions relating to program variables, outputs, and outcomes and unambiguously specify variables and their hypothesized relationships. These questions can be conceptualized as guides for subsequent evaluation designs. Evaluators often categorize these questions as *descriptive*, *relationship*, or *comparison* (Creswell, 2012). A descriptive question may ask how often participants perform a particular action that is associated with a variable of interest (e.g., completing a course). A relationship question may ask how one variable (e.g., course completions) is related to another (e.g., community involvement). A comparison question may ask how one group (e.g., program participants) differs from another (e.g., non-program participants) on outcomes of interest (e.g., the number of relationships in the community).

After writing clear evaluation questions, the skilled evaluator will specify the corresponding research designs aimed at answering those questions. Effective evaluators are skilled at constructing qualitative and quantitative research designs and often use both to triangulate findings and increase confidence in their conclusions. A comprehensive review of research designs is beyond this chapter's scope, but some general methods and design considerations warrant mentioning. When used to help determine the effectiveness of a program, qualitative methods such as in-depth interviews, direct observations, and document analysis can reveal important context and detail (Office of Data, Analysis, Research & Evaluation, 2016). Such methods help illuminate participants' perceptions of key program variables, outputs, and outcomes and often reveal previously overlooked program strengths, weaknesses, and factors affecting program effectiveness.

When qualitative methods are used with quantitative designs, evaluators are best equipped to make causal inferences about a program and observed outcomes (Kirkpatrick, 1994). Quantitative designs can help evaluators determine if variables in the logic model are causally related or whether the program has caused certain observed outcomes. They can also help evaluators eliminate rival hypotheses that suggest something other than the program or a program variable of interest is causing the change. Four commonly used quantitative designs in evaluation work are experiments, quasi experiments, times-series designs, and single-case designs. Choosing one is often determined by the degree of access to data sources and the amount of resources available to the evaluator. For instance, experiments remain the gold standard for causal inference, but they are difficult to implement because they require the evaluator to assign participants randomly to different conditions before comparing these conditions on an outcome. Quasi experiments allow evaluators to compare intact groups along some outcome, but in doing so they provide the evaluator with less confidence to infer causality because they are unable to rule out other influential variables. Time-series designs require evaluators to either collect data on groups for an extended period or have access to previously collected data over an extended period. Generally, evaluators using time-series designs often use institutional (or organizational) data to organize a consecutive series of observations on an outcome before and after the introduction of the program (Shadish, Cook, & Campbell, 2002). If the data show statistically significant changes concurrent with the introduction of the program, the evaluator may infer a causal relationship. A similar design for causal inference is the single-case design, which also collects data over time but from a single person rather than a group or compound unit (Huitema, 2011). When used with proper controls, these designs "can provide a strong basis for establishing causal inference" (Kratochwill et al., 2010, p. 2), that is, evidence of program impact.

When using any of these quantitative designs, skilled evaluators must be able to identify threats to validity that may compromise their conclusions. Three types of validity are particularly important for the evaluator to understand. *Internal validity* refers to "the validity of inferences about whether the relationship between two variables is causal" (Shadish et al., 2002, p. 508). A threat to internal validity, then, is something other than a program or program variable that could have produced the same outcome. Skilled evaluators should work to identify these threats and implement design controls to minimize their impact. *Statistical conclusion validity* refers to the appropriateness of a chosen statistical method for making a causal inference. Often evaluators will work with statistical methods specialists in this area to suggest a method that works for a given design and to determine if the assumptions inherent in that method have been met. Last, *construct validity* refers to the degree to which what is measured is representative of what is sought. For example, an evaluator may be interested in social independence as an outcome for program participants. To measure this, the evaluator creates a questionnaire asking participants to report their level of social independence. Construct validity refers to whether this questionnaire actually measures the construct of interest, social independence. Skilled evaluators work to establish the validity of their measurements, or they select measures that have been previously validated. We discuss this concern later regarding questionnaire development.

After selecting a design and accounting for threats to validity, the evaluator must determine if the data needed to address the evaluation questions are readily available or require collecting. Readily available data often consist of information sources that have historically been of interest to the program (e.g., course enrollment, course offerings, learner retention, faculty attrition, test scores). In some cases, evaluators may find similar data in public databases for useful comparisons. An important consideration when using available test scores, particularly when making comparisons either with other programs or national averages, is understanding the distinction between norm-referenced tests and criterion-referenced tests. Norm-referenced tests determine how well the learner scores on a measure when compared to all learners in a predefined population. Examples of such measures are the Scholastic Aptitude Test, Graduate Record Exam, and reading-level tests. Criterion-referenced tests, in contrast, determine how well the learner scores on some measure when compared to a predetermined criterion. A widely used example of these measures is the General Educational Development test, which determines whether an adult learner passed or failed according to a predefined cutoff score based on the performance of high school graduates. When using norm-referenced measures, evaluators must understand that the program's learners may not represent the population they are being compared to. This is particularly critical when evaluating programs that target marginalized learners or those from historically underrepresented groups. Criterion-referenced test scores, however, are more easily compared across programs because the criteria used to measure each learner's performance are the same across settings.

When evaluation questions require the evaluator to collect new data, they have different considerations. These are particularly noteworthy when the evaluator uses questionnaires to measure learners' perceptions. Skilled evaluators must understand the basics of psychometric standards when using tools such as questionnaires and formalized instruments. We focus here on questionnaires because in our view they represent the sort of informal self-report measures that evaluators are likely to use in adult education settings. When evaluators use questionnaires, they frequently attempt to measure an underlying construct such as learner satisfaction, engagement, or understanding. Often evaluators will pose questions thought to target this construct and ask participants to respond along a numerical continuum called a Likert-type scale (e.g., 1 = *very dissatisfied*, 2 = *dissatisfied*, 3 = *neutral*, 4 = *satisfied*, 5 = *very satisfied*). Responses to questions are then summed, and each participant is given a score thought to illustrate their level of the underlying construct. To meaningfully interpret these scores, though, the evaluators must first illustrate their questionnaire's reliability and validity. *Reliability* refers to a measure's scoring consistency. If the same person completes the questionnaire on multiple occasions and scores similarly, the questionnaire may be said to be reliable. *Validity,* on the other hand, refers to whether a metric is actually measuring the underlying construct it is intended to measure. A questionnaire may be reliable but not valid. It may result in consistent scores from participants, but these scores may be representative of something other than the underlying construct of concern to the evaluator. Although a comprehensive overview of how to determine reliability and validity of a questionnaire is beyond the scope of this chapter, readers may consult Popham (1993).

Once evaluators have formalized their measures, they must determine how to go about collecting the required data. Usually evaluators will collect samples with the intention of generalizing findings to the larger program. However, they must be intentional about their sampling methods and understand which methods allow them to generalize most confidently. Three sampling methods are widely used in evaluations. *Random sampling* involves randomly selecting cases (i.e., participants or observations) from the program. With an adequate sample size, evaluators may generalize their sample findings to the larger program. *Purposeful sampling* involves the selection of cases based on characteristics that are salient to the evaluation question. A final sampling method, *convenience sampling*, involves sampling cases that are the most easily accessible to the evaluator. Although this method offers the fewest challenges for evaluators, it is the most likely to produce biased samples that are unable to be generalize either to the whole program or a subset of the program. A detailed discussion of survey sampling can be found in Rea and Parker (2014).

After data have been collected, the skilled evaluator must analyze those data using coding methods, descriptive statistics, and inferential statistics. Data collected through qualitative designs are generally analyzed using coding methods to develop categories in which elements of participant responses can be classified. Using these categories, the evaluator can then identify similarities, differences, and themes within and between participant responses. A review of coding methods is lengthy, so we refer the interested reader to other sources for more information (e.g., Miles, Huberman, & Saldaña, 2014; Saldaña, 2016).

Quantitative data are analyzed using descriptive and inferential statistics. Generally, evaluators will begin with descriptive statistics to summarize their data. They will calculate measures of central tendency (e.g., the mean, median, or mode) to show the center of the distribution of their observations (Field, 2013). For instance, an evaluator may collect the ages of a sample of learners and determine that the average learner's age in the sample is 34. Measures of dispersion (e.g., standard deviation, variance, or range) should be paired with measures of central tendency to show how widely spread values are within the sample distribution. There is a big difference, for instance, between 2 samples with average ages of 34 but standard deviations of 12 and 2. The sample data with a standard deviation of 12 are more widely distributed, meaning learners' ages differ considerably. Some are much younger than 34, some much older. The sample with a standard deviation of 2, however, shows that most learners' ages are very close to 34.

After calculating descriptive statistics, evaluators interested in making causal inferences must calculate inferential statistics. *Inferential statistics* are used to make inferences about how samples relate to populations. Evaluators often use these to compare samples along some outcome, or to compare outcomes measured at different times. A detailed discussion of these methods is also beyond the scope of this chapter, so we again refer interested readers to other sources (e.g., Field, 2013). There are, however, common tests with widespread uses in evaluation worth mentioning briefly here. A *t*-test, for instance, is an inferential statistical test used to compare the means of two samples. An analysis of variance (ANOVA) is a similar test used to compare three or more samples. A chi-square test of independence is used to determine if there is a relationship among different levels of two different categories (e.g., gender and letter grade). And regression is used to explain how different variables (e.g., a learner's age, income, gender, race or ethnicity) relate to an outcome of interest (e.g., number of classes attended). The skilled evaluator will minimally have a working knowledge of these tests and their applications. Most important, it is our position that common inferential statistics are best paired with other findings (e.g., descriptive statistics and those resulting from qualitative inquiry) and tests illustrating the magnitude of the phenomena of interest (e.g., effect sizes and confidence intervals). Statistically significant differences do not always mean practically significant differences. Given the practical nature of evaluators' work, the latter are generally most important.

Provide Information to Take Action to Improve Program

After determining the degree to which a program is effective or ineffective, the skilled evaluator must communicate the findings so that stakeholders can act to improve the program. Great care is needed to deliver this information in a clear and accessible manner and often requires evaluators to analyze and synthesize disparate data from varied sources, whittling down findings until substantive answers to evaluation questions emerge. Consider, for instance, an evaluator investigating whether program participants grow more engaged with their communities following participation relative to nonparticipants. This evaluator may have gathered extensive focus group, survey, and archival data, each contributing a different yet interrelated takeaway message that converges toward a general conclusion. An effective way of communicating such findings is to create succinct and unambiguous summary statements, such as "Program participants feel more connected to their communities than nonparticipants," "Program participants attend 25% more neighborhood watch meetings than nonparticipants," or "Program participants are 4 times more likely to volunteer for Big Brothers or Big Sisters programs." Together, these statements can be used to support the broader finding that the program increased community engagement. In some cases, it may be necessary to lead with statements suggesting a program's ineffectiveness in reaching targeted outcomes: "Program participants felt no more connected to their communities than nonparticipants."

Statements of key findings are often delivered along with succinct statements of the evaluation's purpose, questions, methods, and recommendations in a one- to five-page executive summary, which provides a way for stakeholders to familiarize themselves quickly with the evaluation's findings in advance of a longer report or presentation. Skilled evaluators should familiarize themselves with strategies for creating aesthetically pleasing executive summaries that incorporate graphics while not overwhelming readers with superfluous text (see Evergreen, 2017).

Stakeholder groups will generally require a formal presentation of evaluation findings that expands on the executive summary and commonly includes a formal report detailing the evaluator's biography, the program's history, aims of the evaluation, methodologies used, the results obtained, and recommendations for change. To convey this information effectively, evaluators will need to develop a communication plan. A well-crafted communication plan provides details on the time, place, and duration of the presentation, as well as the medium (e.g., PowerPoint, Prezi) and activities for helping stakeholders make meaning of content. Simple and accurate graphs are often the best way to present complex quantitative data (Field, 2013), whereas visual tools such as word clouds, concept maps, and Venn diagrams can be used to illustrate qualitative findings. With all presentation materials, careful attention to graphics, color, and content arrangement is warranted.

When developing a communication plan, evaluators should look for ways to involve stakeholders and create opportunities for dialogue. Evaluators should schedule time to discuss how findings confirm or disconfirm stakeholder beliefs. They should incorporate activities that encourage stakeholders to ask questions and share their own interpretations of findings. When discussing the project's implications, evaluators should encourage stakeholders to specify what they see as key implications that have been overlooked. Such activities will often strengthen buy-in and expand the reach of the evaluation by identifying implications with particular interest and relevancy to stakeholders.

In addition to planning for a discussion of implications, a communication plan must include time to work with stakeholders to develop an action plan. When stakeholders are engaged in the process of developing action plans, they see evaluation results as more beneficial to their programs (Gilliam et al., 2002). Action plans should specify what determinate actions stakeholders can use to improve their program. Skilled evaluators will begin this process by offering suggestions while allowing stakeholders to ultimately determine those actions that are most feasible, given available resources and the urgency for change. Evaluators should facilitate this discussion so that stakeholders arrive at potential actions that are observable, informed by evaluation findings, and aligned with program outcomes. Skilled evaluators will also work with stakeholders to establish time frames for implementation and dates for periodic reviews of the program's progress. Arrangements are often made so that evaluators can continue working with the program to evaluate subsequent implementation efforts.

Conclusion

Adult and continuing education programs are typically constrained by funding sources and other stakeholders to produce results that can be tied to program implementation. In this chapter, we provide insight into the influential evaluation models and approaches that have shaped our understanding of evaluation processes and identified the essential skill sets adult educators should possess to fully implement program evaluations.

References

Altschuld, J., & Kumar, D. D. (2010). *Needs assessment: An overview* (Vol. 1). Thousand Oaks, CA: Sage.

Creswell, J. W. (2012). *Educational research: Planning, conducting, and evaluating quantitative and qualitative research* (4th ed.). Upper Saddle River, NJ: Pearson.

Evergreen, S. (2017). Evaluation executive summaries & reports. Retrieved from http://stephanieevergreen.com/evaluation-executive-summaries-reports/

Field, A. (2013). *Discovering statistics using IBM SPSS statistics* (4th ed.). Thousand Oaks, CA: Sage.

Gilliam, A., Davis, D., Barrington, T., Lacson, R., Uhl, G., & Phoenix, U. (2002). The value of engaging stakeholders in planning and implementing evaluations. *AIDS Education and Prevention, 14*(3_supplement), 5–17.

Huitema, B. E. (2011). *The analysis of covariance and alternatives: Statistical methods for experiments, quasi-experiments, and single-case studies* (2nd ed.). New York, NY: Wiley.

Kirkpatrick, D. L. (1994). *Evaluating training programs: The four levels.* San Francisco, CA: Berrett-Koehler.

Kratochwill, T. R., Hitchcock, J., Horner, R. H., Levin, J. R., Odom, S. L., Rindskopf, D. M., & Shadish, W. R. (2010). Single-case designs technical documentation. Retrieved from https://ies.ed.gov/ncee/wwc/Document/229

McDavid, J. C., Huse, I., & Hawthorn, L. R. L. (2013). *Program evaluation and performance measurement: An introduction to practice* (2nd ed.). Thousand Oaks, CA: Sage.

McNicol, S. (2005). The importance of evaluation and evidence-based skills to improving service delivery. *Library and Information Research*, *29*(93), 26–34.

Miles, M. G., Huberman, A. M., & Saldaña, J. (2014). *Qualitative data analysis: A methods sourcebook* (3rd ed.). Thousand Oaks, CA: Sage.

Office of Data, Analysis, Research & Evaluation. (2016). Qualitative research methods in program evaluation: Considerations for federal staff. Retrieved from https://www.acf.hhs.gov/sites/default/files/acyf/qualitative_research_methods_in_program_evaluation.pdf

Popham, W. J. (1993). *Educational evaluation*. Boston, MA: Allyn & Bacon.

Rea, L. M., & Parker, R. A. (2014). *Designing and conducting survey research: A comprehensive guide* (4th ed.). San Francisco, CA: Jossey-Bass.

Robinson, D. G., & Robinson, J. C. (1989). *Training for impact: How to link training to business needs and measure the results*. San Francisco, CA: Jossey-Bass.

Saldaña, J. (2016). *Coding manual for qualitative researchers* (3rd ed.). Thousand Oaks, CA: Sage.

Scriven, M. (1967). The methodology of evaluation. In R. E. Stake (Ed.), *Curriculum evaluation* (Vol. 1, pp. 39–55). Chicago, IL: Rand McNally.

Scriven, M. (1991). Prose and cons about goal-free evaluation. *Evaluation Practice*, *12*(1), 55–63.

Shadish, W. R., Cook, T. D., & Campbell, D. T. (2002). *Experimental and quasi-experimental designs for generalized causal inference*. Belmont, CA: Wadsworth Cengage.

Stake, R. E. (1967). The countenance of educational evaluation. *Teachers College Record*, *68*, 523–540.

Stufflebeam, D. L. (2003). The CIPP model for evaluation. In T. Kellaghan & D. L. Stufflebeam (Eds.), *International handbook of educational evaluation* (pp. 31–62). Boston, MA: Kluwer.

W. K. Kellogg Foundation. (2004). W. K. Kellogg Foundation: Logic model development guide. Retrieved from https://www.bttop.org/sites/default/files/public/W.K.%20Kellogg%20LogicModel.pdf

PART TWO

ASSESSMENT AND EVALUATION PRACTICES IN SPECIFIC AREAS OF ADULT EDUCATION PRACTICE

4

THE GORDIAN KNOT OF ADULT BASIC EDUCATION ASSESSMENT

Untangling the Multiple Audiences and Purposes

Alisa Belzer and Daphne Greenberg

The complexity of describing assessment in adult basic education (ABE) is demonstrated by the fact that we need to begin this chapter by defining the term and that we even had to debate what term we should use. Federal legislation uses the term *adult education* (Workforce Innovation and Opportunity Act, 2014), but this term can include many other fields of study that have nothing to do with basic literacy, numeracy, and language skill development, making it too general. *Adult literacy education*, the term frequently used by researchers, seems too narrow. In fact, there is no routinely used term with a common definition among researchers, practitioners, and policymakers to describe the field of practice that includes adult literacy, numeracy, and language education serving all levels of need and skill from those at the most basic beginning levels to those preparing to make the transition to college. This demonstrates that any term used must cover a broad swath of adult learners and content. For the purpose of this chapter, the term *adult basic education* is meant to cover the broadest array of literacy, numeracy, and language skill levels, interests, and needs.

The complication of terminology is an indicator of the complexity of describing assessment for the field of adult basic education. Given the broad range of stakeholders, purposes, needs, and interests, it is not surprising there is a wide range of assessment tools and approaches. For this chapter, we attempt to comprehensively describe ABE assessment by identifying four broad categories of its use: accountability, diagnosis, credentialing, and population study. Our somewhat nonparallel descriptions of each type of assessment reflect their divergent purposes and audiences. However, the descriptions are followed by a discussion of themes that focus on the opportunities and obstacles those in the field face when it comes to assessment. It is important to note that no assessment used in ABE measures whether individuals are literate or numerate; rather they all describe a continuum of reading, writing, numeracy, and language skills and practices. Understanding these constructs as complex and multifaceted, shaped by context, purpose, task, and text rather than absolutes that can be defined as present or absent, however, signals a need for complex tools and frameworks for measuring and describing them. We conclude with the assertion that no silver bullet assessment is possible or desirable for the field. Therefore, those in the field should have at their disposal a wide range of assessments that effectively reflect learner needs, promote effective practices, and demonstrate impacts to funders. Currently, this type of assessment does not exist.

Assessment for Accountability

Assessment for accountability draws on standardized tests, which can maximize efficiency in terms of time and cost while providing the required data. Its purpose is primarily to demonstrate program effectiveness and a return on investment to funders. In the case of federal ABE funding, this takes place through the National Reporting System for Adult Education (Workforce Innovation and Opportunity Act, 2014). The aggregated assessment data are passed from local programs to the state agency that receives and distributes federal dollars, the state agency passes the data to the U.S. Department of Education, and the U.S. Department of Education summarizes these data and reports on outcomes to the U.S. Congress as required by law. Although assessment for accountability purposes can be used to inform instruction, this is not its primary purpose, and its potential to do so has been critiqued (Guskey, 2003; Supovitz, 2009).

Assessment for accountability for federal funding was first mandated by the Workforce Investment Act (1998) and updated in 2014 when the reauthorization legislation known as the Workforce Innovation and Opportunity Act was passed; both statutes have provided federal funds to support ABE programs. Prior to these statutes, the main focus related to program accountability had been on program inputs. For example, the previous federal statute (National Literacy Act, 1991) had tasked each state with developing "indicators of program quality" (p. 348) as a measure to evaluate program effectiveness. The language that replaced this in the Workforce Investment Act signaled a distinct shift toward accountability for the purpose of demonstrating a return on the investment of federal funds in local ABE programs. This was indicated in Section 212 of Workforce Investment Act Title II that states that a

> comprehensive performance accountability system . . . [should] assess the effectiveness of eligible agencies in achieving continuous improvement of adult education and literacy activities funded under this subtitle, in order to optimize the return on investment of Federal funds in adult education and literacy activities. (p. 999)

This gave rise to the National Reporting System for Adult Education, which was sustained by Title II of the Workforce Innovation and Opportunity Act.

Although states were required to report outcomes following National Reporting System regulations, they were left on their own to design their own assessment and data management systems to be in compliance with this mandate. Regardless of how they chose to do this, all states were required to report outcomes in terms of standardized definitions of gains in reading, writing, numeracy, language learning, academic credential attainment, and employment. States had the option to add additional performance indicators, but few did. States also had the option to use already approved standardized assessments or develop alternatives that would meet "accepted psychometric standards for valid and reliable assessment, including empirically validated scoring rubrics with high inter-rater reliability" (U.S. Department of Education, 2016, p. 60); only Massachusetts did so. This requirement effectively limited burgeoning efforts to develop qualitative assessments of adult literacy that had sprung up during the 1990s that aimed to describe literacy and learning through a sociocultural lens. Advocates of these alternative assessments argued that they could more authentically reflect literacy practices (numeracy was not generally included in these earlier assessments) and more thoroughly describe readers' literacy strengths and challenges (Fingeret, 1992). They could, therefore, provide complex layered and detailed descriptions of growth and improvement and inform learner-centered instruction. Although some program directors eagerly adopted these alternative assessments, others did not have a formal assessment procedure in place, or they used a mishmash of standardized and home-grown assessments; the new accountability system placed so much emphasis on standardized measurement that most program administrators experienced a significant transition in their assessment procedures. As a result, a small handful of assessment instruments are currently being used, including Tests of Adult Basic Education (TABE; 2019), Comprehensive Adult Student Assessment System (CASAS; 2019), and one of several versions of the Basic English Skills Test (BEST;

2019), to report educational gains to the state agency that distributes federal funds.

The most common assessment instrument used for accountability purposes is the TABE, which is a multiple-choice test designed to assess current education levels (as described by grade level equivalents) in reading, mathematics, and language skills. The reading part of the assessment provides short decontextualized passages and informational graphs and tables on a range of topics that are followed by questions designed to assess literal and interpretive comprehension. Various forms of the BEST are the most common assessments used to measure growth among English language learners. BEST Plus measures speaking and listening skills in a face-to-face interview format, and BEST Literacy measures reading and writing skills in a paper-and-pencil format and asks learners to read and write about authentic situations (Center for Applied Linguistics, 2019). The CASAS test is used almost as widely as the TABE and BEST tests; it can be used to assess skills of all learners (including English language learners) at all levels. Like the BEST, it asks learners to complete tasks related to authentic life skills and competencies.

The logic of assessment for accountability is that it will encourage programs to focus on instructional excellence as a way to boost learner achievement. However, this assumes there is a consensus on what counts as achievement in a field with many views of literacy. Until recently, critics have argued that valued outcomes are contested or ambiguous (Merrifield, 1998). However, the Workforce Innovation and Opportunity Act (2014) has now codified a nearly single-minded emphasis on employability (Belzer, 2017; Jacobson, 2016; Pickard, 2016). Nonetheless, the fact that the accountability system was put in place without aligning it with efforts to improve instruction (St. Clair & Belzer, 2007) detracts from its potential to improve achievement.

Additionally, although the accountability system has now been in place for many years, technical challenges to its usefulness still exist including a lack of standardized teacher preparation requirements, which may detract from effective test administration, interpretation, and reporting, and problematic aspects of the assessment instruments (Kruidenier, 2002). For example, the TABE's practice of reporting results in terms of grade-level equivalents has been questioned repeatedly because the grade level notion is based on children's development and has not been validated with adults (e.g., Perin, 1991). It also creates a false assumption that adults are like children by reducing literacy and numeracy assets to a narrow measure of competence that fails to reflect the ways adults develop knowledge and skills and masks the importance of social networks of support that strengthen their ability to carry out tasks that may not be captured in standardized assessment settings (Fingeret, 1983). Without careful interpretation and communication with adult learners, testing can reinforce prior negative schooling experiences and convey false messages about what literacy is. The necessity of fast and efficient testing for accountability purposes means that programs will often lack the capacity to carry out more detailed and informative assessment strategies. Additionally, the fact that states generally meet their federal accountability goals suggests that performance standards may be too low to drive improved outcomes (Condelli, 2007). Research investments in assessments for accountability that have the potential to address these issues have not been made.

Assessment for Diagnosis

Reading, writing, and math involve many underlying skills. Diagnostic assessments can be used to detect and address reasons for difficulties by providing a detailed view of the extent to which individuals are able to deploy these skills. Although standardized tests such as the TABE are often used for accountability purposes and to place students in appropriately leveled classes, these types of tests do not provide enough detailed information about individuals' skill profiles of strengths and difficulties to truly inform instruction and enable teachers to tailor instruction to students' needs. It is beyond the scope of this chapter to detail all the different skills involved in reading, writing, and math, but here we discuss a few of these skills to provide a taste for their complexity and the challenges of assessing them in adults.

Expert reading requires the deployment of many skills. When a reader does this effectively, the end goal of reading—comprehension—is accomplished (Mehta, Foorman, Branum-Martin, & Taylor, 2005). The skills needed include the ability to read known words and sentences quickly and accurately and the ability to decode new and unfamiliar words. Vocabulary is also important in terms of breadth (how many words one understands) and depth (how many meanings for a word one knows). An important vocabulary building block is an understanding of morphemes (the smallest meaningful part of a word; e.g., *ed* and *ing*). Finally, background knowledge and reasoning skills are also critical for comprehension.

Compared to reading, much less is known about the underlying processes of writing. However, we do know that various underlying processes and components are necessary for expert writing, beyond the basic writing skills of handwriting, typing, spelling, punctuation, and sentence construction (National Research Council, 2012). For example, writers need to know how to write different text structures for diverse audiences and purposes, and they need to know how to plan, compose, and revise their writing in an iterative fashion.

ABE research often neglects numeracy. However, similar to reading and writing, many underlying skills are needed for math proficiency such as accurate and fluent number sense, calculation basics, relational understanding, numerical operations, probability, measurement, patterns, mathematical reasoning, conceptual understanding, and problem-solving (Ginsburg, Manly, & Schmitt, 2006).

Motivation is critical to learning in general (Pintrich, 2003). In reading, writing, and numeracy, one's sense of self-efficacy, sense of importance, and sense of self-worth all inform how hard an individual will persist with a difficult reading, writing, or numeracy task; how often they will want to read, write, or engage in numeracy when not required to practice and further develop the skill; and whether an individual will ask for help when needed.

Assessment for diagnosis is used to increase understanding of what learners know and can do regarding these underlying components and to improve instruction; however, there are many challenges to implementing this assessment approach. Tests that assess skills at low levels are not typically normed on adults (Greenberg, 2013), and those that are do not typically include large samples of adults who are struggling with basic skills. The tests that measure basic skill levels for beginning readers assume typical child development; it is unclear whether this is a correct assumption for adults who struggle with basic skills. This assumption is brought particularly into question by the fact that adults perform differently from children on component skill diagnostic assessments (Greenberg, Pae, Morris, Calhoon, & Nanda, 2009). This makes test administration and interpretation of results problematic. Diagnostic tests are also expensive and often require specialized training for proper administration and interpretation, making their use unrealistic in most ABE programs. Another challenge is that diagnostic tests are typically not sensitive enough to capture the amount of progress acquired in the short time most adults spend attending literacy programs (Coben & Alkema, 2017).

An additional issue with diagnostic assessment in ABE is that these types of tests characteristically focus on academic tasks. Sociocultural aspects of reading, writing, and math are generally ignored. It is important to understand when, how, where, and why adults engage in reading, writing, and numeracy activities outside the classroom and to acknowledge that the context can have a significant impact on an adult's ability to use these skills. For example, as Coben and Alkema (2017) state, "The development of . . . proficiency over time is strongly associated with adults' engagement in . . . practices" (p. 23).

Finally, although adults are reading, writing, and doing numeracy tasks using digital tools, research has not yet focused deeply on the underlying skills needed in a digital learning environment, and no diagnostic instruments have been designed to support instruction in this context. For example, using hyperlinks to read information on different Web pages, searching the Internet, revising written text, and using Microsoft Excel formulas, all require different types of skills than traditional paper-and-pencil literacy tasks.

Assessment for Credentialing

Assessment in ABE has also evolved to provide a high school equivalency credential as an alternative for those who leave school before graduating. The prospect of earning a high school credential is one of the most important motivators for many adults who participate in ABE because it can serve as a gateway to employment and higher education. Until recently, getting an alternative high school credential meant just one option: passing the General Educational Development (GED™; McLendon, 2017) test.[1]

The GED™ test was developed in the 1940s for returning GIs who experienced interrupted schooling when entering the military and were unwilling or unable to return to high school to graduate after the war. The GI Bill (Servicemen's Readjustment Act, 1944) enabled returning soldiers to enroll, tuition free, in postsecondary educational institutions, but many first needed a high school diploma. The GED™ provided an easily accessible alternative; it assessed test takers for learning, competence, and proficiency equivalent to what students learn in high school (Rose, 2006).

The GED™ has been revised four times since its inception reflecting changes in high school curricula, the rise of content standards, and the role of the high school credential in the labor market. The 2014 revision was designed to be aligned with the Common Core State Standards Initiative (2019), a set of content standards adopted by most states that specify what twenty-first-century students need to know and be able to do to succeed in college and career settings. This fully computerized GED™ has four parts (language arts, math, science, and social studies) and requires test takers to draw on prior knowledge, uses a constructed-item response model, has extended-item response tasks, and expands from the traditional multiple-choice type questions to several new item formats including fill in the blank, drag and drop, and multiple select. Overall, this latest version of the GED™ focuses more on higher order thinking skills (GED™ Testing Service, 2019) and more rigorous academic content (McLendon, 2017).

When the latest round of GED™ revisions was announced, many in the field were distressed by its computer-based-only administration, increased cost, and its change in organizational affiliation that transformed it from a nonprofit to a for-profit entity. Consequently, the door opened to alternatives, and two other high school equivalency credentialing tests were developed, the Test Assessing Secondary Completion (TASC; Data Recognition

Corporation, 2019) and the High School Equivalency Test (HiSet; Educational Testing Service, 2019). (For a chart comparing the tests, see Zinth, 2015). The tests take between 7 hours and 5 minutes and 7 hours and 45 minutes; the HiSet is the shortest, and the TASC is the longest. The 2 new tests, which are about the same in length, have phased-in alignment with Common Core. The TASC and the HiSet have the same 5 subject area tests as the earlier version of the GED™ (reading, writing, math, science, and social studies) and are available in paper and pencil and computerized versions. Research has not been conducted to analyze the differences in measurement constructs among the tests or their predictive power to assess success in the workplace or higher education.

With 3 options available, states have made a variety of decisions about which high school equivalency tests to offer. At the time this chapter was written, the GED™ was offered in 42 states, the HiSet in 22, and the TASC in 16, but these statistics seem to be in flux. Additionally, several states offer adult diploma programs that recognize experience (assessments of prior learning) and demonstrations of proficiency (competency-based assessments) through platforms such as portfolios or that enable adults to accrue credits in nontraditional adult high school settings. In states where more than 1 assessment is available, the cost is generally the same for any test, but in some cases the GED™ is more expensive. Factors that affect state decision-making regarding which tests to offer include cost, infrastructure requirements, staff capacity to administer the test, and test takers' ability to complete the computer-based GED™.

Effectively assessing for the higher order thinking and academic skills needed to succeed in the modern workplace or in higher education is a substantial challenge (McLendon, 2017). Which route is the best predictor of success, and what is best for learners is yet to be determined. As of 2019, the state agencies that administer high school equivalency programs, instructors, and learners are all struggling to adjust to the significant changes in high school credentialing. This is complicated by the fact that the jury is still out on the value of a high school equivalency credential. Many researchers have critiqued the value of the GED™ (which potentially could be extended to all high school equivalency exams). For example, Tyler's (n.d.) summary of research noted that although having a GED™ increases employment probability and earnings, it does not do so at a rate sufficient to create a pathway out of poverty. Other critiques include that it is too narrowly focused on cognitive skills while neglecting to measure other abilities needed to succeed in the workplace (Brinkley-Etzkorn & Ishitani, 2016).

Assessment for Population Studies

Population studies, such as the Program for the International Assessment of Adult Competencies (PIAAC) are intended to provide countries with "information on how well prepared their adult residents [are] to participate fully in the civic, cultural, and economic life of their countries" (Stein, 2017, p. 30). The first national assessment was conducted in 1985. By adding a sample of adults between the ages of 21 and 25 to the National Assessment of Educational Progress (referred to as the Young Adult Literacy Assessment), the U.S. Department of Education began to collect data on U.S. adults' abilities to perform simulated common adult literacy–related daily tasks. Following passage of the Adult Education Amendments (1988), which required the U.S. Department of Education to report on the literacy skills of U.S. adults, the National Adult Literacy Survey (NALS; National Center for Education Statistics, n.d.) was administered to a much larger adult sample and specifically tested skills related to prose (continuous texts, e.g., newspaper articles), documents (noncontinuous texts, e.g., applications), and quantitative literacy, such as balancing a checkbook (Kirsch, Jungeblut, Jenkins, & Kolstad, 2002). Administration of the NALS was critical in showing that a large-scale survey of U.S. adults was possible (National Center for Education Statistics, n.d).

The same domains tested in the NALS were used in the International Adult Literacy Survey (IALS; Kirsch, 2001). Between 1994 and 1998, the United States participated in this international survey, which was the first large-scale international effort to assess the skills of adults ages 16 to 65. This was later followed by NAAL (Kutner et al., 2007). It included the same NALS prose, document, and quantitative literacy domains, but NAAL also included an assessment of health literacy (the capability to use literacy in health care) as well as fluency (the ability to quickly and accurately identify words, nonsense words, numbers and read passages). In addition, very low-skilled adults were administered the Adult Literacy Supplemental Assessment, which assessed the ability to identify items in pictures and objects such as food boxes instead of prose, document, and quantitative literacy (Baer, Kutner, & Sabatini, 2009).

In 2003 the United States participated in the international Adult Literacy and Lifeskills Survey (Murray, Clermont, & Binkley, 2005). Similar to previous national and international surveys, this one measured prose and document literacy. Instead of assessing quantitative literacy, it assessed numeracy, which focused on a wider and more assorted range of mathematical tasks than the National Assessment of Adult Literacy's quantitative literacy domain assessment items, and it piloted a new domain called analytical reasoning and problem-solving.

In 2011–2012 the United States participated in the international PIAAC survey (Organisation for Economic Cooperation and Development, 2013), which replaced the need for a national assessment. The PIAAC differed from the previous population studies by including a measurement of problem-solving in technology-rich environments. In addition, although previous surveys were completed using paper and pencil, the PIAAC was administered on laptop computers, allowing adaptability as participants received items targeted to their specific literacy levels. There is also a paper-and-pencil test measuring reading component skills for adults who were not familiar with or comfortable using a computer.

Although assessment items have changed over time, a common thread through all the different population studies is that they are designed to focus on the application of skills in authentic adult contexts rather than a narrow set of academic skills. The tasks presented to participants are simulations designed to look like authentic, adult daily-life tasks. This approach, grounded in a sociocultural perspective on literacy, is designed to authentically capture complex and overlapping literacy and numeracy skills rather than measure the ability to complete isolated skills in an artificial context. For example, an item could focus on a parent addressing a child's fever. In day-to-day life, this would engage diverse literacy, numeracy, and problem-solving tasks in a technologically rich environment including taking the child's temperature and reading the thermometer, comparing the result to a chart on the Internet, reading recommended steps to take, and then acting on those steps. However, a weakness in this approach to assessment is that difficulties with task completion related to a given situation do not explain the reasons behind the parent's struggles (e.g., does the parent have difficulty reading the thermometer, searching the Internet, reading or understanding the words in the recommendations?). Therefore, although population studies can paint a broad-brush picture of a population's skills, they do not have specific instructional implications at the local program and classroom levels.

Additionally, St. Clair (2012) has joined others in critiquing population studies on the grounds that, despite efforts to be authentic, they measure the ability to draw meaning from and answer specific kinds of questions about only certain kinds of texts. Finally, neither the extent to which population studies can be used to measure improvement in study countries over time, nor the common claim that designates a minimum literacy level (e.g., Level 3 in the PIAAC) as what is needed to function in contemporary society have been tested. And yet, findings from population studies have been used to influence national ABE policy in some countries (Hamilton & Hillier, 2007; Tett, 2014).

Discussion

Clearly there is a diverse range of assessment purposes, audiences, and instruments employed in ABE. In trying to identify common opportunities and challenges that can be described across this wide array, we note that assessment efficiencies are often introduced at the cost of detail and that this trade shapes practice in ways that are not always in the best interest of learners and learning. Although we have not explicitly tracked an assessment evolution in this chapter, we have implied that assessment has become more systematic and standardized (Gibb, 2015) and more aimed at quantitative measurement of change at the reading component, individual reader, reading program, or societal levels. Gibb (2015) observes that this has been done with the intention of holding educators and systems accountable for an appropriate return on public investment, to advance broad social aims, and to compete globally for a skilled workforce. This has led to a policy discourse of numbers (Gibb, 2015), which can lead practice away from learner-centered, humanistic approaches and toward standardization driven by externally determined goals and outcome measures.

Muth, Sturtevant, and Pannozzo (2017) suggest that assessment choices need not be either-or, but rather that assessment should be conducted through two lenses: postpositivist and social constructivist. The former draws on quantitative, scientifically valid tests that measure reading component skills and can serve a diagnostic purpose, and the latter typically employs qualitative interviews employing open-ended, learner-centered questions about literacy beliefs and practices, which can responsively inform and match instruction to learners' needs and interests. Although Gibb (2015) sees assessment as heading toward standardization, he asserts that both approaches can inform instruction in meaningful ways. However, his suggestion seems to exist outside the realm of accountability, and using and interpreting two approaches is generally unrealistically time-consuming and expensive outside a research context.

No assessment seems to serve more than one purpose (at least not well), but assessment needs are multidimensional. As a result, the expense and time required to conduct assessments that respond to the needs of instructors, learners, and funders are significant; justifiable; and, unfortunately, hard to come by. To dig deep into the many factors that can and should inform instruction requires more time, money, and training than most programs, practitioners, and learners have available. However, even with adequate resources, current assessment tools are relatively blunt instruments. At best, they draw on literacy and numeracy tasks that approximate actual day-to-day practices but seem always to have a ring of artificiality in measuring constructs that are thoroughly shaped by social contexts. At worst, they separate literacy and numeracy tasks from any authentic context in which these skills are practiced in adult life. This puts their results into question as a way to describe learning growth, inform instruction, evaluate the success of programs, or enable comparisons of cognitive skill from one country to another. Assessment practices are shaped by diverse purposes, audiences, and conceptions of literacy, and scarce resources in the field have unfortunately failed to encourage the development of more sophisticated and complex tools. In day-to-day practice, the goal is often to do the most possible for the least amount of money, in the least amount of time, and still meet accountability expectations. Although tools designed to serve these purposes may yield actionable information, the information gleaned often provides a limited view of learners, learning, and skills. Unfortunately, the easier and quicker an assessment is to administer, the less it tends to tell us.

As we indicated earlier, no silver bullet assessment is possible or even necessarily desirable for ABE. Learners, practitioners, and policymakers have different assessment requirements and therefore need a menu of assessments that can show change over time in a wide variety of contexts using a wide variety of measures and descriptions. Given scarce resources and a relatively untrained workforce, administration and interpretation must be neither too expensive nor too difficult. Currently, such a menu of assessments does not exist. Efforts toward creation of this kind of menu are well worth the effort and will help make ABE much more learner centered and descriptions of learning and return on investment far more authentic and valid. However, the value added in authenticity and descriptiveness likely will always be counterbalanced by the policymaker's and the funder's needs for relatively easy to interpret and easy to compare data to inform decisions about return on investment. This tension demonstrates well the competing interests and the Gordian knot that is ABE assessment. Although fast and inexpensive may meet the policymaker's and funder's needs, those of us in the field need to resist falling back on this option to the exclusion of more descriptive and informative assessment, because it neither reflects the reality of how adults interact with literacy, numeracy, and language, nor can it adequately inform instruction.

Note

1. We and this work are not affiliated with or endorsed by American Council on Education (ACE) or GED™ Testing Service. Any reference to GED™ in this chapter is not intended to imply an affiliation with, or sponsorship by, ACE, GED™ Testing Service, or any other entity authorized to provide GED™ branded goods or services.

References

Adult Education Amendments. (1988). Pub. L. No. 100-297, 100th Cong.

Baer, J., Kutner, M., & Sabatini, J. (2009). Basic reading skills and the literacy of America's least literate adults: Results from the 2003 National Assessment of Adult Literacy (NAAL) Supplemental Studies (NCES 2009-481). Retrieved from https://nces.ed.gov/pubs2009/2009481.pdf

Basic English Skills Test. (2019). Assessing adult English language proficiency in the United States. Retrieved from http://wwwcal.org/aea

Belzer, A. (2017). Focusing or narrowing: Trade-offs in the development of adult basic education, 1991–2015. In A. Belzer (Ed.), *Turning points: Recent trends in adult basic literacy, numeracy, and language education* (pp. 11–18). San Francisco, CA: Jossey-Bass.

Brinkley-Etzkorn, K., & Ishitani, T. T. (2016). Computer-based GED testing: Implications for students, programs, and practitioners. *Journal of Research and Practice for Adult Literacy, Secondary, and Basic Education*, 5(1), 28–48.

Center for Applied Linguistics. (2019). Adult English Assessment. Retrieved from http://www.cal.org/areas-of-impact/testing-assessment/adult-english-assessment

Coben, D., & Alkema, A. (2017). The case for measuring adults' numeracy practices. *Journal of research and practice for adult literacy, secondary, and basic education*, 6(1), 20–32.

Common Core State Standards Initiative. (2019). Preparing America's students for success. Retrieved from http://www.corestandards.org/

Comprehensive Adult Student Assessment Systems. (2019). Product overviews: Assessments. Retrieved from https://www.casas.org/product-overviews/assessments

Condelli, L. (2007). Accountability and program quality: The third wave. In A. Belzer (Ed.), *Toward defining and improving quality in adult basic education* (pp. 11–31). Mahwah, NJ: Erlbaum.

Data Recognition Corporation. (2019). Test assessing secondary completion. Retrieved from https://tasctest.com

Educational Testing Service. (2019). ETS-HiSET: The future starts here. Retrieved from https://hiset.ets.org

Fingeret, A. (1983). Social network: A new perspective on independence and illiterate adults. *Adult Education Quarterly*, 33(3), 133–146.

Fingeret, H. A. (1992). Adult literacy education: Current and future directions: An update. Retrieved from ERIC database. (ED3543910).

GED™ Testing Service. (2019). Retrieved from https://ged.com/

Gibb, T. (2015). Literacy and language education: The quantification of learning. *New Directions for Adult and Continuing Education*, 2015(146), 53–63.

Ginsburg, L., Manly, M., & Schmitt, M. J. (2006). *The components of numeracy*. Cambridge, MA: National Center for Study of Adult Learning and Literacy.

Greenberg, D. (2013). Adult literacy: The state of the field. *Perspectives on Language and Literacy*, 39, 9–11.

Greenberg, D., Pae, H. K., Morris, R. D., Calhoon, M. B., & Nanda, A. O. (2009). Measuring adult literacy students' reading skills using the Gray Oral Reading Test. *Annals of Dyslexia, 59*(2), 133–149.

Guskey, T. R. (2003). How classroom assessments improve learning. *Educational Leadership, 60*(5), 6–11.

Hamilton, M., & Hillier, Y. (2007). Deliberative policy analysis: Adult literacy assessment and the politics of change. *Journal of Education Policy, 22*(5), 573–594.

Jacobson, E. (2016). Workforce development rhetoric and the realities of 21st century capitalism. *Literacy and Numeracy Studies, 24*(1), 3–22.

Kirsch, I. (2001). *The International Adult Literacy Survey (IALS): Understanding what was measured.* Retrieved from https://www.ets.org/Media/Research/pdf/RR-01-25-Kirsch.pdf

Kirsch, I., Jungeblut, A., Jenkins, L., & Kolstad, A. (2002). *Adult literacy in America: A first look at the findings of the National Adult Literacy Survey.* Retrieved from https://nces.ed.gov/pubs93/93275.pdf

Kruidenier, J. (2002). *Literacy assessment in adult basic education.* San Francisco, CA: Jossey-Bass.

Kutner, M., Greenberg, E., Jin, Y., Boyle, B., Hsu, Y., & Dunleavy, E. (2007). *Literacy in everyday life: Results from the 2003 National Assessment of Adult Literacy.* (NCES 2007-480). Washington, DC: National Center for Education Statistics.

McLendon, L. (2017). High school equivalency assessment and recognition in the United States: An eyewitness account. In A. Belzer (Ed.), *Turning points: Recent trends in adult literacy, numeracy, and language education* (pp. 41–49). San Francisco, CA: Jossey-Bass.

Mehta, P. D., Foorman, B. R., Branum-Martin, L., & Taylor, W. P. (2005). Literacy as a unidimensional multilevel construct: Validation, sources of influence, and implications in a longitudinal study in grades 1 to 4. *Scientific Studies of Reading, 9*(2), 85–116.

Merrifield, J. (1998). *Contested ground: Performance accountability in adult basic education.* (NCSALL Reports No. 1). Cambridge, MA: National Center for the Study of Adult Learning and Literacy.

Murray, T. S., Clermont, Y., & Binkley, M. (2005). *Measuring adult literacy and life skills: New frameworks for assessment.* Ottawa, Ontario, Canada: Statistics Canada.

Muth, B., Sturtevant, E., & Pannozzo, G. (2017). Performance and beliefs: Two assessments of literacy learners in prison, part II. *Journal of Correctional Education, 68*(2), 62–81.

National Center for Education Statistics. (n.d). History of international adult literacy assessment. Retrieved from https://nces.ed.gov/surveys/piaac/history.asp

National Literacy Act. (1991). Pub. L. No. 102-73, 105 Stat. 33.

National Research Council. (2012). *Improving adult literacy instruction: Options for practice and research.* Washington, DC: National Academies Press.

Organisation for Economic Cooperation and Development. (2013). *OECD skills outlook.* Retrieved from https://doi.org/10.1787/9789264204256-en

Perin, D. (1991). Test scores and adult literacy instruction: Relationship of reading test scores to three types of literacy instruction in a worker education program. *Language and Literacy Spectrum, 1*, 46–51.

Pickard, A. (2016). WIOA: Implications for low-scoring adult learners. *Journal of Research and Practice for Adult Literacy, Secondary, and Basic Education, 5*(2), 50–55.

Pintrich, P. R. (2003). A motivational science perspective on the role of student motivation in learning and teaching contexts. *Journal of Educational Psychology, 95*(4), 667–686.

Rose, A. D. (2006, June). Adult education, assessment and the beginnings of the GED. Paper presented at the Adult Education Research Conference, Minneapolis, MN.

Servicemen's Readjustment Act. (1944). Pub. L. 346. 30 U.S.C. 268.

St. Clair, R. (2012). The limits of levels: Understanding the International Adult Literacy Surveys (IALS). *International Review of Education, 58*(6), 759–776.

St. Clair, R., & Belzer, A. (2007). The challenges of consistency: National systems for assessment and accountability in adult literacy education. In P. Campbell (Ed.), *Measures of success: Assessment and accountability in adult basic education* (pp. 159–206). Edmonton, Alberta, Canada: Grassroots Press.

Stein, S. G. (2017). PIAAC: Focusing adult learning on building adult competence. *New Directions for Adult and Continuing Education, 2017*(155), 29–40.

Supovitz, J. (2009). Can high stakes testing leverage educational improvement? Prospects from the last decade of testing and accountability reform. *Journal of Educational Change, 10*(2–3), 211–227.

Tests of Adult Basic Education. (2019). TABE and TASC test for adult assessment. Retrieved from https://tabetest.com/

Tett, L. (2014). Comparative performance measures, globalising strategies and literacy policy in Scotland. *Globalisation, Societies and Education, 12*(1), 127–142.

Tyler, J. H. (n.d.). So you want a GED? Estimating the impact of the GED on the earnings of dropouts who seek the credential. Retrieved from http://www.ncsall.net/fileadmin/resources/research/brief_tyler2.pdf

U.S. Department of Education. (2016). *Implementation guidelines: Measures and methods for the National Reporting System for Adult Education.* Washington, DC: Author.

Workforce Innovation and Opportunity Act. (2014). Pub. L. No 113–128.

Workforce Investment Act. (1998). Pub. L. No. 105-220, 112 Stat. 93.

Zinth, J. (2015). *GED, HiSET and TASC Test: A comparison of high school equivalency assessments.* Denver, CO: Education Commission of the States.

5

ASSESSMENT AND EVALUATION PRACTICES IN ARMY MILITARY EDUCATION

Royce Ann Collins, COL Ryan Welch, and James B. Martin

T he U.S. military's mission in today's world is to act as a deterrent to aggression and protect the nation as needed. The preparation for such tasks requires dedication and accountability from individuals and organizations. From an education and training standpoint, this accountability often comes in the form of assessment of individual learning and the evaluation of unit training against stated outcomes. Although the entire military establishment focuses on this type of accountability, this chapter discusses the Army's efforts in assessment and evaluation in the education and training arena.

For decades, the Army's culture has included evaluations after every exercise or simulation. These after action reviews (AAR) have created a culture in which Army leaders regularly examine how well individuals and organizations perform in reaching identified objectives. These AARs might occur in a classroom or in the desert sands of California or in a far-off country, but they are always critical examinations of the performance being judged. Just as the best higher learning institutions around the world use assessments of student learning to improve their degree programs or the institution's performance in some other way, the Army takes data from these AARs and uses them as a form of continuous improvement in education and training.

The commitment to quality and assessment is embedded in the Army's culture. This chapter begins with an examination of assessment in professional military education (PME) and its role in the Army's preparation. The

Command and General Staff College is used as a case study to illustrate the assessment-embedded culture. In the second half of this chapter, the transfer of learning assessment is illustrated by focusing on the Army's system to evaluate organizational performance using training evaluations at the National Training Center (NTC) in California. Although some administrators and faculty of colleges and universities may view assessment of learning as an add-on to responsibilities, the military illustrates how a culture of quality can be embedded as part of the fabric.

Background

During a presentation at the 2011 annual conference of the Higher Learning Commission, Mark Milliron, at that time deputy director for postsecondary improvement of U.S. programs at the Bill & Melinda Gates Foundation, proposed an end-to-end learning pathway that would take students from high school through community college or a four-year college and into the workforce with a progressive and sequential approach to education in America (Kem, LeBoeuf, & Martin, 2016). This pathway makes sense but is very difficult to put into practice with the diverse educational entities that would have to come together to implement it. In contrast, the Army controls the learning pathway in PME for soldiers of every rank from the time they enter the service until they depart or retire. The U.S. Army Training and Doctrine Command (2011) learning concept identified the military's version of the end-to-end learning pathway as the career-long learning continuum and laid out the progression of formal military education throughout a career and the educational model that is used to accomplish this education. A key component of the Army learning concept was the need for improved assessments throughout PME and that the importance of these appropriate assessments "cannot be overstated" (p. 22).

The Army maintains accountability for its assessment system through its quality assurance program, which accredits the various schools in the Army on a recurring basis. Regional accreditors, which require the same level of assessment as they do for other higher education institutions, also accredit a few schools in the Army's system. Two of the Army's schools, the Army War College and the Army Command and General Staff College (CGSC) are also accredited by the Joint Staff, which performs as a programmatic accreditor for awarding a specific level of Joint educational credit. All these accreditations have the same requirements for assessment and evaluation that are common in civilian educational institutions.

The reality for Army education and training is that the Army's mission is to prepare soldiers and organizations to perform in high-stakes environments.

The learning occurring during these activities is essential in meeting the Army's mission and saving lives in potential combat situations. The assessments used provide a grade to a student but are also critical in determining the quality of education and training and the assessments' effectiveness in preparing those being assessed for their real-world missions.

Assessment and Evaluation in PME

PME refers to rank-specific education that occurs throughout a soldier's career. Much of the time spent in professional development in the early years of a career is very focused on training courses. These courses aid in developing specific skills, technical and more general, that are critical to the performance of tasks for more junior soldiers and leaders

The most commonly cited training course is basic rifle marksmanship in which soldiers are taught to effectively fire their assigned weapons and are then assessed through a straightforward test involving their competency at hitting the targets presented. Not all soldiers will master this skill quickly, and the Army has simulation training systems that allow soldiers to practice over and over again, without expending ammunition that is only available in restricted amounts, until they are able to meet the required standards. Similar training assessments occur in other areas, such as welding or driving a truck. The assessments of student learning here are the actual performance of welding tasks or the observed performance of a truck driver on the open road.

Assessing tasks that cannot truly be performed in a training environment are very challenging. In a combat situation, a medic treats soldiers who are actually wounded, but how is such a task effectively assessed? The Medical Education Training Center in San Antonio trains combat medics for all military services. To train and assess soldiers in the most realistic of scenarios, the center has created physical scenarios with battlefield sounds and smells where medics are assessed on closed-circuit cameras on their performance in caring for wounds on high-tech mannequins. Each training scenario is observed from a control room, from which the operator can manipulate the mannequin so it appears to talk and respond to questions. Working in a mock village with dim lighting, loud noises, and the smells of a combat environment rather than the sterile environment of a classroom provides the best opportunity to assess how well a student would perform in a real situation. The assessment of specific tasks through application-type examinations provides the Army with direct assessment data on these institutional training programs. How well students perform and data derived from their testing can be directed into the curriculum planning process to create continuous improvement in the school's program of instruction.

It is more difficult to assess the career-long learning continuum of an educationally focused PME. When a soldier begins to assume formal leadership roles, the Army's professional development opportunities provide education in outcomes that include critical thinking, leadership, and planning activities. The enlisted soldiers have a progressive and sequential process of PME that is referred to as the Noncommissioned Officer Education System (NCOES) and provides institutional education and training at each progressive rank. As soldiers progress to a leadership position as a sergeant, they attend the Basic Leaders Course and receives formal instruction to attain specific learning outcomes. This type of formal instruction continues at each new rank and responsibility level as long as the soldier remains in the Army. Noncommissioned officers who attain the upper reaches of the enlisted ranks must attend the Sergeants Major Course (SMC), a formal 10-month period of education that prepares them to perform as the senior enlisted soldier and advise the commanders of large military organizations.

For officers, the PME world begins when they are a captain and continues as long as they stay in service. The most senior course in PME that all officers must attend is the Command and General Staff Officers Course (CGSOC), taught at the CGSC. Officers must complete this portion of PME through resident or nonresident education regardless of their specialty or whether they are in the active, reserve, or National Guard components. The resident campus is just outside the Kansas City metropolitan area. Nonresident education takes place at satellite campuses across the United States and in a distance learning program. As this is the most senior school attended by all officers, the CGSC is used as a case study in assessment and evaluation in the PME portion of the Army's system.

Command and General Staff College

The CGSC is the largest school of its kind in the Army and the Department of Defense. It is accredited by three different entities: the Higher Learning Commission (regional), the Joint Staff (programmatic), and the Army (specialized). These accreditations provide the formal impetus for a vibrant assessment and evaluation program at the college, along with the informal impetus of continuous academic improvement (Joint Institutional Research and Evaluation Coordinating Committee, 2017; Suskie, 2015; Walvoord, 2010). As one would expect from a higher education institution, the CGSC has a formal system of direct and indirect assessment measures that feed into a formal system (Accountable Instructional System) of curriculum change and improvement (Walvoord, 2010). The CGSC faculty are not unlike faculty at any other accredited college or university and are experts in military operations with all the appropriate academic credentials.

Instead of dividing the academic experience into semesters, the CGSOC spans a 10-month period. The curriculum is a collection of academic experiences or themes. The CGSOC creates discrete pieces of content grouped into 2 major components. For clarity in this chapter, each of the smaller unique instructional components in the two major components are referred to as a course. They may vary in length and differ from semester courses. Although most students just complete the 10-month CGSOC graduate-level academic program, some students opt to work for additional credit hours to complete a master of military arts and sciences.

Army leaders, Joint regulations, and the CGSC faculty identify the learning outcomes for the CGSOC, which has established a culture of evidence (Suskie, 2015), and institutional-level learning outcomes. The CGSOC has nested its learning outcomes in these college-level outcomes. The faculty creates and presents the curriculum organized to meet these outcomes and plays the central role in the creation of appropriate assessment instruments to determine student performance and provide data for curricular improvement. Curriculum maps are created to demonstrate where each learning outcome is assessed.

The college has a Quality Assurance Office that provides assistance and advice to the faculty and leadership on assessment and evaluation issues, along with direct support of the academic program by maintaining the college's survey system. This formal system is used to collect indirect assessment data from students, faculty, graduates, and supervisors in the field. All the indirect assessment data are funneled into the college's curricular change system (Accountable Instructional System) and are used in the program review process.

The formal survey system in support of the CGSOC takes many forms of indirect assessments. Indirect assessments include student, faculty, and graduate surveys. At the end of every course in the program, half the student body (about 600 students at the resident campus) is surveyed to gather information on the curriculum to determine how well the content aided students in meeting the learning outcomes and how well the faculty facilitated the learning process. This holds true for the resident campus and the satellite campuses where the curriculum is taught in various parts of the United States. These surveys are also provided to the students studying the program in a distance-learning modality so that comparisons can be made between the different modalities of the courses to ensure appropriate quality across the board. Faculty surveys occur less often but are taken at the end of major component breaks or after specific major events. Graduates are surveyed at the end of the first year after their graduation to investigate how well they believe the CGSOC prepared them for their next Army assignment and then again at five years from graduation, after they have moved to higher levels of leadership and responsibility. Finally, the leadership of major Army formations (equivalent to supervisors of graduates) are surveyed to gather their opinions on how well graduates of the CGSOC perform in the environment of the operational Army.

In addition to these indirect measures of student performance, where the college asks for student, faculty, and supervisor opinions on how well the curriculum and faculty aided in meeting the learning outcomes, the college focuses on direct measures of assessment to see how well students can demonstrate mastery of the learning outcomes. The CGSC faculty use many of the same techniques found in assessment across the United States and focus most of their effort on formative assessments that aid students in their learning and development. The major difference between CGSC and the civilian sector is the number of faculty who are available to assess and mentor students. Based on guidance from the Joint Chiefs of Staff (2015), the college maintains a 4:1 student-to-faculty ratio at all times. This concentration of faculty allows a relatively rapid turnaround of assessment instruments and the ability to mentor students to improve their performance. It also allows regular advising and mentoring designed to improve performance when students return to the operational Army. In comparison with other graduate schools, the large faculty and the fact that this is the student's full-time job for a year partially result in the high retention rate this graduate-level program achieves.

Along with the various formative assessments common to other graduate programs, the CGSOC uses a large summative assessment to determine student mastery of learning outcomes. At the end of the initial instructional period (about 15 weeks), students are required to take an online written comprehensive examination of the content up to that point. Because a number of the Joint outcomes in the officer's PME policy require preparation at the knowledge level of Bloom's (1956) taxonomy, this method works to determine the level of student learning on these Joint outcomes. Following this written portion, about 2,200 students at the resident and satellite campuses participate in individual oral comprehensive examinations to assess their mastery of learning outcomes after the Common Core portion of the CGSOC. This dual-format examination provides the college with summative evidence to determin the efficacy of the curriculum and the teaching methodology.

The comprehensive examination is explained to the students on their first formal day of classes. They are given a number of sample questions and a guarantee that some of them will be on the comprehensive examination. An apparent result of this transparency has been an increased level of student participation in the day-to-day classroom presentations as reported by the teaching faculty. Cohort groups of 16 students that stay together throughout the year-long program are free to prepare together in any way they desire. Interviews with students revealed a wide variety of methods they used to practice. In one group, for example, each student chose a sample oral comprehensive examination question each week and provided an answer prior to the comprehensive exams.

After the completion of the first major component of the CGSOC, the content and the management of the curriculum change significantly. Rather than focusing on communication, Joint topics, critical thinking, national security affairs, and other broad topics, students concentrate on execution of the planning process they will use in the operational Army. The CGSC has 96 identical classrooms that house the cohort groups mentioned earlier. All these classrooms are equipped with the appropriate technology to replicate the digital systems used in the operational Army at the brigade (about 4,000 personnel) and division (about 16,000 personnel) levels. Students spend the next few months planning military operations at different echelons and in different geographical environments, replicating the work they will have to perform after their graduation from the CGSOC. They are assessed by their performance in individual assignments, which are part of the larger planning process, and by their performance as members of different planning cells as the cohort works its way through different scenarios. Each course closes with an application-based exercise, often using digital simulations, in which students perform the same planning and decision-making tasks they will be doing in their next duty assignments. This assessment of activities and the use of digital systems that are consistent with what the operational Army uses are deliberately intended to produce the increased transfer of learning.

Students at the CGSOC may opt to complete the master of military arts and sciences during the course of their study. This requires additional electives, writing and defending a thesis on an appropriate topic, and completing a final oral comprehensive examination on the entire year-long curriculum. As part of the college's Quality Initiative Project for the Higher Learning Commission (2019), the faculty used the comprehensive examination of master's students as a means to examine the quality of students' critical thinking without creating a new and possibly intrusive assessment. Although the college has a large faculty, additional assessments take time away from other critical efforts. With the quality initiative, faculty used a digital audio recorder to capture each of the oral comprehensive examinations over a 2-year period. These recordings were archived and then examined by a volunteer group of faculty members using a rubric focused on assessing the level of critical thinking displayed by the students while they responded to questions during the oral examination. The initial faculty panel focused on the content of the questions and on awarding the students an appropriate grade for their examination, whereas the second panel looked beyond each student and sought to identify trends in the 200-plus recordings they examined. The results provided the college with data on how well students met the college-level learning outcome concerning critical thinking without creating a requirement for another assessment to gather the data.

This ongoing attempt to use assessments for multiple purposes is being tested using the comprehensive examinations with the entire class. Although the examination was intended to broadly examine the students' ability to demonstrate mastery in the entirety of the first major portion of the course, it is now being used to measure specifically the students' ability to meet the Joint learning outcomes required for programmatic accreditation. Up to this point, the college has shown its Joint accreditors where each outcome is taught and has pointed to the formative assessments in the various courses to demonstrate assessment of student learning. Moving to use assessments for multiple purposes, the comprehensive examination questions are now being nested in the appropriate joint learning outcomes, and the performance data for each learning outcome are being examined to determine more specific direct assessment results.

Colleges and universities have long used portfolios as a way to assess student improvement over time. The CGSOC has required students to keep portfolios for a number of years simply as a way to catalog their performance and not in an organized fashion for assessment. A pilot under way at the CGSOC and SMC, mentioned earlier, is using electronic portfolios to catalog student artifacts and then gather the students' reflections on their improvement.

Furthermore, the SMC is examining using the portfolio in a unique way. The faculty of the SMC have chosen to look beyond the resident SMC and are formulating plans to examine the use of electronic portfolios across the breadth of the NCOES. Rather than examining the growth of a student in a single course in the NCOES, in this program soldiers begin an electronic portfolio at the Basic Leaders Course and then maintain that portfolio throughout their progressive education at each successive level. Portfolios like these allow the Army to assess a soldier's development and growth over a 15- to 20-year time span and provide interim assessments to improve professional performance.

Assessment data's most important role is providing appropriate data to improve program performance and quality (Suskie, 2015). Just as the Army's culture has driven AARs across the spectrum of training, the college has a formal process to gather evidence for academically focused AARs and program reviews. Within 45 days of completion of a course in the CGSOC, the assessment data are analyzed and provided to the military and academic leadership of the school and college. Faculty who have responsibility for the course present their analysis and recommend methods for improvement during its next iteration. The leadership provides guidance, and the faculty embarks on making the design changes to the curriculum. Once these design changes have taken shape, they are presented to the leadership, and the formal course redesign is undertaken. The course is taught again in its next iteration, direct and indirect assessment data are gathered, and the analysis cycle begins again as part of the curricular change model. This system brings together assessment data gathered each year and provides reliable information to improve the course the following year. As the Army requires instructors of every course to conduct a full program review every three years, the Quality Assurance Office works with the course directors to gather a wider range of information during each program review, which is then fed into the AIS to provide even more granularity of data for the faculty to analyze and use to improve the education process at the college.

The education of adults in our society is largely focused on the provision of knowledge and skills that will aid them in their working environment (Kazis et al., 2007). Because of this requirement, the ability to create improved transfer of learning from the classroom to the workplace is highly valued. The knowledge and skills taught in the NCOES or at the CGSC are not really about providing grades or degrees, although both are present in some respect. The real purpose of PME is to create adaptive and innovative soldiers and leaders who can perform their necessary functions in support of the Army's larger mission. Performing well in important leadership or staff positions matters more for officers who graduate from the CGSOC than their class standing. The real test of PME and its assessment system is whether the training and education make a more successful soldier after leaving school.

The Army measures success once students return to their units by evaluating how well units can perform their assigned mission tasks under combat conditions. This is a direct assessment type of situation where a unit commander is not asked if they believe the unit is ready, but instead students are sent to a training center to be placed in a stressful, real-life situation and evaluated on the unit's performance. The second half of this chapter focuses on the Army's system to evaluate organizational performance using training evaluations at the NTC in California as an example of direct assessment.

Assessment and Evaluation in High-Intensity Military Training

The number one priority for the Army is readiness—the ultimate account-ability metric for the Army's stakeholders, namely, the American public and its military leadership. Readiness is measured across the force by a unit's ability to collectively accomplish its Mission Essential Task List (METL) as prescribed by the Department of the Army (Headquarters, U.S. Department of the Army, 2016a). In each METL task, subtasks, conditions, and standards for execution of each ensure that units are able to plan, prepare, and execute missions across the range of military conflict. Although these tasks and conditions are prescriptive in nature, warfare is a human endeavor. Chaos and confusion are hallmarks of armed conflict requiring soldiers and leadership to think and adjust on their feet and "prevail in conditions of ambiguity" (NTC, 2017, para. 2).

The NTC is located about 150 miles northeast of Los Angeles. As the Army's preeminent training center, the mission of the NTC is to conduct "tough, realistic, Unified Land Operations with Unified Action Partners to prepare Brigade Combat Teams and other units for Combat" (NTC, 2017, para. 1). Covering a landmass roughly the size of Rhode Island, the NTC provides the optimal environment to execute and assess land and air forces in their combat missions. Although no amount of simulation or replication can accurately create a wartime environment, the NTC's high-tech tracking systems, virtual and constructive training environments, and engagement replication provide a second-to-none training opportunity for units.

The NTC places units in an austere desert environment where they are subjected to an independently thinking, highly capable opposing force that presents Army forces with multiple dilemmas to test units' mastery of fundamental skills and identify gaps in training and expertise. The harsh environment of the Mojave Desert not only stresses a unit's ability to demonstrate proficiency in its METL tasks but also exercises leaders' critical thinking skills, application of military doctrinal principles, and decision-making ability in an ambiguous, free-flowing combat scenario.

The NTC hosts rotational units from all over the United States. Army brigades are continually assessed from their arrival date, after deploying by sea, air, and rail. Units are received, staged to move to their initial objectives, moved onward, and integrated into multiple scenarios against a hybrid threat enemy that uses criminal, insurgent, special operations, and conventional forces. Operations Group staff (the organization tasked to evaluate unit performance) at the NTC ensure that mission-essential subtasks are evaluated and units given a snapshot assessment of training proficiency at the end of their 21-day iteration to identify areas for immediate improvement.

While conducting training rotations, daily assessments are generated by a highly professional, experienced, and hand-selected staff of observer-coach-trainers (OCTs) certified by the NTC command to objectively grade actions against training and evaluation outlines. The outlines serve as a baseline rubric or checklist to account for performance measures contained in field manuals, training circulars, and Army training doctrine (Headquarters, U.S. Department of the Army, 2016a). The OCTs shadow key leaders and small units throughout their operations at the NTC 24 hours a day. Observer coach teams observe, conduct internal reviews of procedure, and analyze the unit's understanding of what the enemy is doing versus what the actual enemy array on the ground is doing through tracking, instrumentation, and firsthand observations.

After every major action or milestone, OCTs conduct sit-down AARs with the units being evaluated to ensure that observations, limited evaluations, and assessments are conveyed; responsibility to remedy deficiencies is assigned; and best practices are emphasized to build on success in future iterations. Although the training and evaluation outlines and task proficiency standards provide objective criteria for determining task proficiency, assessments allow leaders to take into account the subjective nature of training. Leaders' assessments combine their professional observations with other information to develop an overall assessment of the unit's ability to accomplish its mission (Headquarters, U.S. Department of the Army, 2016a).

It is important to understand that the definition of *assessment* in military doctrine differs from the commonly understood higher education definition focused on assessment of student learning. The governing publication for military operational doctrine that focuses on training defines *assessment* as "determination of the progress toward accomplishing a task, creating a condition, or achieving an objective" (Headquarters, U.S. Department of the Army, 2016b, p. Glossary-2). Assessment precedes and then occurs during the other activities of the operations process. Assessment involves deliberately comparing forecasted outcomes with actual events to determine the overall effectiveness of force employment. More specifically, assessment helps the commander determine progress toward achieving the desired end state, attaining objectives, and performing tasks (Headquarters, U.S. Department of the Army, 2017b).

The objective of these assessments is to shape future training opportunities at the units' home station and ultimately improve performance for future evaluations. Figure 5.1 shows the Army's training and evaluation process.

The NTC bears responsibility for only the first three steps of the training and evaluation process shown in Figure 5.1. AARs are developed with the military's assessment methodology in mind—determine what the end

Figure 5.1.   Process of evaluating and assessing training proficiency and reporting training.

Note. From *Leader's Guide to Objective Assessment of Training Proficiency*, p. 6, by Department of Army, 2017, https://home.army.mil/irwin/index.php/about/mission

state of the operation was meant to be, what was planned, what actually happened, and then compare outcomes with the desired end state. This enables units to see themselves organizationally and understand gaps in procedure, leadership deficiencies, or doctrinal misunderstanding. More important, it reinforces what the unit did well to ensure best practices are not lost for future training iterations or employment in actual combat situations.

Observations and lessons learned do not reside solely with the evaluated unit. Trends and findings are collated, and specific unit information is redacted then sent to Army professional publications, the Center for Army Lessons Learned databases, and Army branch-specific (e.g., aviation, infantry, etc.) publications to enhance total force awareness of trends and best practices in operating procedures.

Although evaluations merit some weight in the Army's determination of readiness, the amount of time units spend at Fort Irwin does not allow a comprehensive evaluation of all soldier or unit tasks and capability. The size, scope, and duration of the exercise simply does not allow units to perform all their mandated METL tasks. Per the Army's training doctrine, the ultimate responsibility for evaluation of training resides with the command (Headquarters, U.S. Department of the Army, 2016a). The NTC provides assessments to frame future evaluations for the command to make the final determination of readiness.

Through the provision of AARs and OCT feedback, the NTC is able to objectively assess the unit's ability to apply doctrine, implement operational processes, and exercise appropriate leadership that influences decisions on resourcing and training forces for optimum readiness. Continuous feedback, coaching, and external assessment of unit performance and tactics to defeat a highly capable enemy are the most beneficial aspects of what the NTC does: "We do not teach units WHAT to think, we teach them HOW to think" (National Training Center, 2017, para. 2).

Globalization and the resulting velocity of instability in the world demand a level of readiness to project power and operate in ambiguous environments never before seen in the history of military operations. The ebb and flow of recruitment, new technology, training opportunities, and budgetary constraints all directly influence the readiness of military units today. Accurate assessment of capability and unit readiness directly informs funding for manning, training, and equipment at the highest echelons of the military.

The chief of staff of the Army, General Mark A. Milley, stated "Readiness is the Army's top priority" (Association of the United States Army, 2016, para. 1); "there is no other number one. . . . We train like we fight, and our Army must always be ready to fight tonight"; he added, "Readiness deters our most dangerous threats" (para. 6).

From humanitarian relief to homeland security to counterinsurgency to more traditional combat operations across the globe, the military's approach to assessment and evaluation of unit performance has to be sufficiently broad, adaptable, and flexible to apply to all Army specialties across the spectrum of conflict. Without the ability to see itself in terms of planning, preparation, and execution of operations, the Army cannot remain the best-trained and ready force in the world—the quality U.S. taxpayers expect from its military. Training and military education assessment remains a critical capability that the Army must continually reinforce to maximize the benefit of Army training events and ensure that units remain relevant and ready for any potential conflict.

Conclusion

This chapter is intended to show how a culture of evidence is demonstrated by the many ways the Army assesses training, education, and performance (Suskie, 2015). The military is committed to quality on many levels. Once again, the military training and education systems make a significant contribution to higher education through examples of embedded accountability and quality assessment: "The goal of assessment is information-based decision making" (Walvoord, 2010, p. 4). This case study of the Army's training, PME, and the ultimate transfer of learning to the workplace demonstrates how data are used to inform curricular changes, incorporate faculty and leadership in the decision-making process, and improve student performance. It is an example of how assessment can be systematic and institutionalized over a lifelong learning continuum. Perhaps adult education programs and higher education institutions may gain some insights on how to make continuous improvement a higher priority.

References

Association of the United States Army. (2016). Milley: Readiness wins, deters wars. Retrieved from https://www.ausa.org/news/milley-readiness-wins-deters-wars

Bloom, B. S. (1956). *Taxonomy of educational objectives: The classification of educational goals by a committee of college and university examiners.* New York, NY: McKay.

Headquarters, U.S. Department of the Army. (2016a). *Fm 7-0: Train to WIN in a complex world.* Retrieved from https://armypubs.army.mil/epubs/DR_pubs/DR_a/pdf/web/ARN9860_FM%207-0%20FINAL%20WEB.pdf

Headquarters, U.S. Department of the Army. (2016b). Army doctrinal reference publication. *(ADRP) 3.0, Operations.* Washington, DC: Author. Retrieved from https://usacac.army.mil/sites/default/files/publications/ADRP 3-0 OPERATIONS 11NOV16.pdf

Headquarters, U.S. Department of the Army. (2017a). *Leader's guide to objective assessment of training proficiency.* Washington, DC: U.S. Army.

Headquarters, U.S. Department of the Army. (2017b). Operations, field manual 3-0. Retrieved from https://armypubs.army.mil/epubs/DR_pubs/DR_a/pdf/web/ARN6687_FM%203-0%20C1%20Inc%20FINAL%20WEB.pdf

Higher Learning Commission. (2019). Quality initiative. Retrieved from https://www.hlcommission.org/Accreditation/quality-initiative.html

Joint Chiefs of Staff. (2015). *CJCSI 1800.01E: Officer professional military education policy.* Retrieved from http://www.jcs.mil/Library/CJCS-Instructions

Joint Institutional Research and Evaluation Coordinating Committee. (2017). *Student learning and program effectiveness during a program of accreditation for joint education.* Washington, DC: U.S. Army.

Kazis, R., Callahan, A., Davidson, C., McLeod, A., Bosworth, B., Choitz, V., & Hoops, J. (2007). *Adult learners in higher education: Barriers to success and strategies to improve results.* [Employment and Training Administration Occasional Paper No. 2007-03]. Washington, DC: U.S. Department of Labor, Employment and Training Administration.

Kem, J. S., LeBoeuf, E. J., & Martin, J. B. (2016). Answering the hottest question in army education: What is army university? *The Journal of Continuing Higher Education, 64*(3), 139–143.

National Training Center. (2017). Fort Irwin, California. Retrieved from https://home.army.mil/irwin/index.php/about/mission

Suskie, L. (2015). *Five dimensions of quality: A common sense guide to accreditation and accountability.* San Francisco, CA: Jossey-Bass.

U.S. Army Training and Doctrine Command. (2011). *The U.S. Army learning concept for 2015.* Retrieved from https://sill-www.army.mil/DOTD/divisions/pdd/docs/Army%20Learning%20Model%202015.pdf

Walvoord, B. (2010). *Assessment clear and simple: A practical guide for institutions, departments, and general education* (2nd ed.). San Francisco, CA: Jossey-Bass.

6

ASSESSMENT AND EVALUATION IN CONTINUING PROFESSIONAL EDUCATION

Paul E. Mazmanian, Meagan W. Rawls, and J.K. Stringer

I n his treatise on the meaning of adult education, Lindeman (1926) examined relationships of life, learning, and occupation. "A fresh hope is astir," he said,

> From many quarters comes the call to a new kind of education with its initial assumption affirming that *education is life*—not merely preparation for an unknown kind of future living. Consequently all static concepts of education which relegate the learning process to the period of youth are abandoned. The whole of life is learning, therefore education can have no endings. . . . This new venture is called *adult education* not because it is confined to adults but because adulthood, maturity, defines its limits. (p. 6)

Lindeman said adult education demonstrated value to society and to the individual worker because,

> In this world of specialists every one will of necessity learn to do his work, and if education of any variety can assist in this and in the further end of helping the worker to see the meaning of his labor, it will be education of a high order. (p. 7)

It is sensible, in turn, that those who accept responsibility for the education of adults must become well versed and proficient in the methods of assessment to help learning and evaluation improve educational activities.

Although this chapter addresses assessment and evaluation in the broadly defined area of continuing professional education, many of our examples draw more particularly from the health professions, in part because that field represents our experience and also because health care is well represented in the literature of assessment and evaluation of continuing professional education. The foundations of adult education not only support but also influence our perspectives on continuing professional education. The ideals of self-direction, lifelong learning, and improvement drive the enterprise of assessment and evaluation in continuing professional education, and we describe professionals at their practical interface with curriculum and instruction and professional education and revisit the role of credentials as markers of competence. In this chapter we frame the education and work of professionals through professionalism and professionalization, and we recognize the evolving armamentarium of tests and measures for use by the individual practitioner and for implementation by the adult educator specializing in continuing professional education. We conclude with a brief discussion of portfolios, neuroimaging for more holistic assessment, and the development of big data for measuring and promoting program improvement.

Professions and Professionals: What Is a Profession?

More than 60 years ago, Cogan (1955) wrote, "To define 'profession' is to invite controversy" (p. 105). In his review of previous studies, Cogan said there is

> a rather extensive literature of definitions of profession . . . [with] . . . no general agreement on any "authoritative" statement. . . . So many advantages have accrued to [the] profession, so many claims to it are made by so many people, that the cutting edge of a definition—be it ever blunt—is almost sure to draw cries of protest from many aspirants to the title. (p. 105)

Later reviews of the literature tend to confirm Cogan's conclusion as they encourage additional debate to improve understandings of the influence of governmental policy, the economy, values, organization, knowledge, and expertise in the work and construction of professions (Cervero, 1988; Muzio & Ackroyd, 2005; Saks, 2012).

With no commonly held answer to the question of what constitutes a profession, three conceptual approaches have proven useful for interpreting the work of those who guide our businesses, manage and account for our money, settle our civil disputes, diagnose and treat our individual and community health needs, and protect our national interests through military defense (Cervero,

1988; Houle, 1980). The static approach requires professions to (a) involve intellectual operations, (b) derive their material from science, (c) involve definite and practical ends, (d) possess an educationally communicable technique, (e) tend to self-organization, and (f) be altruistic (Flexner, 1915). The process approach offers gradation; all occupations are seen as existing on a continuum of professionalization with several fundamental questions to enable a more detailed judgment of members' status. Questions may concern the degree to which providers control their practice, the extent to which the occupation is working toward its further refinement, or what members are doing to increase control of their practice. In contrast with the static and process approaches, the socioeconomic approach assumes there is no such thing as an ideal profession, and no criteria are necessary to define one. The word *profession* is ascribed in honor; it is a collective symbol, socially constructed and socially granted, suggesting that the members of a select line of work are highly valued by society (Cervero, 1988; Freidson, 1988). Fundamental philosophical differences extend into the practical and political realms where adult educators are supposed to help ensure the ongoing competence of professionals to meet individual, social, and institutional standards (Cervero & Wilson, 2001; Elias & Merriam, 2005). Different fields hold differing expectations of performance with various approaches to learning and assessment applied throughout professional education (Ericsson & Pool, 2016).

Professional Education

Figure 6.1 shows an emerging model of professional education, revised from Houle's (1980) classic model of professional education, with adjustments for

Figure 6.1.   An emerging model of professional education, including assessment and continuous certification of competence.

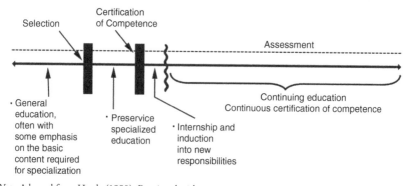

Note. Adapted from Houle (1980). Reprinted with permission.

continuous certification of competence, concurrent with continuing education; internship, for a more detailed description of the period aligning with induction into new responsibilities; and assessment, extending throughout professional education and credentialing.

Houle (1980) suggested individuals choose an occupation for myriad reasons; although some have the choice made for them at birth or early in life, others pursue occupations to enhance their social standing or in response to a calling, and some choose an occupation as a result of chance or circumstance. Regardless of the many reasons influencing a person's choice of occupation, sometime after the choice is made, formal education and assessment for progress begin (see Figure 6.1). The process ordinarily includes basic college courses, often with some narrowing focus on the selected area of occupational study, for example, when a college student is enrolled in a premedical or prelaw curriculum (Cervero & Daley, 2016; Houle, 1980). Later the student's choice of occupation is ratified by their acceptance in a course of study that calls for deep immersion into specialized content, acquisition of specific skills, and adoption of a discrete and complex value system. This formal process is reinforced by a differentiated lifestyle that separates the individual psychologically, if not always physically, from the general public and permeates their thought with a distinctive point of view (Houle, 1980).

At the end of formal preparatory study and the reorientation of values, initial judgments are made about the competence of the individual, first by those who have guided the previous course of study and then, in most cases, by some greater authority: the organized profession, the state, or both (Houle, 1980). Although selection and certification of competence are clear steps in the process of professional education, the period between initial certification and continuous certification involves a more gradual transition. It includes the performance of recently learned skills, formal internship, informal supervision, and acculturation into the new field by fellow workers. It may include an internship in a library, museum, social services agency, or a medical residency based in a hospital, the purpose of which is to present challenges for learning in the work environment while adapting and innovating in response to challenges in practice (Cutrer et al., 2017; Ericsson & Pool, 2016; Fox, Mazmanian, & Putnam, 1989). Then, somewhat early in adulthood, the professional person becomes established in their practice, and soon after, the need to keep up to date with new developments, change plans, solve problems, and remove obstacles is considered a requirement by members of the profession itself, by employing organizations, and by society in general (Houle, 1980; Jundt, Shoss, & Huang, 2015). Although decisions to learn are made chiefly by individual practitioners, the reliance on continuous assessment and lifelong learning enables all those with a stake in professional education to focus on learning for competence, service provision, and benefits to clients and communities (Cervero & Wilson, 2001; Cutrer et al., 2017; Fox et al., 1989; Nowlen, 1988).

Credentials and Competence

Continuing professional education has multiple stakeholders in ensuring competent performance: adult and continuing educators; faculty members across disciplines; professional associations; regulatory agencies; employers of professionals; private entrepreneurs engaged in providing continuing professional education; public consumers of professional services; and, not insignificantly, professionals themselves (Queeney, 2000). To reduce the risk of failing to maintain competence, many professions, states, employers, or accrediting organizations require participation in continuing education to qualify for and maintain licensure, certification, or registration to practice (Cervero & Daley, 2016; Mazmanian & Davis, 2018). In exchange for the privilege to practice, many professions require successful assessment of knowledge and skills, in addition to participation in continuing professional education (Cervero, 2001). Examples include airline transport pilots (Electronic Code of Federal Regulations, 2019), nuclear reactor operators (U.S. Nuclear Regulatory Commission, 2019), and select physician specialists (American Board of Medical Specialties, 2019).

For those involved in professional education, training, workforce development, or employment, the term *credential* is synonymous with verification of qualification or competence, an indication that an individual, a group, or an organization has been evaluated by a qualified and objective third-party credentialing body and has met standards that are defined, published, psychometrically sound, and legally defensible (Durley, 2005). Professions ordinarily influence and are influenced by three major types of credentials: licensure, certification, and registration. Licensure is the mandatory process a governmental agency conducts to grant time-limited permission to an individual to engage in a given occupation after verifying that they have met predetermined and standardized criteria. For example, to protect the public from the unprofessional, improper, unlawful, fraudulent, and incompetent practice of medicine, all 50 states, the District of Columbia, and territories of the United States have a medical practice act that defines the practice of medicine and delegates the authority to enforce the law to a state medical board (Federation of State Medical Boards, 2019). Certification is a vehicle that a profession or occupation uses to differentiate among its members, using standards, sometimes developed through a consensus-driven process, based on existing legal and psychometric requirements. It is a voluntary process of a nongovernmental entity to grant recognition and use of a credential to an individual after verifying that they have met predetermined and standardized criteria. For example, to become a certified public accountant in the United States, the candidate must sit for and pass the Uniform Certified Public Accountant Examination, which is set by the American Institute of Certified Public Accountants (n.d.) and administered by the National Association of State Boards of Accountancy. Registration is similar to licensure as it is a governmental agency's process to grant a time-limited status on a registry, determined by specified knowledge-based requirements (e.g., experience, education, examinations), thereby authorizing those individuals to practice. For example, teachers in Australia are registered and receive additional leadership certification opportunities based on student and teacher performance (Australian Institute for Teaching and School Leadership, n.d).

Notwithstanding such heavy confidence in continuing professional education participation to ensure competent performance, accreditation systems have been developed to monitor and strengthen the quality of educational activities available to participating learners. Accreditation is the voluntary process of a nongovernmental agency to grant time-limited recognition to an institution, organization, business, or other entity after verifying that it has met predetermined and standardized criteria (Durley, 2005). Accreditation offers those in professions an opportunity to reflect on concerns and act on evidence with standards to guide program decisions. For example, as evidence revealed a limited role of lectures in effecting change in physician behavior (Davis et al., 1999), the Accreditation Council for Continuing Medical Education moved to require that accredited providers analyze changes in learners' competence, performance, or patient outcomes achieved as a result of the program's educational activities. In such a manner, programs and learners were challenged to move beyond simple measures of attendance, or seat time, to higher levels of measured learning, behavior, and outcomes. In addition, the Accreditation Council for Pharmacy Education, the American Nurses Credentialing Center, and the Accreditation Council for Continuing Medical Education adopted standards to ensure their independence of influence from commercial support in needs assessment, determination of objectives, selection and presentation of content, selection of people and organizations to control content, selection of educational methods, and evaluation of the activity (Accreditation Council for Continuing Medical Education, 2019). The Institute for Credentialing Excellence (2019) is an example of a membership organization that develops standards for certification and certificate programs. In subject areas such as test development and delivery and assessment-based certification, the Institute for Credentialing

Excellence can accredit a program to ensure it is accountable to stakeholders and has met stringent standards set by the credentialing community itself.

As continuing professional education becomes more integrated into discussions of policy and regulation, those with responsibility for planning, assessment, and evaluation of programs must recognize the strengths and weaknesses of tools used to measure competence and performance in practice and appreciate the relative social and economic value of continuing professional education in credentialing individuals and professions to practice (Ross-Gordon, Rose, & Kasworm, 2017). It is essential for continuing professional education leaders to recognize the longer term influences of selection, early professional education, professional school course work, internships, and continuing education on performance, including outcomes for the diverse publics that receive professional services. Working with multiple stakeholders to account for the complexity of change in practice and to determine the value of improvement associated with continuing professional education is core to the mission of the adult educator focused on building professionalism in varied occupations, including continuing professional education itself (Mazmanian & Davis, 2018; Queeney, 2000).

Professionalism, Action, and Outcomes

An inquiry into the nature of professionalism (Irby & Hamstra, 2016) found three frameworks that contribute to our understanding of students' behavior during earlier experiences of professional education, especially those stretching from selection to initial certification of competence (see Figure 6.1). The frameworks also help explain behavior during the induction of professionals to new responsibilities, extending through continuing education and continuous certification.

First, the value-based framework is the oldest, with proponents of lifelong learning evident as far back as the first century CE (Rancich, Pérez, Morales, & Gelpi, 2005) and with advocates today continuing to advance the notion that appropriate action results from the right values and ethical principles being internalized until habits are created. In value-based professionalism, the learner is viewed as a moral agent who must put aside self-interest to act in the best interest of the patient or client receiving services. For education and training, internal values and the humanism of the learner are seen as strengths in securing a commitment to core values and actions that are guided by moral reasoning. Second, with its focus on developmental trajectories and evolving and changing identities, the professional identity framework suggests that appropriate action results from learners having been sensitized in advance to situations in which they might encounter negative role models. Socialization into communities of professionals, learning through observation of role models, and interactions with others are expected to facilitate performance. Third and contrastingly, the behavior-based framework suggests that appropriate action results from clear expectations, carefully delivered feedback, and reinforcement from external sources, including coaches and role models. Although self-assessment and feedback align with all three frameworks, major strengths of the behavior-based model includes its utility, its focus on milestones, competencies, and measurement of knowledge and behavior to enable certification of competence and sanction of unprofessional behavior.

In the space designated internship and induction into new responsibilities (Figure 6.1), the perspective of the learner shows evidence of transformation. Away from the context of classroom teaching, prescribed subject matter, and summative tests of knowledge in preparation for service, the learner's most immediate priorities take on central importance: They include providing service; solving problems in practice with increasing self-direction; and decreasing supervision in contexts that require ethical behavior, moral development, professional identity formation, and competent performance (Dreyfus, 2004; Holmboe, Ten Cate, Durning, & Hawkins, 2018).

A Framework for Assessment and Evaluation

Even as the scrutiny of professionalism grows more visible, and participation in continuing professional education courses gains popularity as a requirement for professional credentials to regulate practice privileges, limited attention has been paid to whether participation in continuing professional education actually makes a difference in professional performance. Of late, demands for better assessment of learners and evaluation of continuing professional education programs have been amplified with calls for continuing professional education leaders to move beyond measures of participants' acquisition of knowledge and satisfaction with participation in continuing professional education activities to identify and clarify relationships between continuing professional education participation and improved professional practice (Baker, 2009; Ericsson, 2009; Ericsson & Pool, 2016; Hawkins & Durning, 2018; Mazmanian & Davis, 2018). The intent includes optimal alignment of assessment with learner objectives; methods of instruction, including feedback; and reliable evaluation of program goals (Cervero & Daley, 2016; Coady, 2015; Ericsson & Pool, 2016; Fenwick, 2009; Fisher & Spikes, 2017; Hawkins & Durning, 2018; Knox, 2016; Mazmanian & Davis, 2018; Prados, Peterson, & Lattuca, 2005; Queeney, 2000; Wittnebel, 2012).

Table 6.1 compares an expanded version of Moore's (2011) outcomes framework for assessment of continuing medical education with the Kirkpatrick and Kirkpatrick (2006) model, which was developed initially for evaluation of training programs. Moore's seven levels of outcomes for planning and assessing continuing medical education activities are juxtaposed with Kirkpatrick and Kirkpatrick's more widely recognized model for evaluating training programs through four levels of outcomes: reaction, learning, behavior, and results of learners' performance. Table 6.1 aligns outcomes with data sources and methods of assessment. The generic descriptions of outcomes are linked with assessment methods and presented for extrapolation and use in the continuing education of similarly prepared professions and professionalizing occupations.

Beginning with documented attendance as a data source for measuring participation at Level 1 (Moore, 2011), the framework advances toward higher order tests of attitudes, knowledge, and behavior. At Level 2, participants' satisfaction with the setting and delivery of the continuing education activity is measured, as is the learner's reaction, as seen in Kirkpatrick and Kirkpatrick (2006) model. In this model, learning is Level 2, which is changes in knowledge, skills, or attitude. Kirkpatrick and Kirkpatrick's Level 2 extends comparatively through Moore's Level 4, competence. In Moore's framework, declarative knowledge (Level 3A) is the degree to which participants state what the continuing medical education activity intended for them to know. Procedural knowledge (Level 3B) is the degree to which participants state how they do what the continuing medical education activity intended them to know how to do. In Moore's framework, competence is the outcome measured at Level 4. It is defined as the degree to which participants show in an educational setting how they do what the continuing medical education activity intended them to do. For Kirkpatrick and Kirkpatrick, behavior is expressed as change in behavior or performance in applying knowledge, Level 3. At Level 5 in the Moore framework, participants demonstrate performance as the degree to which they do what the continuing medical education activity intended them to do in practice. Kirkpatrick and Kirkpatrick's Level 4 is results, or outcomes that align with Moore's Levels 6 and 7. At Level 6, Moore describes patient health as the degree to which the health status of patients improves because of changes in the practice behavior of the continuing professional education participant. At Level 7, community health is the degree to which the health status of a community of patients changes because of adjustments in the practice behavior of continuing medical education participants.

TABLE 6.1

Moore's Expanded Outcome Framework and Kirkpatrick and Kirkpatrick's Model Compared for Planning of Continuing Education Activities

Moore's Outcomes	Kirkpatrick and Kirkpatrick's Level	Description	Assessment Method
Participation LEVEL 1		The number of learners who participate in the educational activity	Documentation of attendance
Satisfaction LEVEL 2	Level 1: Reaction	The degree to which expectations of participants were met regarding the setting and delivery of the educational activity	Questionnaires/surveys completed by attendees; focus groups; self-report/portfolio
Learning: Declarative Knowledge LEVEL 3A	Level 2: Learning	The degree to which participants state *what* the educational activity intended them to know	Pre- and post-tests; true/false and multiple choice questions; self-assessment/self-report of knowledge gain; portfolio
Learning: Procedural Knowledge LEVEL 3B		The degree to which participants state *how* to do what the educational activity intended them to know how to do	Pre- and post-tests; short fill-in questions; essays, case-based discussion; self-assessment/self-report; portfolio
Competence LEVEL 4		The degree to which participants *show* in an educational setting *how* to do what the educational activity intended them to be able to do	Direct observation in educational setting; checklists of task perfomance or global ratings (e.g., peer assessment); tests of individual differences and organizational learning environment; self-assessment/self-report of competence; portfolio

(Continues)

TABLE 6.1 (*Continued*)

Moore's Outcomes	Kirkpatrick and Kirkpatrick's Level	Description	Assessment Method
Performance LEVEL 5	Level 3: Behavior	The degree to which participants *do* what the educational activity intended them to be able to do in their practices	Direct observation in the clinical setting; patient charts; quality of care process measurement; chart–stimulated recall; multi-source feedback; tests of individual differences and organizational learning environment; selfassessment/self-report of performance; portfolio
Patient Health LEVEL 6	Level 4: Results	The degree to which the health status of patients improves due to changes in the practice behavior of participants	Quality of care health status measures recorded in patient charts; tests of individual differences and organizational learning environment; portfolio; patient self-report of health status
Community Health LEVEL 7		The degree to which the health status of a community of patients changes due to changes in the practice behavior of participants	Tests of individual differences and organizational learning environment; community/population health outcome measures, including epidemiological studies by government agencies and academic researchers; portfolio

Note. From Kirkpatrick and Kirkpatrick (2006) and Moore (2011).

The selection of evidence-based tools for conducting assessments in continuing professional education is deep and wide ranging. It includes general support for periodic written examinations for qualification or certification of competence; direct observation; feedback of information from multiple sources; tests of individual differences such as cognitive and psychomotor abilities or skills, personality traits, motives, values, and interests (Chernyshenko, Stark, & Drasgow, 2011); continued examination of congruence and compatibility between adults and their work environments (Kristof-Brown & Guay, 2011); and self-assessment examinations. The best tools to use depend on who will use the information, how it will be used, and for what purposes. Each intended test score should be clearly stated, and appropriate validity evidence in support of each intended interpretation should be provided (American Educational Research Association, 2014). Validation can be thought of as an evaluation of the coherence and completeness of the interpretation or use argument and of the plausibility of its inferences and assumptions (Kane, 2013). The relative value of the argument is strengthened or weakened by the quality of measurement demonstrated through consistency with best practices for reliability and validity evidence.

Defining and Refining the Value of Continuing Professional Education

Despite the availability of knowledge to assess individuals and evaluate continuing professional education programs, many practitioners and scholars of continuing professional education believe implementation has been slow (Coady, 2015). Confusion over terminology may explain some of the apparent lag. For example, in health professions education, continuing professional education is recognized as a subset of continuing professional development. Continuing professional education is typically associated with didactic learning methods, such as lectures and seminars taking place in auditoriums or lecture halls, and is often viewed merely as a path to maintaining licensure or certification through the accumulation of credits (Institute of Medicine, 2010; National Academies of Sciences, Engineering, & Medicine, 2017). In contrast, continuing professional development embraces a wider array of learning formats, more workplace based with methods driven by learners as a way of maintaining, improving, and broadening knowledge and skill throughout one's professional life credits (Institute of Medicine, 2010; National Academies of Sciences, Engineering, & Medicine, 2017). It is not uncommon for the terms *continuing education, continuing professional education*, and *continuing professional development* to be used interchangeably.

For instance, most states and the District of Columbia require continuing education or continuing professional development credits for teachers to maintain certification and licensure. Both terms are used throughout the profession (Institute of Medicine, 2010). The National Council of Examiners for Engineering & Surveying (2019) endorses uniform continuing professional competency to promote continuing education for ethics and methods of business practice or operations. The American Bar Association describes continuing legal education as professional development, a way to maintain the highest standards of professional knowledge and to ensure public trust in lawyers (Institute of Medicine, 2010).

Using a workshop format, the National Academies of Sciences, Engineering, & Medicine (2017) explored the business case for high-value continuing professional development. The National Academies looked at formal and informal tools, methods, and models for educating the current clinical workforce (e.g., faculty development, preceptor training, workplace learning, and continuing education). The workshop included discussions of (a) what constitutes the business case, including costs and who pays for training and (b) what signals high-value continuing professional development (e.g., improved efficiency, better quality and safety, and a social return on investment). Stakeholders converged around a business case assessing the value of continuing professional development calculated as value = (quality + outcomes) ÷ cost. Consistent with Lindeman's (1926) perspectives on life, learning, and occupation, the continuing professional development activities generated for analysis during the workshop included a wide range of individual, interpersonal, and professional roles; changing professional responsibilities; job performance of individuals in response to or in anticipation of changes; and career development, to not only map clinical, organizational, and social changes but also negotiate a way through them (Cutrer et al., 2017; Cutrer et al., 2018; Fox et al., 1989; Jundt et al., 2015; Karle, Paulos, & Wentz, 2011).

National Academies of Sciences, Engineering, & Medicine (2017) identified the following major approaches to analyzing the costs and benefits of a continuing professional development program: (a) simple calculation of the per-participant cost, for example, the total costs of the venue, materials, staffing, and food divided by the number of participants; (b) an analysis including nonmonetary benefits, for example, if a specific continuing professional development program costs more than another option but is more time efficient, the extra money may be worth the time savings; and (c) a cost analysis that takes into account future revenue gains that are owed to the program. For example, a physician who is trained through continuing professional development on a procedure will be able to generate future revenue by performing the procedure, and this revenue may justify the initial expense of continuing professional development. It was a central understanding of the National Academies of Science, Engineering, and Medicine report that those who provide and study continuing professional development must provide sound explanations and realistic expectations for the value of their work, inasmuch as the science to explain outcomes is incomplete and the causal linkages uncertain.

Although there is no singularly correct model for valuing or evaluating continuing professional education programs, the need for evaluation is undiminished. Guiding improvement efforts that meet the needs and requirements of program stakeholders, including funders, accreditors, learners, and the public, and support development of the evidence base on best practices continue to be core responsibilities of evaluators and adult educators in continuing professional education (Hawkins & Durning, 2018; Knox, 2016; Queeney, 2000). A high-quality evaluation plan requires an accurate description and clear definition of the goals and objectives of the evaluation, engagement of stakeholders, and a range of structural, process, and outcomes measures to develop a comprehensive view of the program, including the extent to which it is attaining its goals and how the program can be improved. Those goals may include better participation and satisfaction of learners. They may also include measurement of demonstrated skills, professional performance, and outcomes for individuals and communities of clients and learners (Fisher & Spikes, 2017; Prados et al., 2005). In the final analysis, evaluators must ensure that the values, experience, moral character, and professional identity of individual professionals are assessed reliably and that the evaluation process provides accurate, comprehensive, and actionable feedback on which continuing professional education leaders can base program improvement activities (Hawkins & Durning, 2018; Mazmanian & Davis, 2018).

Emerging Pathways for Assessment and Evaluation

Three sets of activity constitute emerging pathways for assessment of individuals and evaluation of programs in continuing professional education. Portfolio uses self-assessment for learning and improvement. Neuroimaging isolates biomarkers in growing recognition of a biopsychosocial (Durning et al., 2016) approach to learning and development.

Self-Assessment

Leaders in continuing professional education recognize the importance of developing a better understanding of how knowledge becomes meaningful in practice. They also see that professionals develop and change their practice with the intent of continually meeting clients' needs and expectations. Yet those very same professionals may not hold a clear understanding of how knowledge learned in a continuing professional education activity becomes meaningful in practice (Daley, 2001). With self-assessment widespread throughout the reflective process, its use in regulation continues to be carefully considered with the current evidence pointing toward its value as a component of continuing professional education and continuous quality improvement (Davis et al., 2006). It is understood that self-assessment can play a major role in performance improvement so long as it is not treated as the mechanism through which performance improves. Its main value may be seen in the broader judgments, self-monitoring of how well one performs in an area generally, and how one determines in the moment whether one is performing in a way that is yielding the outcomes desired (Eva, Regehr, & Gruppen, 2012; Price, 2018).

Portfolio

Because of its success in creating reflective opportunities and feedback across all stages of professional education, the use of a portfolio continues to hold promise for resolving important issues in assessment and learning (Ivers et al., 2012; Janke, 2012). The portfolio approach aligns with major concepts of formative assessment, summative assessment, and improvement, as well as professional identity formation, virtue-based professionalism, and behavior-based professionalism. Portfolios may include log books or files, but they also involve active collection of work, assessments, and products of the learner gathered over time to provide evidence of professional development, annotated by the learner's reflection on learning outcomes (O'Sullivan, Carraccio, & Holmboe, 2018). Reflection is the critical difference between a portfolio and a log book or file. Every aspect of selecting, annotating, and writing reflective statements for a portfolio calls on learners to consider their practice in a critical fashion.

Purpose determines the content and creation of the portfolio and how the evidence will be interpreted and judged (Driessen, 2017; Klenowski, 2011). The content of the portfolio may be mostly or wholly determined by the learner. However, when the goal requires valid determination of competence and performance, the portfolio must involve a collaborative effort between educators and learners, requiring frontline faculty willing to serve as assessors, evidence-based assessment tools, and direct observation in the workplace over time. Partnership between the learner and the assessor must be built on a relationship that supersedes the recipient's sensitivity to receiving formative feedback and performance reports and allows the learner to gauge their progress toward competence (Driessen, 2017; O'Sullivan et al., 2018; Powell & Carraccio, 2018).

Neuroimaging

Knowing how professionals think is important to optimizing their learning. Professionals make decisions regularly, and some decisions involve higher risks than others. Trying to understand the full range of conditions that support or impede decision-making draws the attention of the investigator away from the more narrowly focused psychological and sociological approaches that inform assessment and evaluation toward a more holistic model accounting for biological factors (Engel, 1977) that can influence professional performance and well-being (Williams, 2018). Although its original intent was to improve the diagnosis and treatment of structural and functional abnormalities correlated with illness (Brammer, 2009), neuroimaging has been used to help confirm the validity of assessment tools (Durning et al., 2016) and to test for differences in performance between groups. For example, a study found that resident physicians were more susceptible to burnout effects on clinical reasoning, suggesting they need more cognitive and emotional support to improve quality of life and to optimize performance and learning (Durning et al., 2013). Neuroimaging has shown that decision-making and conflict in decision-making can be identified, imaged, and modeled in the human brain. There appears to be a neurophysical mechanism fundamental to value-based decisions wherein the brain weighs costs and benefits by combining neural benefit and cost signals into a single, difference-based neural representation of net value, which is accumulated over time until the individual decides to accept or reject an option (Basten, Biele, Heekeren, & Fiebach, 2010). Human choices have been successfully attributed to the dopaminoceptive system. Humans can structure their search for and use of relevant information by adaptively selecting decision strategies. Effective connectivity between sensory and reward-related brain structures is positively affected by value as long as the specific sensory information is considered relevant to the decision (Gluth, Rieskamp, & Büchel, 2014). It is sensible to conclude when working with professionals that assessment should be relevant to practice. In a group of medical students scanned by functional magnetic resonance imaging during a review of clinical vignettes, comparisons were made for recall tasks versus reasoning tasks; problem-solving questions induced medical students to use higher cognitive functions and lowered emotional stress (Chang, Kang, Ham, & Lee, 2016). Assessment decisions at any stage of professional identity formation should take into account the role of stress on desired measures (Mazmanian & Davis, 2018).

As accreditation, certification, licensing, and employing organizations turn toward continuous quality improvement and focus on developing as systems of learning, they collect data on the individuals, workforce, organizations, and populations they serve. They use employment testing for employee selection, placement, promotion, and prediction of future job behaviors with the goal of influencing organizational outcomes such as efficiency, growth, productivity, and motivation and satisfaction. Measured personality characteristics, interests, values, preferences, and work styles are used with the goal of providing self-insight to employees and information to educational planners (American Educational Research Association, 2014).

Many of the educational innovations deriving from such work relate to Web-based technologies that involve static learning for online courses. More adaptive and intelligent Web-based systems promise solutions for more individually rich learning environments. For example, studies in cognitive psychology demonstrate that subjects who engage in effortful, deliberate attempts to recall information show better learning, retention, and transfer than subjects who spend time repeatedly studying the same material. This effect, "test-enhanced learning," occurs when the retrieval practice occurs (Green, Moeller, & Spak, 2018). Several member boards of the American Board of Medical Specialties are engaged in a collaborative research effort to explore longitudinal assessment, which builds on test-enhanced learning with regular, spaced delivery of a limited number of questions on practice-relevant content on a computer or mobile Internet platform. Participating physicians may indicate relevance of the content to their practice and confidence in their answer prior to receiving feedback, including critiques, on each question (Price, Swanson, Irons, & Hawkins, 2018).

The American Medical Association established the AMA Physician Masterfile in 1906, which includes current and historical data for more than 1.4 million physicians, residents, and medical students in the United States. A record is created when an individual enters a U.S. or Canadian medical school accredited by the Liaison Committee on Medical Education, an accrediting body sponsored by the Association of American Medical Colleges and the American Medical Association. As a physician's training and career develop, certification information is added to the Masterfile record; it is never removed, even in the case of a physician's death. Data are shared with organizations and agencies that verify physicians' credentials and are concerned with workforce planning (American Medical Association, 2019).

The following examples demonstrate the power, feasibility, and implications for individual assessment and program evaluation with the use of a large database such as the Masterfile. To help determine whether its program was meeting its goal of producing high-quality physicians, the Uniformed

Services University performed a retrospective analysis of its U.S. graduates (1980–2009), and the Masterfile was used to describe their practice characteristics compared with a national cohort of U.S. medical school graduates. The Uniformed Services University was able to determine that its graduates were practicing in primary care and specialty care in all 50 states, extending services beyond their military obligation to include practice in federal hospitals and agencies (Cervero et al., 2018). In another project, 3,638 surgeons and 1,237,621 patients, representing 214 residency programs, were studied over a 2-year period to determine whether there were differences in non-university-based residency programs and university-based residency programs. Using the AMA Masterfile for demographic and training information and a separate claims database for evidence including inpatient mortality, complications, and prolonged length of stay after surgery as outcomes measures, the study found surgeons trained in non-university-based residency and university-based residency programs have distinct practice patterns and no observed differences in inpatient outcomes between the 2 groups (Sellers et al., 2018).

Looking Ahead

It is not uncommon for adult educators leading assessment, evaluation, or planning of continuing professional education activities to be without formal training in the discipline they serve. For example, a director of assessment and evaluation in continuing engineering education may have no formal training in electrical engineering, and a university-based director of continuing legal education may never have earned the juris doctor degree. Regardless of role, external or internal to the planning, assessment, or evaluation, it is best for adult educators in continuing professional education to become familiar with the history, terminology, current developments, key publications, regulatory requirements, culture, and major contributions, of not only the professions and professionals they serve but also adult education as the field they represent. It is essential for adult educators involved in continuing professional education to carry out fundamental program planning, evaluation, and cost analysis and to help other individuals and organizations accomplish their work through more advanced systems of assessment for learning and improvement. It will be important to strengthen understandings of the individual professional's decision-making at home, at work, and as a member of a professional work force. Big data sets placed in motion by vast computational power promise opportunities for predictive analytics to complement more standard social and psychological tools in use by those conducting individual assessment and program evaluation (Mazmanian & Davis, 2018). To serve at the interface of adult education, continuing professional education, assessment, and evaluation, the leader must exercise a level of expertise in research design, measurement techniques, instrument development, sampling, organizational systems, and data analysis while recognizing that leadership must involve carefully constructed feedback and trusting collaborations to maximize learning and improvement. Because there are few certification requirements for those involved in continuing professional education, leaders must indicate an ongoing commitment through self-assessment, lifelong learning, and shared knowledge, demonstrated typically through conference attendance, presentations, service to professional and community boards, peer-reviewed journals, books and publications, and also through successful project implementation with the individuals and organizations they serve.

References

Accreditation Council for Continuing Medical Education. (2019). Standards for commercial support. Retrieved from http://www.accme.org/news-publications/news/joint-accreditation-interprofessional-continuing-education-creates-new-logo

American Board of Medical Specialties. (2019). Steps toward initial certification and MOC. Retrieved from http://www.abms.org/board-certification/steps-toward-initial-certification-and-moc/

American Educational Research Association. (2014). *Standards for educational research and psychological testing.* Washington, DC: Author.

American Institute of Certified Public Accountants. (n.d.). Become a CPA. Retrieved from https://www.aicpa.org/becomeacpa.html

American Medical Association. (2019). AMA physician Masterfile. Retrieved from https://www.ama-assn.org/practice-management/masterfile/ama-physician-masterfile

Australian Institute for Teaching and School Leadership. (n.d). About certification. Retrieved from https://www.aitsl.edu.au/teach/understand-certification-and-halt-status/about-certification

Baker, E. L. (2009). Influence of learning research on assessment. In K. A. Ericsson (Ed.), *Development of professional expertise: Toward measurement of expert performance and design of optimal learning environments* (pp. 333–355). New York, NY: Cambridge University Press.

Basten, U., Biele, G., Heekeren, H. R., & Fiebach, C. J. (2010). How the brain integrates costs and benefits during decision making. *Proceedings of the National Academy of Sciences, 107*(50), 21767–21772.

Brammer, M. (2009). The role of neuroimaging in diagnosis and personalized medicine: Current position and likely future directions. *Dialogues in Clinical Neuroscience, 11*(4), 389–396.

Cervero, R. M. (1988). *Effective continuing education for professionals.* San Francisco, CA: Jossey-Bass.

Cervero, R. M. (2001). Continuing professional education in transition, 1981–2000. *International Journal of Lifelong Education, 20*(1/2), 16–30.

Cervero, R. M., & Daley, B. J. (2016). Continuing professional education: A contested space. *New Directions for Adult and Continuing Education, 2016*(151), 9–18.

Cervero, R. M., Torre, D., Durning, S. J., Schreiber-Gregory, D., Reamy, B. V., Pangaro, L. N., & Boulet, J. R. (2018). Staying power: Does the Uniformed Services University continue to meet its obligation to the nation's health care needs? *Military Medicine, 183*(9–10), e277–e280.

Cervero, R. M., & Wilson, A. L. (2001). *Power in practice: Adult education and the struggle for knowledge and power in society.* San Francisco, CA: Jossey-Bass.

Chang, H. J., Kang, J., Ham, B. -J., & Lee, Y. -M. (2016). A functional neuroimaging study of the clinical reasoning of medical students. *Advances in Health Sciences Education, 21*(5), 969–982.

Chernyshenko, O. S., Stark, S., & Drasgow, F. (2011). Individual differences: Their measurement and validity. In S. Zedeck (Ed.), *American Psychological Association handbook of industrial and organizational psychology* (Vol. 2, pp. 1–50). Washington, DC: American Psychological Association.

Coady, M. J. (2015). From Houle to Dirkx: Continuing professional education (CPE), a critical state-of-the-field review. *Canadian Journal for the Study of Adult Education, 27*(3), 27–41.

Cogan, M. L. (1955). The problem of defining a profession. *The Annals of the American Academy of Political and Social Science, 297*(1), 105–111.

Cutrer, W. B., Miller, B., Pusic, M. V., Mejicano, G., Mangrulkar, R. S., Gruppen, L. D., . . .Moore, D. E. (2017). Fostering the development of master adaptive learners: A conceptual model to guide skill acquisition in medical education. *Academic Medicine, 92*(1), 70–75.

Cutrer, W. B., Atkinson, H. G., Friedman, E., Deiorio, N., Gruppen, L. D., Dekhtyar, M., & Pusic, M. (2018). Exploring the characteristics and context that allow master adaptive learners to thrive. *Medical Teacher, 40*(8), 791–796.

Daley, B. J. (2001). Learning and professional practice: A study of four professions. *Adult Education Quarterly, 52*(1), 39–54.

Davis, D., O'Brien, M. A., Freemantle, N., Wolf, F. M., Mazmanian, P., & Taylor-Vaisey, A. (1999). Impact of formal continuing medical education: Do conferences, workshops, rounds, and other traditional continuing education activities change physician behavior or health care outcomes? *Journal of the American Medical Association, 282*(9), 867–874.

Davis, D. A., Mazmanian, P. E., Fordis, M., Van Harrison, R., Thorpe, K. E., & Perrier, L. (2006). Accuracy of physician self-assessment compared with observed measures of competence: A systematic review. *Journal of the American Medical Association, 296*(9), 1094–1102.

Dreyfus, S. E. (2004). The five-stage model of adult skill acquisition. Retrieved from http://www.bumc.bu.edu/facdev-medicine/files/2012/03/Dreyfus-skill-level.pdf

Driessen, E. (2017). Do portfolios have a future? *Advances in Health Sciences Education, 22*(1), 221–228.

Durning, S. J., Costanzo, M., Artino, A. R., Dyrbye, L. N., Beckman, T. J., Schuwirth, L., . . .van der Vleuten, C. (2013). Functional neuroimaging correlates of burnout among internal medicine residents and faculty members. *Frontiers in Psychiatry, 4*(131), 1–7.

Durning, S. J., Costanzo, M. E., Beckman, T. J., Artino, A. R., Roy, M. J., van der Vleuten, C., . . .Schuwirth, L. (2016). Functional neuroimaging correlates of thinking flexibility and knowledge structure in memory: Exploring the relationships between clinical reasoning and diagnostic thinking. *Medical Teacher, 38*(6), 570–577.

Durley, C. C. (2005). The NOCA guide to understanding credentialing concepts. Retrieved from http://www.cvacert.org/documents/CredentialingConcepts-NOCA.pdf

Electronic Code of Federal Regulations. (2019). Airline transport pilot privileges and limitations. Retrieved from https://www.ecfr.gov/cgi-bin/text-idx?SID=4348 0f59479f9a1019f8298ad787a84e&node=14:2.0.1.1.2.7.1.12&rgn=div8

Elias, J. L., & Merriam, S. B. (2005). *Philosophical foundations of adult education* (3rd ed.). Melbourne, FL: Krieger.

Engel, G. L. (1977). The need for a new medical model: A challenge for biomedicine. *Science, 196*(4286), 129–136.

Ericsson, K. A. (2009). Enhancing the development of professional performance: Implications from the study of deliberate practice. In K. A. Ericsson (Ed.), *Development of professional expertise: Toward measurement of expert performance and design of optimal learning environments* (pp. 405–431). New York, NY: Cambridge University Press.

Ericsson, A., & Pool, R. (2016). *Peak: Secrets from the new science of expertise.* New York, NY: Houghton Mifflin Harcourt.

Eva, K. W., Regehr, G., & Gruppen, L. D. (2012). Blinded by "insight": Self-assessment and its role in performance improvement. In B. D. Hodges & L. Lingard (Eds.), *The question of competence* (pp. 131–154). New York, NY: Cornell University Press.

Federation of State Medical Boards. (2019). About FSMB. Retrieved from https://www.fsmb.org/about-fsmb/

Fenwick, T. (2009). Making to measure? Reconsidering assessment in professional continuing education. *Studies in Continuing Education, 31*(3), 229–244.

Fisher, H. B., & Spikes, W. F. (2017). Exploring programmatic issues which affect continuing legal education in Kansas. Retrieved from http://newprairiepress.org/aerc/2017/papers/32

Flexner, A. (1915). Is social work a profession? Retrieved from https://ia800208.us .archive.org/27/items/proceedingsofnat42natiuoft/proceedingsofnat42natiuoft .pdf

Fox, R. D., Mazmanian, P. E., & Putnam, R. W. (Eds.). (1989). *Changing and learning in the lives of physicians.* New York, NY: Praeger.

Freidson, E. (1988). *Profession of medicine: A sociology of applied knowledge.* Chicago, IL: University of Chicago Press.

Gluth, S., Rieskamp, J., & Büchel, C. (2014). Neural evidence for adaptive strategy selection in value-based decision-making. *Cerebral Cortex, 24*(8), 2009–2021.

Green, M. L., Moeller, J. J., & Spak, J. M. (2018). Test-enhanced learning in health professions education: A systematic review: BEME Guide No. 48. *Medical Teacher, 40*(4), 337–350.

Hawkins, R. E., & Durning, S. J. (2018). Program evaluation. In E. S. Holmboe, S. J. Durning, & R. E. Hawkins (Eds.), *Evaluation of clinical competence* (2nd ed., pp. 303–328). Philadelphia, PA: Elsevier.

Holmboe, E. S., Ten Cate, O., Durning, S. J., & Hawkins, R. E. (2018). Assessment challenges in the era of outcomes-based education. In E. S. Holmboe, S. J. Durning, & R. E. Hawkins (Eds.), *Evaluation of clinical competence* (2nd ed., pp. 1–19). Philadelphia, PA: Elsevier.

Houle, C. O. (1980). *Continuing learning in the professions.* San Francisco, CA: Jossey-Bass.

Institute for Credentialing Excellence. (2019). Accreditation through ice: A benchmark of quality. Retrieved from file:///C:/Users/pemazman/Downloads/ICE%20Accreditation%20Brochure.pdf

Institute of Medicine. (2010). *Redesigning continuing education in the health professions.* Washington, DC: National Academies Press.

Irby, D. M., & Hamstra, S. J. (2016). Parting the clouds: Three professionalism frameworks in medical education. *Academic Medicine, 91*(12), 1606–1611.

Ivers, N., Jamtvedt, G., Flottorp, S., Young, J., Odgaard-Jensen, J., French, S. D., & Oxman, A. D. (2012). Audit and feedback: Effects on professional practice and health care outcomes. *Cochrane Database Systematic Review, 6*(6), CD000259.

Janke, K. K. (2012). Preparing health professional students for continuing education and continuing professional development. In G. J. Neimeyer & J. M. Taylor (Eds.), *Continuing professional development and lifelong learning: Issues, impacts, and outcomes* (pp. 3–12). New York, NY: Nova Science.

Jundt, D. K., Shoss, M. K., & Huang, J. L. (2015). Individual adaptive performance in organizations: A review. *Journal of Organizational Behavior, 36*(S1), S53–S71.

Kane, M. T. (2013). Validating the interpretations and uses of test scores. *Journal of Educational Measurement, 50*(1), 1–73.

Karle, H., Paulos, G., & Wentz, D. K. (2011). Continuing professional development: Concept, origins, and rationale. In D. K. Wentz (Ed.), *Continuing medical education: Looking back, planning ahead* (pp. 281–290). Hanover, NH: Dartmouth College Press.

Kirkpatrick, D. L., & Kirkpatrick, J. D. (2006). *Evaluating training programs* (3rd ed.). San Francisco, CA: Berrett-Koehler.

Klenowski, V. (2011). Portfolio assessment. In K. Rubenson (Ed.), *Adult learning and education* (pp. 198–204). Oxford, UK: Elsevier.

Knox, A. B. (2016). *Improving professional learning: Twelve strategies to enhance professional performance*. Sterling, VA: Stylus.

Kristof-Brown, A. L., & Guay, R. P. (2011). Person-environment fit. In S. Zedeck (Ed.), *American Psychological Association handbook of industrial and organizational psychology* (Vol. 3, pp. 1–50). Washington, DC: American Psychological Association.

Lindeman, E. (1926). *The meaning of adult education*. Retrieved from https://archive.org/stream/meaningofadulted00lind#page/5/mode/2up

Mazmanian, P. E., & Davis, D. A. (2018). Projecting the future of continuing professional development. In W. F. Rayburn, M. G., Turco, & D. A. Davis (Eds.), *Continuing professional development in medicine and health care: Better education, better patient outcomes* (pp. 385–406). Philadelphia, PA: Wolters Kluwer.

Moore, D. E. (2011, June). *The value proposition for CME: The importance of an outcomes-based approach*. Paper presented at a meeting of the Global Alliance for Continuing Medical Education Conference, Munich, Germany.

Muzio, D., & Ackroyd, S. (2005). On the consequences of defensive professionalism: Recent changes in the legal labour process. *Journal of Law and Society, 32*(4), 615–642.

National Academies of Sciences, Engineering, & Medicine. (2017). Exploring a business case for high-value continuing professional development. Proceedings of a workshop. Washington, DC: National Academies Press.

National Council of Examiners for Engineering & Surveying. (2019). CPC tracking FAQs: What is the NCEEs continuing professional competency (CPC) standard? Retrieved from https://ncees.org/cpc/faqs/

Nowlen, P. M. (1988). *A new approach to continuing education for business and the professions*. New York, NY: American Council on Education, Macmillan.

O'Sullivan, P., Carraccio, C., & Holmboe, E. (2018). Portfolios. In E. S. Holmboe, S. J. Durning, & R. E. Hawkins (Eds.), *Practical guide to the evaluation of clinical competence* (2nd ed., pp. 270–287). Philadelphia, PA: Elsevier.

Powell, D. E., & Carraccio, C. (2018). Toward competency-based medical education. *New England Journal of Medicine, 378*(1), 3–5.

Prados, J. W., Peterson, G. D., & Lattuca, L. R. (2005). Quality assurance of engineering education through accreditation: The impact of engineering criteria 2000 and its global influence. *Journal of Engineering Education, 94*(1), 165–184.

Price, D. W. (2018). Maintenance of board certification, continuing professional development, and performance improvement. In W. F. Rayburn, M. G., Turco, & D. A. Davis (Eds.), *Continuing professional development in medicine and health care: Better education, better patient outcomes* (pp. 191–202). Philadelphia, PA: Wolters Kluwer.

Price, D. W., Swanson, D. B., Irons, M. B., & Hawkins, R. E. (2018). Longitudinal assessments in continuing specialty certification and lifelong learning. *Medical Teacher, 40*(9), 917–919.

Queeney, D. S. (2000). Continuing professional education. In A. L. Wilson & E. R. Hayes (Eds.), *Handbook of adult and continuing education* (pp. 375–391). San Francisco, CA: Jossey-Bass.

Rancich, A. M., Pérez, M. L., Morales, C., & Gelpi, R. J. (2005). Beneficence, justice, and lifelong learning expressed in medical oaths. *Journal of Continuing Education in the Health Professions, 25*(3), 211–220.

Ross-Gordon, J. M., Rose, A. D., & Kasworm, C. E. (2017). *Foundations of adult and continuing education.* San Francisco, CA: Jossey-Bass.

Saks, M. (2012). Defining a profession: The role of knowledge and expertise. *Professions and Professionalism, 2*(1), 1–10.

Sellers, M. M., Keele, L. J., Sharoky, C. E., Wirtalla, C., Bailey, E. A., & Kelz, R. R. (2018). Association of surgical practice patterns and clinical outcomes with surgeon training in university- or nonuniversity-based residency program. *Journal of the American Medical Association Surgery, 153*(5), 418–425.

U.S. Nuclear Regulatory Commission. (2019). Licensing process for operators. Retrieved from https://www.nrc.gov/reactors/operator-licensing/licensing-process .html

Williams, B. W. (2018). Assessing and remediating the struggling physician. In W. F. Rayburn, M. G., Turco, & D. A. Davis (Eds.), *Continuing professional development in medicine and health care: Better education, better patient outcomes* (pp. 287–301). Philadelphia, PA: Wolters Kluwer.

Wittnebel, L. (2012). Business as usual? A review of continuing professional education and adult learning. *Journal of Adult and Continuing Education, 18*(2), 80–88.

7

ASSESSMENT AND EVALUATION IN HUMAN RESOURCE DEVELOPMENT

Lilian H. Hill, Sharon E. Rouse, and Cyndi H. Gaudet

Assessment and evaluation are central to effective practice in human resource development (HRD). Composed of three main activities, career development, learning and development, and organizational development, HRD involves processes organizations use to provide employees with relevant opportunities to learn needed skills to meet current and future job requirements. Providing training to employees is intended to modify their knowledge, skills, and behavior to improve their work performance and contribution to organizational goals (Jasson & Govender, 2017). Poell and Van Der Krogt (2017) described HRD as an "instrument to improve the internal labor market and support organizational change" (p. 215). In a knowledge-based global competitive economy, HRD is an interdisciplinary field that emphasizes learning critical to the development of specialized expertise, communication, collaboration, and transformational learning needed to elevate employees' focus beyond task achievement to systems improvement (McGuire, 2014). Its purpose is to integrate learning capacity and a learning culture into business strategy to achieve high-quality organizational performance (McGuire, 2014). Walton and Valentin (2014) recognized the multiplicity of possible definitions for HRD and recommended caution because of the complex nature of the constructs under consideration, namely learning, development, and performance.

This chapter addresses assessment and evaluation processes as they are used in HRD. The vocabulary of assessment in HRD is different from the terminology in chapters 1 and 2. The term *assessment* is most often used in the context of needs assessment. Performance feedback may be the concept most closely aligned with the way assessment is defined in this book and can be described as a process in which employees receive feedback intended to improve their learning, skills development, and work performance. Evaluation is designed to address the effectiveness of HRD interventions and extends beyond program evaluation to an examination of the program's ability to assist organizations to meet their vision, mission, and goals. The chapter begins with a discussion of needs assessment and analysis and follows with a consideration of performance analysis and the critical nature of learning transfer to employee and organizational effectiveness. A section on evaluation first describes Kirkpatrick's (1994) widely referred to four-level model, along with its critiques and modifications. Evaluation is then discussed in relation to HRD interventions' contributions to organizational goals and return on investment (ROI). The chapter concludes with a brief section on future directions and critical HRD.

Needs Assessment or Analysis

As an investigative and decision-making process, needs assessment in HRD practice is used for determining the training and human performance interventions to be developed in response to an observed need and discerning what kind of intervention would be most useful. Needs assessment can be thought of as formative evaluation conducted to form the basis of designing training or human performance interventions. A needs assessment process is often implemented when an organization's administrators become concerned about problems with their products, services, and internal or external context. Needs assessment can discern "educational needs, performance problems, new opportunities, . . . areas for improvement, . . . societal issues, customer demands, and images of ideal practice" (Caffarella & Daffron, 2013). It can integrate knowledge of organizational strategy and goals, address current and future skills gaps, and point out changing business and societal conditions. Needs assessment can be used to diagnose and investigate contexts that precipitate problems, investigate innovative ways of accomplishing work, and identify compliance needs. Needs assessment should be future oriented and proactive. Formal, structured needs assessment may use several of the following: questionnaires, observations, task and job analysis, documentation of work processes, focus groups, tests, performance reviews, and consideration of social indicators (Caffarella & Daffron, 2013, p. 134). In a formal needs analysis, HRD professionals need strong research and statistical skills to implement data-gathering steps and conduct needs analysis at multiple levels of an organization (Lee, 2019).

Needs assessment, sometimes known as needs or performance analysis, is implemented to characterize performance gaps of employees, analyze sources of discrepancy, and identify potential training and nontraining solutions (Lee, 2019). Christensen (2018) differentiated needs assessment from needs analysis by stating that needs assessment identifies the gap between current and desired results whereas a needs analysis involves subsequent steps of putting identified needs in order of priority based on costs of training or consideration of the consequences of not providing training. Causes of performance gaps may be external to the organization, and training is not always the appropriate solution. Christensen makes a cogent argument for differentiating between needs and wants and for inclusion of business priorities in the needs analysis process.

Multiple models for needs assessment include instructional systems design (ISD); analyze, design, develop, implement, and evaluate (ADDIE); training performance system (TPS); and rapid needs assessment, among others. Most of these models incorporate needs assessment and evaluation in a recursive process. For example, ISD, originally designed by the military for training large numbers of people in standardized tasks, is based on behaviorist conceptions of learning, begins with the assumption that training is required and employs rigorous and standardized methodology (Lee, 2019; Swanson & Holton, 2008). ISD has five phases: analyze, design, develop, implement, and control. Analysis takes into account job tasks and functions and constructs behavioral job performance measures. Design involves creating learning objectives and tests, and it sequences learning structures. Development of learning activities, materials, and management plan precedes implementation of instruction and of the management plan. Finally, control requires external and internal evaluations to structure revisions of the instructional system, if needed. Otherwise known as analyze, design, develop, implement and evaluate (ADDIE), the model is commonly used for developing systematic training. However, the initial model was found to be too rigid for HRD practice and was adapted by allowing the steps to be followed in any order, entry at any point in the model, and integration of cognitive learning into a practice based on behavioral learning. More than 100 variations of the model exist (Lee, 2019; Swanson & Holton, 2008).

Based on the ADDIE model, TPS proposed by Richard Swanson adds more nuance and detailed analysis. Swanson and Holton (2008) describe TPS as "a process for developing human expertise for the purpose of improving the organization, process, and human performance" (p. 237). The analyze stage involves (a) consideration of the meaning of effective job performance for the organization and (b) job and task analysis that reveals the requirements of procedural, systems, and knowledge work by studying subject matter experts. Design is similarly broken into steps of creating the training program and individual lessons intended to support employees' acquisition of workplace expertise. Develop involves planning training materials and pilot-testing training modalities. Pilot-testing training methods and materials is essential to training effectiveness and efficiency. Implement means putting a particular training program into practice, including managing training activities and their delivery to intended participants. Fidelity to intended training outcomes requires training expertise and appropriate preparation. Finally, evaluate refers to analyzing training effectiveness using a results-oriented system that takes into account job performance, learning, and participant satisfaction. TPS focuses most on whether the organization, the work processes, and the individuals working in the organization perform better, and to a lesser extent it is invested in participant satisfaction. Evaluate also refers to reporting the results of training to managers, decision-makers, and stakeholders, particularly when the desired outcomes of the training are work and job performance improvement.

Critiques of the ISD model, and its multiple iterations, are that it draws extensively on individual learning theories rooted in behaviorism and is, therefore, inadequate to address cognitive and constructivist learning and the complexities of social interactions and culturally influenced behaviors. Nor does ISD acknowledge contributions of professional expertise and professionals with more discretion and autonomy over what and how to learn (Poell, 2012; Weinstein & Shuck, 2011). Changing work expectations requires extensive communication and collaboration among individual employees and work systems. Rather than training individual employees in discrete, standardized tasks, HRD is now responsible for supporting employees in a global knowledge economy where task ambiguity and employee discretion are prevalent. According to Weinstein and Shuck (2011), "High-performance work systems require a combination of employee technical preparedness, individual worker empowerment, and effective and authentic communication, often facilitated by flattened and networked organizations" (p. 287).

Lee (2019) proposed a rapid needs assessment model accomplished by "limiting the amount of data collected and analyzed, using existing information and data, or anticipating training needs for common business problems without collecting additional data" (p. 63). The model involves the following steps:

(1) identifying the purpose and scope of the needs assessment, (2) preliminary analysis for identifying problems and boundary conditions, (3) developing hypothetical interventions, (4) elaborating, revising, and prioritizing hypothetical interventions, and (5) confirming the optimal interventions. (p. 67)

Lee asserted that this model differs from previous needs assessment models by engaging clients in decision-making and the interactive, cyclical process between proposing hypothetical interventions and adjusting to fit actual conditions that include the (a) organizations' mission, values, culture, and resources; (b) relationships between clients and participants; and (c) individual conditions that include expertise, prior knowledge, and skills of participants. Testing of the model indicated it is feasible, applicable to practice, and grounded in evidence. Lee indicated further study is required to determine the validity of the model.

Weinstein and Shuck (2011) said that models based on ISD, such as ADDIE and TPS, have not been adapted to the work requirements of the twenty-first century. Instead, they recommended a social ecology model, based in Broffenbrenner's (1979) ecological learning theory, in which individuals are encapsulated in nested, interacting relationships in the "immediate family, work groups, community, and formal and informal institutions of society" (p. 292) as a more robust mode of explaining and influencing human behavior. They further indicate that "the social ecological framework views individual behavior as effected and affecting multiple dimensions in the environment" (p. 292). Needs analysis should investigate not only individual learning but also interactions with others, sociocultural contexts, individuals' relative power to effect change, occupational or professional norms, communities of practice, and political and religious influences. Weinstein and Shuck (2011) advocated for the integration of social learning theories to develop more encompassing knowledge of workplace learning.

The potential benefits of effective needs analysis may not be realized because a formal process is perceived as time-consuming and expensive, action is preferred to research, there is an overreliance on existing information, or there is a lack of management support. Lee (2019) said that many HRD professionals lack the requisite skills to conduct effective needs assessment, and rigorous academic-style needs assessments are too time consuming and cumbersome for organizational conditions that require agile decision-making. Further, a formal needs assessment may not be necessary when an educational program is mandated by state or federal policy or when a client strongly desires implementation of a particular program (Lee, 2019).

Learning Transfer

Learning transfer, also known as knowledge transfer or training transfer, is a crucial element in economic and social development that serves to promote innovation, improve business practices, and organizational sustainability. Although training is not the appropriate solution for every organizational performance problem (Christensen, 2018), it is extremely important for recipients of training be able to effectively apply and use new knowledge in work (Caffarella & Daffron, 2013). Because training investments are intended to bear results in changed or improved work practices, the concept of learning transfer is critical to HRD. The more central knowledge assets are to an organization's mission, the more important knowledge transfer becomes (Benito-Bilbao, Sánchez-Fuente, & Otegi-Olaso, 2015).

Learning transfer is often conceived of in behavioral terms, meaning employees' learning can be observed in results of changed knowledge, skills, and behaviors and ultimately in amendments in work practices. However, learning transfer is a complex and multidimensional process influenced by training conditions, knowledge complexity, and posttraining climate and conditions. Factors influencing learning transfer include "learner characteristics, professional backgrounds, learner motivation, program design and delivery, and organizational strategies" (Caffarella & Daffron, 2013, p. 212). Intellectual and emotional characteristics of individual learners, social relationships among peers, knowledge complexity, tools and instruments used in work, the external context, and corporate and management strategy all play a role in rendering learning transfer possible (Benito-Bilbao et al., 2015). von Treuer, McHardy, and Earl (2013) stated that "*affective* organisational commitment, job involvement and utility perceptions are predictors of motivation to learn and transfer learning" (p. 606). Other factors may influence learning transfer including learner readiness, resistance to change in the work setting, peer and manager or supervisor support for change, and mismatches between training and work-setting conditions (Cho, Jo, Park, Kang, & Chen, 2011; Ruona et al., 2002).

Just because employees have gained knowledge during a program does not mean they are able or willing to apply it in their daily work (Dean & Ripley, 2016). Taylor, Evans, and Pinsent-Johnson (2010) said that knowledge learned in one setting often "fails to be recognised or utilised fully in . . . the work-site" (p. 348). Caution must also be used in interpreting measures of learning transfer. For example, some measures of learning transfer are implemented with higher level workers and do not report the experiences of workers with lower literacy skills who may have difficulty interpreting the vocabulary used in a scale designed to measure learning transfer.

Learning transfer does not happen automatically. In planning for learning transfer, opportunities should be identified, and barriers to transfer should be minimized. Caffarella and Daffron (2013) proposed a model for analyzing opportunities for learning transfer that investigates interactive factors including workplace climate, learning context, learner characteristics, the planning process, and design and delivery of training. They characterize the process as nonlinear and multifaceted. To eliminate learning transfer barriers, changes in work conditions may need to be made before initiating training. For example, if an organization intends to introduce a complex software system to be used in multiple organizational functions, work to ensure the system is working correctly should precede software training for employees. Caffarella and Daffron (2013) described a framework for planning learning transfer that advises planning for transfer before, during, and after training occurs and suggest specific actions for program planners, instructors and facilitators, learners, and other key players.

Taylor and colleagues (2010) questioned the metaphor in learning transfer and instead refer to it as *learning recontextualization*. Moving knowledge from a context in which it was originally generated into different settings requires recontextualization in which the meanings of knowledge, practices, and experiences may be changed as they are moved from their origins and integrated into the curriculum and teaching of a training program. Learners also change as they recontextualize knowledge and integrate it into work practices. Recontextualization may occur in content, pedagogy, the workplace, and the learner as they make sense of the process. Taylor and colleagues found that social capital in the form of trust, reciprocity, tolerance, and respect for others plays a large role in whether learning will be integrated in practice.

Performance Feedback

Performance feedback is the assessment practice most closely aligned with the definitions of *assessment* in chapter 1. HRD is involved in planning, determining content, and creating systems for performance improvement, whereas human resource management may support managers in conducting performance appraisals and providing feedback. Sommer and Kulkarni (2012) indicated that performance feedback serves as a critical managerial tool for improving individual and organizational effectiveness. It can be used to measure "capability, competence, efficiency and effectiveness" (Sangwa & Sangwan, 2017, p. 768). In addition to providing individuals with information about their current work performance, feedback supports employee engagement with organizational goals and contributes to employees' view of their future prospects in the organization. In turn, supporting employee engagement fosters a positive organizational culture (Kissack & Callahan, 2010; Shuck, Reio, & Rocco, 2011).

Performance improvement appraisals are implemented to make critical decisions regarding employees' developmental needs, promotion pathways, and succession planning, meaning appraisals are how organizations identify and prepare future leaders (Sommer & Kulkarni, 2012). Individuals tasked with conducting performance reviews should use direct communication strategies that are considerate, timely, and delivered appropriately with sensitivity for confidentiality. Constructive performance feedback employs a positive tone, avoids threat, supports employee engagement, elicits potential, and improves employees' skill levels. Sommer and Kulkarni (2012) distilled several theoretical models to formulate principles of constructive feedback: (a) emphasize problematic behavior over personal weaknesses, (b) make explicit references to standards for performance, and (c) provide clear strategies for remedying poor performance. They reported that employees perceive constructive feedback as a fair process that minimizes manager-employee conflict. In contrast, poorly conducted performance appraisals contribute to employees' alienation and detachment, decreased work performance, and intentions to leave the organization.

New challenges for performance feedback relate to the integration of technology in work practices, security of information, continual changes in technology, cyber attacks, and changing regulations supporting security of information (Ritzman & Kahle-Piasecki, 2016). Employees are often considered the weakest link in information security when they are ill informed about prevention techniques; indulge in poor password management or inappropriate Web browsing; or become subject to phishing attempts, data compromises, criminal behavior, or espionage. Such security threats prompt organizations to provide continuous technology and training support. Ritzman and Kahle-Piasecki (2016) identified security-related stress experienced by employees under pressure to maintain organizational information security as a factor that must be taken into account in performance improvement. In addition to learning and development of interventions, effective performance improvement is supported by interrelated organizational policies, communications, and organizational culture.

Performance Improvement

Claims for the importance of performance analysis are rooted in assertions that training by itself is only 10% effective (Holland, 2016). Holland noted that as much as $162 billion was invested annually in "leadership and management training [that] typically doesn't yield the ROI in improved organizational effectiveness and performance that companies expect" (para. 2). Based on a comparison of different models of performance analysis, Christensen (2018) asserted that the models situate needs assessment and training as only one of several tools that can be employed in mediating identified performance gaps. For example, Van Tiem, Moseley, and Dessinger (2012) proposed a change management model that recommends examination of organizational factors related to the organization's vision, mission and goals, and environmental factors including regulatory, competition, and work flow influences on work, as well as evaluation of worker knowledge, skills, and performance capacity to analyze an identified performance gap to find potential causes. Processes for identifying effective interventions may include consideration of job analysis and work flow and design, performance support, organizational design, and learning, among others. Implementation of interventions are exemplified by creating partnerships, networking, process consulting, project management, and finally employee development. Other models of performance improvement reviewed by Christensen incorporated analysis factors that included the organization's capacity, systems design, expertise, performance review, outcome metrics, culture, business environment, and external environment. In a study using citation network analysis, Cho et al. (2011) found that key themes in the human performance technology literature were performance, instructional design, performance support, organization and workplace, and transfer of training.

Performance management systems for large-scale organizations should "provide direction, encourage dialogue, promote inclusivity, ensure relevancy, and support the mission" (Armitage & Parrey, 2013, p. 27). Large-scale, multinational organizations maintain complex performance systems for thousands of employees located in different regions and nations who have different cultural values even though they work in a specific organizational culture. For example, company offices in the United States and overseas may display the same talismans of company culture while at the same time employees wear different national clothing and adhere to different belief systems.

Organizational executives are questioning the value and results of performance management systems, and directors of some multinational organizations have decided to discontinue formal performance appraisal systems that require intensive investments of effort and time (McElgunn, 2019). Organizations require more agile, iterative evaluation processes that not only investigate past performance but provide foundations for future performance in the face of changing work conditions. Instead of unwieldy, standardized annual reviews, HRD professionals advocate for frequent check-ins with managers, quarterly or project-related assessments, and annual compensation meetings designed to recognize and coach effective performance in a process that maintains confidentiality and transparency (Buckingham & Goodall, 2013; McElgunn, 2019). Armitage and Parrey (2015) indicated some performance management systems are decades old and in need of updating. More agile, iterative systems are being implemented that focus on identified competencies, frequent feedback, coaching, and linking skills development to organizational goals.

Evaluation

Effective evaluation of HRD interventions should serve as a foundation for good decision-making. The value of HRD initiatives may lie in the benefits they bring to employees, improved work processes, or successful organizational outcomes (Russ-Eft, 2014). Organizations generally support measurement of effectiveness and efficiency of HRD initiatives; however, the complexity of these interventions and the site of measurement render effective summative evaluation difficult (Han & Boulay, 2013). It is difficult to directly link learning to changes in performance. The usefulness of evaluation results rest in the comprehensiveness of the evaluation process and credibility of information it produces.

Participation Reaction Measures

Kirkpatrick's (1994) four-level model of evaluation based in participant reactions (Level 1), learning (Level 2), on-the-job behaviors (Level 3), and results from behavior change (Level 4) is widely discussed in training literature. Phillips (1997) and Phillips and Phillips (2009) added a fifth level related to ROI. In an electronic survey of 704 learning managers conducted by Patel (2010), most respondents reported they used the combined Kirkpatrick-Phillips model for training evaluation. They indicated 92% of training evaluations conducted used a participation reaction form (Level 1), 80% involved measurement of learning (Level 2), more than 50% measured learners' changed behavior (Level 3), and 37% evaluated results (Level 4). Only 18% of evaluations measured ROI (Level 5). Survey respondents reported that although they valued higher level evaluation, they also experienced barriers to higher level evaluations including difficulties attributing learning solely to training interventions and evaluation results not being comparable across functional areas within the organization (Patel, 2010).

Patel's (2010) survey may have overestimated the percentage that measured behavior change and ROI. Other estimates indicate that fewer than half of HRD interventions are evaluated based on objective performance measures (Ruona et al., 2002). Few comprehensive evaluations are actually conducted, and they may be devised at the end of a program rather than being part of a thorough program planning process in which program evaluation is closely linked to program and learning objectives from the outset (Caffarella & Daffron, 2013; Dean & Ripley, 2016). Han and Boulay

(2013) found that "evaluation efforts overwhelmingly assess participant reactions and rarely identify bottom-line impacts or returns on investment" (p. 6). Han and Boulay said that Kirkpatrick's model serves as a classification tool, or taxonomy, and the basis of common language about evaluation for HRD practitioners rather than a reflection of practice. Wang, Dou, and Li (2002) asserted that "if HRD is to grow as a discipline and a profession, it is vital to develop a rigorous and comprehensive evaluation and measurement system" (p. 211).

Criticisms of Kirkpatrick's model pertinent to HRD are that it emphasizes participant reactions, is not fully implemented, and leaves out important information that can contribute to poor decision-making (Dean & Ripley, 2016; Swanson & Holton, 2008). Several people have proposed an additional level of the model related to ROI. Han and Boulay (2013) indicated that "understanding and quantifying impact is essential for the credibility of HRD intervention and an increasing necessity for organizations choosing among various investment options for their continuous improvement" (p. 6). Despite the use of quantitative data to measure financial and performance outcomes, they say that the model "fails to account for the complex system of influences on training outcomes that exist in organizations" (Han & Boulay, 2013, p. 7). Dean and Ripley (2016) indicated that evaluation is critical for measuring effectiveness of performance improvement interventions and that management is receptive to results expressed in relation to the bottom line.

Systems Models of Evaluation

The dissatisfaction with the Kirkpatrick four-level or Kirkpatrick-Phillips five-level models have prompted consideration of other evaluation models (Han & Boulay, 2013). For example, the performance learning evaluation system proposed by Swanson (1996) relates performance to business and financial results, learning to mastery of information, demonstration of workplace expertise, and satisfaction of employees participating and stakeholders sponsoring the program. Dean and Ripley (2016) described performance learning evaluation as a practical and valid method for reporting performance results used in varied settings including business, industry, and government. Knowledge mastery can be measured on tests, and application of knowledge gained in the program can form the basis of improved expertise. Therefore, demonstrating and assessing skillful workplace behaviors can assist workers to meet behavioral outcomes. Although the goal for knowledge mastery and expertise demonstration can be close to 100%, participant and stakeholder satisfaction goals can be somewhat lower "because learning and most performance improvement efforts require change and change is not comfortable"

(Dean & Ripley, 2016, p. 42). Reports generated by this system should be kept short and emphasize results and performance improvement.

Wang et al. (2002) also proposed a systems approach for evaluation based on detailed analysis of industrial psychology and economics. They introduced mathematical models intended to isolate HRD's contributions to economic returns. They indicated that ROI models adapted from accounting are inadequate for measuring complexities of human behavior. ROI equations derived from accounting require all inputs to be translated into their dollar value, but intangible outcomes such as customer satisfaction, job satisfaction, or learning and subsequent performance improvement are difficult to reduce to monetary terms. Another difficulty with measuring ROI is the difficulty of differentiating intervening variables from the influence of HRD interventions. Wang and colleagues' proposed model combines objective information about sales, production levels, profitability, and employee turnover with training records and job satisfaction surveys. They asserted that organization staff could access much of the information from records they already maintain. Statistical procedures can be applied to estimate the relative contributions of each input included in the equation. Han and Boulay (2013) indicated the model is complex in implementation, particularly because the systematic data collection required does not always occur in practice, and many organizations' analyses processes are not sophisticated enough to account for all variables related to ROI. HRD interventions are barely "susceptible to quantitative evaluation" (Sakalas & Liepė, 2011, p. 905).

A systems model of evaluation for HRD can be implemented in recognition of "multiple factors throughout the system [that] can influence an evaluation" (Russ-Eft, 2014, p. 584). At its core, the model begins with the evaluation process including planning and designing the evaluation, budgeting, collecting and analyzing data, and reporting evaluation results (Russ-Eft & Preskill, 2009). The model identifies internal and external influences on the process. The political context includes evaluator characteristics such as competence and previous experience and takes into account the intended uses of evaluation results by stakeholders who may be organizational leaders sponsoring the evaluation or government agencies that mandate reporting of evaluation results. A surrounding layer includes the organizations' mission, vision, and strategic goals; leadership and infrastructure; and communication systems for disseminating evaluation findings. The outermost layer takes account of external factors including "competition, customer expectations, workforce diversity, legal requirements, technology, and the global context" (Russ-Eft, 2014, p. 550). The model is intended to situate evaluation within an ongoing meaning-making process for enhancing knowledge and decision-making.

Future Directions

Concerns have been raised about HRD as a tool of management used to control workers, but Kuchinke (2010) emphasized that human flourishing should be at the heart of HRD activities. The Academy of Human Resource Development's (2018) code of ethics is based on general "principles of (a) competence, (b) integrity, (c) professional responsibility, (d) respect for people's rights and dignity, (e) concern for others' welfare, and (f) social responsibility" (2018, para. 10). Bierema and Callahan (2014) documented HRD's drift from its original roots in humanist philosophy supporting employee development and organizational health to a performance orientation toward management goals based in productivity and profitability. Although HRD interventions may support healthier workplaces, employee engagement, and employee decision-making, at the same time workers are now responsible for driving their own career development, seeking and paying for education, and acquiescing to increased organizational surveillance of their activities. Bierema (2015) indicated that

> critical HRD questions the performative, shareholder orientation of traditional HRD, and critiques its view of workers as commodities, omission of discussions of power, and failure to provide alternative conceptions of the field that are more inclusive and concerned with social responsibility and sustainability. (p. 119)

Needs assessment, performance analysis, and evaluation have been essential tools for HRD and remain so even as employee characteristics and working conditions are changing. In 2014 Oxford Economics conducted 2 surveys of business executives and employees in 27 countries and found that organizations are increasingly hiring contingent, intermittent, and consultant employees, which prompts increased needs for training and different compensation mechanisms (Oxford Economics, 2019). Different work-flow patterns such as telecommuting, job sharing, and flextime influence employee relationships with each other and with management as do changing expectations and decreased loyalty among employees. Difficulty in recruiting employees with sufficient base-level skills or specialized skills is becoming more prevalent. Communications technology has provided opportunities for employees to work from home, share jobs, and be more entrepreneurial by entering into a portfolio of contracts. Employee diversity in age, nationality, and demographics was a concern of business executives. Overall, the Oxford Economics report recommended that organizations in the future should

- prepare for increasing diversity, changing employee demographics, and evolving definitions of work;
- gain a better understanding of incoming millennial employees;
- enhance employee engagement by providing the incentives and benefits that people actually want;
- improve executive leadership skills and cultivation; and
- foster a culture of continuous learning that develops talent and empowers workers while capturing and retaining vital knowledge. (Oxford Economics, 2019)

Other changes include "increased interest in addressing complex problems such as social exclusion, environmental concerns, and Indigenous well-being" (Podger, 2017, p. 112). Complex challenges including increased employee diversity, cultural conflicts, and employee mobility require new approaches to assessment, evaluation, and accountability. Changes from vertical to more horizontal management structures change relationships among employees and management. Greater demands for organizational social responsibility and accountability create the urgency for the development of different metrics of effectiveness.

References

Academy of Human Resource Development. (2018). Standards on ethics and integrity. Retrieved from https://www.ahrd.org/page/standards_on_ethics

Armitage, A., & Parrey, D. (2013). Reinventing performance management: Creating purpose-driven practices. *People & Strategy, 36*(2), 26–33.

Benito-Bilbao, J., Sánchez-Fuente, F., & Otegi-Olaso, J. R. (2015). Mapping the connection between knowledge transfer and firm competitiveness: An empirical research in the Basque country. *Journal of Technology Management & Innovation, 10*(4), 45–56.

Bierema, L. L. (2015). Critical human development to enhance reflexivity, change discourse, and adopt a call-to-action. *Human Resource Development Review, 14*(2), 119–124.

Bierema, L., & Callahan, J. L. (2014). Transforming HRD: Framework for critical HRD practice. *Advances in Developing Human Resources, 16*, 429–444.

Broffenbrenner, U. (1979). *The ecology of human development: Experiments by nature and design.* Cambridge, MA: Harvard University Press.

Buckingham, M., & Goodall, A. (2013). Reinventing performance management. *Harvard Business Review, 93*(4), 40–50.

Caffarella, R. S., & Daffron, S. R. (2013). *Planning programs for adult learners: A practical guide* (3rd ed.). San Francisco, CA: Jossey-Bass.

Cho, Y., Jo, S. J., Park, S., Kang, I., & Chen, Z. (2011). The current state of human performance technology: A citation network analysis of *Performance Improvement Quarterly*, 1988–2010. *Performance Improvement Quarterly, 24*(1), 69–95.

Christensen, B. D. (2018). From needs assessment to needs analysis. *Performance Improvement, 57*(7), 36–44.

Dean, P. J., & Ripley, D. E. (2016). *"Richard A. Swanson, Ed.D.: The PLS evaluation system."* *Performance Improvement, 55*(8), 40–46.

Han, H., & Boulay, D. (2013). Reflections and future prospects for evaluation in human resource development. *New Horizons in Adult Education and Human Resource Development, 25*(2), 6–18.

Holland, R. (2016, July 25). Companies waste billions of dollars on ineffective corporate training. *Forbes.* Retrieved from https://www.forbes.com/sites/hbsworkingknowledge/2016/07/25/companies-waste-billions-of-dollars-on-ineffective-corporate-training/#7ec48cf84d22

Jasson, C. C., & Govender, C. (2017). Measuring return on investment and risk in training – a business training evaluation model for managers and leaders. *Acta Commercii, 17*(1), 1–9.

Kirkpatrick, D. L. (1994). *Evaluating training programs: The four levels.* San Francisco, CA: Berrett-Koehier.

Kissack, H. C., & Callahan, J. L. (2010). The reciprocal influence of organizational culture and training and development programs. *European Journal of Training and Development, 34*, 365–380.

Kuchinke, K. P. (2010). Human development as a central goal for human resource development. *Human Resource Development International, 13*(5), 575–585.

Lee, J. (2019). Rapid needs assessment: An evidence-based model. *European Journal of Training and Development, 43*(1/2), 61–75.

McElgunn, T. (2019, January 30). Performance management trends for 2019. *HR Morning.* Retrieved from https://www.hrmorning.com/performance-management-trends-2019/

McGuire, D. (2014). *Human resource development* (2nd ed). Thousand Oaks, CA: Sage.

Oxford Economics. (2019). Workforce 2020: Building a strategic workforce for the future. Retrieved from https://www.oxfordeconomics.com/workforce2020

Patel, L. (2010). Overcoming barriers and valuing evaluation. *Training and Development, 64*(2), 62–63.

Phillips, J. J. (1997). *Measuring return on investment in training and performance improvement programs.* Woburn, MA: Butterworth Heinemann.

Phillips, J. J., & Phillips, P. (2009). Using ROI to demonstrate performance value in the public sector. *Performance Improvement, 48*(4), 22–28.

Podger, A. (2017). Enduring challenges and new developments in public human resource management. *Review of Public Personnel Administration, 37*(1), 108–128.

Poell, R. (2012). Organizing human resource development: Towards a dynamic network approach. *Human Resource Development International, 15*(5), 525–528.

Poell, R. F., & Van Der Krogt, F. (2017). Why is organization human resource development so problematic? Perspectives from the learning network theory (Part II). *Learning Organization, 24*, 215–225.

Ritzman, M. E., & Kahle-Piasecki, L. (2016). What works: A systems approach to employee performance in strengthening information security. *Performance Improvement, 55*(8), 17–22.

Ruona, E. A., Leimbach, M., Holton, E., & Bates, R. (2002). The relationship between learner utility reactions and predicted learning transfer among trainees. *International Journal of Training and Development, 6*(4), 218–228.

Russ-Eft, D. F. (2014). Human resource development, evaluation, and sustainability: What are the relationships? *Human Resource Development International, 17*, 545–555.

Russ-Eft, D., & Preskill, H. (2009). *Evaluation in organizations: A systematic approach to enhancing learning, performance, and change.* New York, NY: Basic Books.

Russ-Eft, D., & Preskill, H. (2005). In search of the Holy Grail: Return on investment evaluation in human resource development. *Advances in Developing Human Resources, 7*(1), 71–85.

Sakalas, A., & Liepė, Ž. (2011). Evaluation methods of investment in human capital. *Economics and Management, 16*, 900–906.

Sangwa, N. R., & Sangwan, K. S. (2017). Leanness assessment of organizational performance: A systematic literature review. *Journal of Manufacturing Technology Management, 29*(5), 768–788.

Shuck, B., Reio, T. G., & Rocco, T. S. (2011). Employee engagement: An examination of antecedent and outcome variables. *Human Resource Development International, 14*(4), 427–445.

Sommer, K. L., & Kulkarni, M. (2012). Does constructive performance feedback improve citizenship intentions and job satisfaction? The roles of perceived opportunities for advancement, respect, and mood. *Human Resource Development Quarterly, 23*(2), 177–201.

Swanson, R. A. (1996). *Performance learning satisfaction evaluation system: The application of the three-domain evaluation model to performance improvement, human resource development, organization development, and training and development.* Minneapolis, MN: Human Resource Development Center. Retrieved from http://richardswanson.com/hrdrcreports/Swanson(1996)PerfLearnSatis.pdf

Swanson, R. A., & Holton, E. F. (2008). *Foundations of human resource development* (2nd ed). San Francisco, CA: Berrett Koehler.

Taylor, M., Evans, K., & Pinsent-Johnson, C. (2010). Work-based learning in Canada and the United Kingdom: A framework for understanding knowledge transfer for workers with low skills and higher skills. *Research in Post-Compulsory Education, 15*(4), 347–361.

Van Tiem, D. M., Moseley, J. L., & Dessinger, J. C. (2012). *Fundamentals of performance improvement: Optimizing results through people, processes, and organizations.* San Francisco, CA: Pfieffer.

von Treuer, K., McHardy, K., & Earl, C. (2013). The influence of organisational commitment, job involvement and utility perceptions on trainees' motivation to improve work through learning. *Journal of Vocational Education & Training, 65*(3), 606–620.

Walton, J., & Valentin, C. (2014). Introduction: Framing contemporary HRD practice and theory. In J. Walton & C. Valentin (Eds.), *Human resource development: Practices and orthodoxies* (pp. 1–16). New York, NY: Palgrave Macmillan.

Wang, G. G., Dou, Z., & Li, N. (2002). A systems approach to measuring return on investment for HRD interventions. *Human Resource Development Quarterly, 13*(2), 203–224.

Weinstein, M. G., & Shuck, B. (2011). Social ecology and worksite training and development: Introducing the social in instructional system design. *Human Resource Development Review, 10*(3), 286–303.

8

A FRAMEWORK FOR COMMUNITY CAPACITY BUILDING

The Role of Assessment and Evaluation

Elizabeth A. Roumell, Corina Todoran, and Nima Khodakarami

S ince the late 1990s, federal and state policies have increasingly continued to require greater accountability, increased cooperation, and partnerships among education and social service sectors, organizations, and agencies and more systematic assessment and evaluation plans. Legislation and policies continue to require improved organizational interoperability, data-driven decision-making, and comprehensive evaluation, as well as detailed implementation plans and scalable programming rooted in assessment and institutional measures. In light of these policy and programming trends over the past 20 years, we present a conceptual framework for analyzing a community or an organization's capacity for carrying out new initiatives, assessment plans, and evaluation.

In the public and institutional discourse regarding assessment, evaluation, and accountability programs, there is a growing need for applied models and conceptual frameworks to help improve the effectiveness in designing and implementing initiatives in organizations and communities. Horner, Sugai, and Fixsen (2017) argue that "too often effective practices are proposed without attention to the breadth of systems variables and implementation tools needed to facilitate adoption, reliable use, and sustainability over time, and generalization across settings, and staff" (p. 26). Program development and evaluation models that are community focused and participatory in nature (Biglan, 1995; Gregory et al., 2012; Nastasi & Hitchcock, 2016; Nastasi, Moore, & Varjas, 2004) are available, but they are not necessarily presented in a way that takes the current parameters of agency requirements and multiple partnerships into consideration, nor do they adequately describe the capacity-building process for collaborative program implementation and system evaluation.

In the fields of adult education, workforce education, and human resource development, it is in our best interest to identify frameworks and processes that are congruent with the demands of relevant funding agencies. It is also critical to propose implementation and evaluation strategies that systematically work toward building the organization's capacity for carrying out new initiatives and programming in a maintainable progression.

This chapter covers the key role capacity development plays in the overall implementation and evaluation process. It provides a brief overview of capacity building, the strategic process, and introduces the capacity-building framework, which consists of eight dimensions. The following sections provide some basic definitions, an explanation of how capacity building fits into the broader processes of implementation and evaluation, a systems thinking orientation to capacity building, and a detailed presentation of the framework. We argue that capacity building and assessment are an important addition to the process of program development, integral to the implementation of new initiatives, and a process that overall improves and complements evaluation design.

Terminology Defined

In this book, *assessment* refers to the measurement of individual student learning that may be used for screening, diagnosis, feedback, monitoring progress, and designing educational interventions, whereas *evaluation* involves the further application of learning assessments and program data to make judgments for program improvement and provide information to stakeholders, regional and professional accrediting bodies, and accountability systems (Galbraith & Jones, 2010). Subsequently, accountability systems are extensions of evaluation, designed to produce evidence to verify that education was conducted appropriately; progress was made; and that resources, particularly taxpayer monies, are used efficiently (Tusting, 2012).

For the purpose of understanding how the notion of capacity building fits into a system of assessment and evaluation, we first build on this book's definition of *evaluation*. A thorough program evaluation involves data collection from multiple sources to appraise overall program impact including acceptability, social and ecological validity, implementation (integrity or fidelity), outcomes, sustainability, and institutionalization. This includes not only inferences about the program across time, participants, settings, and contexts (Shadish, Cook, & Campbell, 2002) but also the organization's capacity to meaningfully translate those findings into improved practice. This chapter addresses the importance of capacity building in the overall program development and evaluation process.

Capacity development, as presented here, is understood as the process through which individuals, programs, and organizations obtain, strengthen, and maintain the capabilities necessary to design and implement new initiatives over time. Capacity development is an analysis of

> desired organizational capacities against existing capacities which generates an understanding of capacity assets and needs that can serve as input for formulating programming responses that address organizational capacities that could be strengthened and help optimize existing capacities that are already strong and well founded. (United Nations Development Program, 2008, p. 4)

Horner et al. (2017) delineate community or organizational capacity as the ability to address the following elements in program or initiative implementation:

1. Formal policies that indicate the primary objectives for developing the requisite resources and skills for those carrying out initiatives and for the organization as a whole
2. Human resources procedures that recruit and hire individuals with documented competence required for implementation, orient all new personnel to the aspects of systemic support, and establish accountability measures
3. Data systems that allow the leadership team, vital administrators, and implementing staff to assess the progress and quality of implementation
4. Training and coaching capacity that allows improved adoption and consistent use of the new initiatives
5. Technical expertise in the organization to assist key personnel in implementing practices with the accuracy and sophistication needed for the establishment and operation of sustainable programming
6. Relevant resources and processes for implementation that can be used as examples, how-to guides, and to demonstrate the value of new practices

Because many new federal, state, and independently funded projects related to workforce development and adult education now require multiple agencies or multiple organizational partnerships and collaborations, the model we are presenting uses the term *community* to represent the plurality of organizations and partnerships that can be involved in program implementation that serve a wide and diverse population of adult learners.

Capacity Building and Evaluation

The importance of the systematic study of program implementation stems from the need to more actively bridge theory and practice in organizations and communities. *Implementation science* is a widely used term that encompasses the development of a knowledge base for understanding and applying effective interventions and community programs across disciplines including medicine, psychology, education, prevention, and public health. Implementation science is the enactment of empirically supported interventions, programs, and practices in naturalistic settings (i.e., in programs, organizations, and communities) and the factors that influence their success. Eccles and Mittman (2006) define *implementation science* as the scientific study of "methods to promote the systematic uptake of research findings and other evidence-based practices into routine practice, and, hence, to improve the quality and effectiveness of public services" (para. 2). The American Psychological Association extended this definition to "understanding the processes and factors related to successful integration" (Foman et al., 2013, p. 80) of evidence-based initiatives with particular attention to core program components, adaptations to the local context, and attention to culture and climate in the community.

Evidence-based practice, as defined by the American Psychological Association Presidential Taskforce on Evidence-Based Practice (2006), is the integration of the best available research with clinical expertise in the context of individual characteristics, context, culture, and preference. The concept of evidence-based initiatives is widely applied, but a more comprehensive process framework that works more effectively toward building implementation capacity is required for the successful implementation and evaluation of initiatives.

Many kinds of novel initiatives have been validated in different contexts, but it is still necessary to consider how to tailor the approaches when introducing them into a different local community and context. Translational research deals with the adaptation and introduction of novel interventions into new and varying cultural contexts. For example, this process would apply when an isolated rural community adopts an educational intervention that was developed and tested in an urban setting. These investigations are related to program acceptability, social and ecological integrity, effectiveness, and necessary adaptations across cultural and contextual variations. Community programming and evidence-based initiatives are most effective when they are well matched with their target population's level and kind of need and are contextually appropriate and culturally relevant (social and ecological validity). The primary concerns of such an investigation are to identify how programs can be successfully adopted and implemented and to get local stakeholders actively involved in a more systematic process of needs assessment, capacity building, and evaluation to improve overall implementation across contexts (Alkin, 2013).

It is critical to establish clarity on the kind and appropriateness of an initiative the community wants to implement, but it is also necessary to determine whether the community and organizations have sufficient capacity to effectively carry out the initiative. A capacity assessment also assists in establishing a more clearly defined implementation process, as well as developing indicators that can be used to mark progress. A capacity-building assessment that employs a consistent framework complements and can be combined with any data-driven strategic program development process and can also be coordinated with or integrated into program evaluation design. The next sections provide further details on building and assessing capacity, a synopsis of strategic process, and a description of the framework in more depth.

Building Capacity

Community capacity development is not a one-off intervention or readiness assessment but an intentional and iterative process of design, application, learning, and adjustment. First, our capacity framework outlines a five-step cycle that broadly coincides with the steps of a program planning cycle. Approaching capacity development through this process lens is a rigorous and systematic way of supporting program improvement by improving the consistency, coherence, and impact of programming initiatives. It also helps promote a common frame of reference for programmatic capacity development. Second, the capacity development process effectively requires identifying the key capacities that already exist and the additional capacities that may be needed to reach objectives. A capacity analysis can also set the baseline for continuous monitoring and the evaluation of progress against relevant indicators and help create a solid foundation for long-term planning, implementation, and sustainable results (United Nations Development Program, 2008).

Capacity assessments can be conducted at different points of a planning or programming cycle. For example, a capacity-building analysis can be used as a departure point when preparing to design or implement new curriculum, standards, or policies; conducting an accreditation process; or elaborating on a new assessment or evaluation plan. Often capacity assessments are conducted in response to a felt and expressed need for capacity development, for example, at a broader systemic level (region, state, district, etc.), a holistic organizational level, in an administrative unit or department, or in a single program. A capacity-building analysis is conducted to determine or clarify the types of capacity that need to be addressed and how to improve implementation and programming. Such an analysis can be prepared in advance of a new initiative or be a part of the first phase of program or project development to establish or confirm its direction. If a capacity analysis was not conducted during the formulation of a strategy, program, or project, it can be initiated during implementation or even during the review stage if there is to be a follow up on the program. According to United Nations Development Program (2008)

> a capacity assessment can serve a variety of purposes. It can provide the starting point for formulating a capacity development response; act as a catalyst for action; confirm priorities for action; build political support for an agenda; offer a platform for dialogue among stakeholders; and provide insight into operational hurdles in order to unblock a program or project. (p. 6)

The Strategic Community Process

The strategic process we present is similar to that of the U.S. Department of Labor (2016), whose six key elements are to build cross-agency partnerships and clarify roles, identify industry sectors and engage employers, design education and training programs, identify funding needs and sources, align policies and programs, and measure system change and performance.

Our process model can generally be considered to be an itemized explanation of the process behind the first three key elements. The strategic process has five ongoing stages that provide a structure for data-based decision-making, which makes use of evidence-based strategies and programs. The steps in the strategic process are the following: a rigorous phase of data collection and needs and capacity assessment to identify the issues at hand; organization and buy-in from the key implementing agents; collective and participatory community decision-making based on the findings of the needs and capacity assessment process; involvement of key implementing agents in community capacity building; and the implementation, monitoring, and evaluation phase in which data are collected again to conduct a summative assessment of the intervention, make adjustments where needed, and provide information and evidence to facilitate future strategic planning.

The strategic process also closely mirrors the conventional analysis, design, development, implementation, and evaluation process (Hund, 2016) commonly taught in training and development and program planning, which is adapted here to better integrate community participation throughout the processes of data collection, analysis, stakeholder identification, and strategic planning. The strategic process foregrounds program maintainability and cultural congruence with the community and emphasizes the importance and value of these in effective community capacity building and implementation.

Gregory et al. (2012) stressed the importance of integrating cultural competence into programming and interventions through attention to community culture, organizational culture, and the cultural competence of partners (i.e., researchers, program developers, agents, stakeholders, and implementers). May's (2013) implementation theory emphasizes the importance of individual and collective action in the dynamic systems context, taking into account that program success is multidimensional and dynamic. The proposed strategic process and capacity framework we are presenting encompass and address the sustainability and cultural factors of program acceptability; social validity; program integrity; implementer competence; institutionalization; sustainability and maintainability; and the use of data and evaluation for adjusting goals and outcomes according to the local culture, values, and needs (Nastasi & Hitchcock, 2016).

Sustained implementation efforts that are grounded in this strategic process and apply the framework to analyze each of the capacity dimensions can also be used to gather information that can help detect the kinds of change and impact of an intervention. The capacity-building domains constitute a conceptual basis for data collection to determine capacity-building needs and for indicating the level of community capacity development. The eight dimensions are presented in Table 8.1, and then we expand on the framework by defining the eight dimensions that make up the capacity-building assessment.

Capacity-Building Framework

The capacity-building model is derived and synthesized from the Plested, Edwards, and Jumper-Thurman (2006) community readiness model, which assesses a community's capacity for implementation; the Hardee, Feranil, Boezwinkle, and Clark (2004) conceptual framework, which identifies the six main components of policy analysis; and also the Council for Adult and Experiential Learning (2008) adult learning policy review framework, which provides a schema for evaluating policies related to adult-oriented education and training. The elements of each model were

TABLE 8.1

Descriptions of the Capacity-Building Framework Domains

Dimensions	Description
Community climate	The prevailing attitude of the community regarding the issue that is intended to be addressed, ranging from perceived helplessness to responsibility and empowerment
	General community knowledge about the influencing factors and causes of the problem the intervention is intended to address
	General community knowledge about current local efforts to address the issues and their effectiveness and the expansion of efforts to all segments of the community, including programs and policies
Leadership and stakeholders	The support and buy-in of appointed and elected leaders and influential members of the community (key stakeholders)
Resources	The availability of local resources to support intervention efforts including people, expertise, time, money, space, information and data, media, and dissemination
	Infrastructure and capacity—the social-structural resources available to implementation agents (i.e., social norms, roles, materials, and cognitive resources in the system)
	Potentials—social cognitive resources (beliefs and values) available to implementation agents and the agents' capacity to link social-cognitive and social-structural resources to bring about action (i.e., intervention)
	Contributions—what the agents, individually and collectively, do to implement the intervention
Evaluation and data use	Regular collection and use of data to continually guide decision-making. Which data are needed, and what data are available? How are data currently used in planning? How are data collected, analyzed, and reported for strategic planning purposes?
	Program integrity—or fidelity or adherence—refers to the extent to which the program is implemented as designed
	Program impact refers to the outcomes of effects of the intervention, both intended and unintended

(Continues)

TABLE 8.1 (*Continued*)

Dimensions	Description
Planning and maintainability	Establishment of collaborative groups (including coalitions, advisory, and planning) and regular cross-system coordinated planning to ensure long-term sustainability; coordinated collaboration among government and funding agencies, private sector, nonprofit, or other sectors; maintainability addresses the extent to which programs can continue without external support and the ability to maintain efforts
Evidence-based approaches	Recognition of the importance, encouragement, and promotion of evidence-based practices
Cultural competence and congruence (ecological validity)	Recognition of the importance, encouragement, and promotion of audience-appropriate practices that are congruent with the needs of the participants and needs of the community
	Program acceptability—the perspectives of stakeholders regarding the feasibility, importance, probable success, and congruence with shared worldviews
	Social validity—the extent to which the program and intended outcomes are socially valued in the target context and everyday lives of the recipients; the cultural relevance of program goals and outcomes and their consistency with values, beliefs, behavioral norms, and language of the target group
	The knowledge, attitudes, and skills of the implementers, necessary competencies to implement the program with integrity and to adapt to program needs in a way that is responsive to and meets contextual and cultural needs of the recipients
Implementer competence	Capability—the likelihood that the agents responsible for implementation can operationalize the intervention based on feasibility and actual contextual fit
	The current state of the agents and qualified specialists responsible for performing the strategy implementation
	Are there sufficient, well-trained personnel and encouragement of multidisciplinary training?

pooled, compared, and merged into a more comprehensive framework for examining and evaluating a community's ability and preparedness for the implementation of new interventions. Additionally, we included the critical components of the Nastasi and Hitchcock (2016) model for culture-specific interventions. The eight components are shown in Table 8.1.

All the capacity domains provide useful information to help identify possible impediments to successful implementation. However, meaningful program implementation requires data resources that provide relevant, usable, and accessible data that can be used at every level of the system. The capacity dimension of *evaluation data use* includes knowledge about the sources and kinds of data that are available; an understanding of how various kinds of data can be used as indicators for the desired outcomes; personnel who are capable of performing the appropriate data collection, maintenance, and analyses; and leaders who can interpret and effectively use the information to further guide the implementation process (Horner et al., 2017). Building the capacity for systematic data use and evaluation cannot be overemphasized as the entire strategic process and implementation procedures hinge on how organizations use information throughout the planning, implementation, and evaluation process. This is also particularly critical for efforts that are multiagentic and built on partnerships that may have multiple goals and outcomes. The domain of data use also informs interorganizational and community learning (Mariotti, 2012) and depends on the frequency and depth of assessment and analysis. The capacity of the leadership to effectively use data along with the implementer's and agents' capacity to generate, collect, maintain, and contribute useful data throughout the process are instrumental and invaluable.

To approach the analysis of the community capacity data collected, the suggested point of departure is Bronfenbrenner's (1989, 1999) developmental-ecological perspective, which views the community or organization in terms of multiple nested systems. There is the *microsystem*, or the immediate context, where the program agents and the community participants directly interact. Locally, this could be a grant recipient team or local program providers or the resource development team. This system is further embedded in, interacts with, and is influenced by the surrounding systems. The *mesosystem* is the relationship among the various ecological systems (e.g., system funding agencies or departments and their organization) and the *macrosystem*, which is made up of the larger community and inherent values, beliefs, and norms of the broader infrastructure, culture, and framework where the programming is being implemented. The *chronosystem* includes any historical and other social developmental influences that may additionally have an impact on program implementation (Nastasi & Hitchcock, 2016).

This nested interactive systems perspective (Wandersman et al., 2008) helps key program actors better understand the interactions between organizations and system levels and their roles and scope of influence throughout implementation. This systems analytic approach parsimoniously pulls the capacity-building dimensions together for a more nuanced community capacity analysis. Identifying the interactive systems calls attention to the following primary systems of consideration that interact to influence implementation and dissemination of community programming: (a) the synthesis and translation system, including those responsible for program design, translation, and planning; (b) the delivery system, including the site of delivery and agents' capacity to execute the interventions; and (c) the support system, which provides technical assistance and consultation to enhance the capacity for successful implementation and sustainability. Some of the capacity-building domains directly influence these three systems: familiarity with the programs and initiatives, organizational climate, funding and other resources, and macro-level organizational policies that can either help or hinder implementation. The eight capacity assessment domains address each of the critical components of these three systems and how they interrelate to build implementation infrastructure and community capacity. Moreover, the multisystemic analytic approach also requires consideration of collaboration across stakeholders, which is appropriate for an analysis that takes into account the coordination of different organizational levels and partners.

Applying the Process and Framework

Often implementation becomes hurried with the focus overly narrowed on programming efforts, and the initial exploration stages of the strategic process are treated only superficially. The following are the stages in the strategic process in capacity building: (a) conduct the capacity assessment, (b) build community buy-in, (c) select the appropriate strategies to build capacity, (d) plan strategically for program implementation, and (e) design the evaluation of the initiative. Too often the first three stages are skimmed over and not adequately performed, even though they lay an essential foundation for building community capacity for successful implementation. Ideally, prior to launching a new program initiative, data need to be collected and analyzed for each of the eight capacity-building dimensions to establish a baseline capacity assessment, identify areas for planning and development, and prioritize efforts. The eight dimensions of community capacity building can be squarely established in the initial community process of a thorough, participatory needs assessment.

The capacity-building dimensions can be examined using qualitative or survey data to describe the main factors that make program implementation possible. A variety of techniques can be used to collect unique data and mine available information to provide indicators and descriptions for each of the eight dimensions. Commonly used data collection techniques include stakeholder interviews, community focus groups, community coalition building, surveys, and Delphi studies, among others. Community or organizational data, state data resources, and national data repositories such as the U.S. Department of Labor Statistics (n.d.) Bureau of Labor Statistics states' databases, or databases like the Integrated Postsecondary Education Data System (National Center for Education Statistics, n.d.) are also resources that can be used. For the purpose of mobilizing and educating key local stakeholders, in-person interviews can also be used to collect information for each of the eight community capacity dimensions and are an effective place to begin the needs assessment stage of the process, to establish baseline community capacity measures for evaluation, and to obtain buy-in from key players for implementation.

In the initial process of identifying the stakeholders and seeking their input and advice, the leadership can generate an opportunity to inform and educate key stakeholders about the community's needs. This process also becomes an opportunity for building community buy-in, informing additional critical leaders, mobilizing resources, and coordinating efforts in building partnerships for addressing the targeted needs. These initial stages of the process are where the community program leadership and stakeholders build and reinforce communication networks, and learning and training needs can be identified for all involved. The first stages also offer leadership the prospect of influencing the community's perceptions and knowledge about planned efforts and encouraging the community climate by building receptivity to the initiatives. The initial phases of the capacity analysis also provide space for collecting participant information and perspectives that can serve as the basis for translational research for the programs and make adjustments to address cultural congruence and ecological validity for the programming. The initial stages of the strategic process and analysis should be thorough, not superficial.

By conducting a preliminary analysis that addresses each of the eight capacity-building dimensions, the leadership team can move directly into the next phase of examining the current infrastructure and capacity for implementation and identifying actionable areas. Leadership can identify additional sources of data, areas where training is needed (perhaps in data analysis or for the agents using strategies in the community), or a clearer picture of the community climate regarding an issue and the kinds of information dissemination that may be necessary to garner community interest and support.

When these dimensions have been adequately assessed, it becomes easier to identify the approaches that are more likely to have the intended impact, which then feeds forward into the continued strategic planning process. For example, if the community stakeholders do not appear to be receptive to a new program or curriculum, or the community climate is simply cold on an issue, then a preparation stage like a public media-driven strategy focused on information dissemination and community education may be a more appropriate and feasible departure point than an intervention that targets a selective community-based services strategy or individually based intervention programs that could be prone to failure in a nonreceptive climate. If the eight capacity-building dimensions are properly taken into consideration and used to plan the structure and design of implementation, then the leadership is less likely to encounter the surprises and obstacles that often hinder the success of new programs and initiatives.

Additionally, using a framework that addresses the capacity dimensions develops a natural scaffolding for the ongoing collection of data for evaluation purposes. This provides a useful structure for developing leadership planning agendas, not to mention meeting data and evaluation requirements of funding agencies, where a baseline can be established and indicators identified to measure progress related to building community capacity. Using the capacity-building framework also feeds into future planning and building networks, boosting maintainability, strengthening the fidelity of program implementation, and encouraging the cultural congruence of community programming.

Capacity-Building Domains

Through conducting a needs assessment and a community stakeholder analysis, the capacity framework helps develop an illustration of the community climate where the programming is to be carried out. It is essential to understand the community social climate, perceptions, and perceived needs to develop effective programming that is socially valid and acceptable. To do so, it is important for the leadership and implementing agents to develop a nuanced understanding of their audience. The needs assessment process involves, in part, discovering more about the community participants as well as the broader community audience, and their perceptions related to the initiative.

Knowledge in the community about current programs is also part of the climate assessment. To address this dimension, it is important to find out about the community's general knowledge about the local programs and services available, how to identify sources and resources, and how they become informed about the services and programs that are being promoted. It is also important to understand the community's receptivity toward the programs to be implemented. Are there social stigmas around an issue or particular kinds of services? For example, what cultural values, beliefs, and perceptions would influence the community's receptivity to individualized services, and would community members be willing to seek such programming and services? Are the implementing agents resistant to the changes and initiative? If stakeholders do not perceive a real problem or need in their community, then implementers may need to focus on educating the community about the opportunities before proceeding with new policies, programs, or interventions.

Leadership

It is also important to gauge the climate of the leading stakeholders and key players as part of the initial needs assessment process. Doing a stakeholder analysis and gathering information from the key leaders on the community climate is critical for a number of reasons. With a clear picture of how initiatives are viewed by the community leadership, it is easier to identify the approaches and interventions that are more likely to garner support and succeed. Gathering information from leadership also generates an opportunity to raise awareness and to educate and inform key stakeholders about a new initiative and possible actions that could be taken in the community. Identifying and assessing the climate among leadership can also be a unique opportunity to identify, obtain buy-in from, and potentially mobilize new stakeholders. This is sometimes called coalition building in which leaders seek partnerships across various agencies and organizations in the community that may also be invested in the potentials of the proposed initiatives.

Resources

Assessing community capacity is also a process of establishing the capability of the leadership and the community to effectively implement a program initiative. It is likely that the agents responsible for implementation can implement the intervention based on feasibility and actual contextual fit for the identified community participants. A close examination of the resources and social infrastructure in the community is necessary. The notion of capacity, in general, also includes the social and structural resources available to the implementing agents (i.e., social norms, roles, materials, and cognitive resources in the system). This directly influences the amount of material and social resources available for implementation.

When looking at the kinds of resources available for community program implementation, more than space, time, and funding need to be taken into consideration. Contributions consist of what the agents, individually and collectively, are able to do to implement the intervention cognitively (e.g., sense making, reflexive monitoring) and behaviorally (collective action), which are essential components in building community infrastructure and implementation capacity. For example, it may become obvious that agents responsible for program implementation need some additional training and development related to the program, assessment, and data analysis and evaluation techniques. Examining the element of contributions includes further investigation into the learning communities, coalitions, and learning networks that begin to emerge (Harold & Fedor, 2008). The implementing agents, leadership, and stakeholders need to continue to cultivate the local networks and communication lines to build momentum and further activate human and material resources for mobilization and implementation (Gay & Hembrook, 2004). Potentials are to the social cognitive resources (beliefs and values) available to implementation agents and the agents' capacity to link professional knowledge and systems resources to bring about collective action (i.e., the intervention). Examining potentials provides the opportunity to identify currently held perceptions and beliefs that may further or hinder implementation efforts and to affect those perceptions where needed.

Evidence-Based Interventions

Recognition of the importance, encouragement, and promotion of evidence-based practices is also essential for effective implementation. The selection of an appropriate evidence-based initiative is essential. It is counterproductive to use limited resources to implement interventions that are contextually inappropriate or have limited impact. The leadership team needs to be able to identify and assess the essential components of possible evidence-based initiatives and their potential contribution to the desired outcomes. In the interest of efficiency and effectiveness, the implementing agents need to know the minimum practice requirements for producing intended outcomes. Interventions should not only be appropriate but also be carried out as intended (fidelity) over time (maintainability) and by competent staff who also have access to relevant technical assistance. The leadership team needs to be able to establish a plan and measures for ensuring that those involved can knowledgeably participate in implementation, which requires attention to the various levels of functional units in the embedded systems (Nastasi & Hitchcock, 2016). The various system levels have a multiplier effect in building community and organization capacity and can become critical factors influencing the quality and overall success of an initiative (Fixsen, Naoom, Blase, Friedman, & Wallace, 2005).

Cultural Competence and Congruence

Building community and social infrastructure capacity for successful implementation encompasses components of acceptability and social validity and adjusting goals and outcomes where needed. To implement programs that are successful and locally relevant, it is essential to consider the degree to which the intervention is socially germane and culturally congruent in the participating community (Nastasi & Hitchcock, 2016). Interventions that have been deemed appropriate in some settings may not have social validity and cultural congruence when implemented elsewhere. Although this point may appear obvious, when it comes to educational programming that is funded by the state, federal agencies, or perhaps other kinds of organizations, the aspects of program fidelity (implementing the program the way it was designed and tested) may be prioritized above the consideration of contextual congruence and cultural fit. This is why each of these dimensions should be addressed from the initial needs and capacity-building assessment stage and throughout the entire implementation process. The perspectives of local stakeholders regarding the feasibility, importance, probability of success, and congruence with shared worldviews are critical and tie in closely with the notions of cultural relevance and program fit.

In this domain, social validity refers to the extent to which the intervention and intended outcomes are socially valued in the target context and everyday lives of the participants; in other words, the cultural relevance of program goals and outcomes and their consistency with values, beliefs, behavioral norms, and the language of the target group (Nastasi & Hitchcock, 2016). This also ties into a number of the domains assessed in the framework, including climate, culture and context, leadership, cultural relevance, and the development of community collaborations and human and intellectual resources throughout the community. Conducting a capacity assessment attending to each of the domains can improve the social validity of interventions. For example, social validity could mean that educational programming fits the needs of the identified community or that career and technical training are well aligned with workforce needs in the region.

Planning and Maintainability

The sustainability and maintainability of selected strategies and interventions are crucial. Program implementation should be geared toward building the community's capacity to carry the initiative and its benefits forward beyond the initially defined implementation stages. Sustainability is often framed in terms of financial stability beyond a granting period and multiple funding streams, but additional capacity issues such as adequate personnel, local expertise, and the sustained interest of community networks must also be taken into consideration. Institutionalization refers more broadly to the extent to which programming has become integral to the community, reflecting that systematically building infrastructure and capacity is necessary for maintainable outcomes (Nastasi & Hitchcock, 2016). For example, if new technologies or pedagogies are introduced into programs, have they become integral and routinely used by staff and educators for the intended purposes? Is training available for teachers, are the technologies supported, and how will learners receive the support they need in using the technologies? Do all the learners have the resources and access they need to master the necessary skills to perform well during the intervention? Will the practices become routine, or is their use temporary and not aligned with the overall aims and curriculum?

Implementers' Competence and Capability

It is essential to identify and build the intellectual and social capital in the workforce necessary for effective programs. This dimension includes the implementers' competence, composed of their knowledge, attitudes, and the skills necessary to carry out the intervention with integrity and to adapt to program needs in a way that is responsive to and meets the contextual and cultural needs of the participants. The development of implementers' competence traverses several dimensions and includes a combination of areas including competencies in strategic information use, cooperative planning and coalition building, the execution of interventions that have been validated, and the quality of the education and development of human resources in the system (Horner et al., 2017). Implementers' competence and the ongoing development of workforce professionals are crucial in establishing an infrastructure and the capacity to effectively initiate and implement interventions in a way that is fitting and suitable to the local community.

Evaluation and Data Use

Implementers at various levels should be able to perform real-time, formative, and summative analyses to assure equitable program adjustments and benefits. Data should inform decision-making, progress monitoring, and action planning and are critical for improvement and reform efforts in carrying out new programs and initiatives. Program planning, which involves assessment, evaluation, and accountability systems, is a cyclical process that provides ongoing opportunities to gauge results and make adjustments. Systematic data use throughout the strategic cycle serves to document the impact of interventions, verify the consistency of results, and validate the efficacy of the initiative (Govindarajan & Trimble, 2013). In this sense, assessment and evaluation become integrated into a more formative rather than soley summative appraisal, and capacity assessment helps take a pulse to judge the health of the systems carrying out the interventions and programs.

Conclusion

The purpose of presenting a strategic process and capacity-building framework is to underscore that the sustained use of effective practices in communities and organizations is more likely to be effective if the implementation process begins with active investment in and purposefully developing a community's overall capacity for implementation. Efforts at implementing new practices without attending to system-level development and support structures often result in unsuccessful initiatives, limited outcomes, and poor program sustainability.

The common temptation to go straight to the implementation stages is counterproductive. It is also tempting to delay developing the areas of systemic capacity until after a new initiative has already been put in place, especially when new practices promise to yield desired results. Unfortunately, without adequately developed support systems and multilevel buy-in, the required professional expertise, coordinated partnerships, networks and planning, and strategies for program sustainability, too often the result will be an effective intervention that quickly fades, playing into the unfortunate cycle of adopt-and-replace programming. Not attending to the initial stages of the strategic process and not paying due attention to each capacity-building dimension also run the risk of initiating programs that are not culturally congruent, potentially resulting in unintended and unanticipated negative consequences.

In response to the Workforce Investment and Opportunity Act (2014) that requires adult learning, career training, and workforce development sectors to employ career pathways models and to engage in multitiered systems program implementation, we propose this conceptual framework for structuring and building community capacity. The strategic process and capacity-building model neatly combine key aspects for program planning, capacity building, and evaluation design. We believe the process and framework accommodate the current policy parameters and the multitiered implementation needs of the Workforce Innovation and Opportunity Act and similar mandates, and together they contribute to intentional systemic capacity building for improved adult educational programming.

References

Alkin, M. C. (2013). *Evaluation roots: A wider perspective of theorists' views and influences* (2nd ed.). Thousand Oaks: CA: Sage.

American Psychological Association Presidential Taskforce on Evidence-Based Practice. (2006). Evidence-based practice in psychology. *The American Psychologist, 61*(4), 271–285.

Biglan, A. (1995). *Changing cultural practices: A contextualist framework for intervention research*. Reno, NV: Context Press.

Bronfenbrenner, U. (1989). Ecological systems theory. In R. Vasta (Ed.), *Six theories of child development: Revised formulations and current issues* (pp. 187–249). Greenwich, CT: JAI Press.

Bronfenbrenner, U. (1999). Environments in developmental perspective: Theoretical and operational models. In S. L. Friedmand & T. D. Wachs (Eds.), *Measuring environment across the lifespan: Emerging methods and concepts* (pp. 3–28). Washington, DC: American Psychological Association.

Council for Adult and Experiential Learning. (2008). *State policies to bring adult learning adult learning into focus: A companion guide*. Chicago, IL: Author.

Eccles, M. P., & Mittman, B. S. (2006). Welcome to implementation science. *Implementation Science, 1*, Article 1.

Fixsen, D. L., Naoom, S. F., Blase, K. A., Friedman, R. M., & Wallace, F. (2005). Implementation research: A synthesis of the literature. Retrieved from http://nirn.fpg.unc.edu/sites/nirn.fpg.unc.edu/files/resources/NIRN-MonographFull-01-2005.pdf

Foman, S. G., Shapiro, E. S., Codding, R. S., Gonzales, J. E., Reddy, L. A., Rosenfield, S. A., . . .Stoiber, K. C. (2013). Implementation science and school psychology. *School Psychology Quarterly, 28*(2), 77–100.

Galbraith, M. W., & Jones, M. S. (2010). Assessment and evaluation. In C. E. Kasworm, A. D. Rose, & J. M. Ross-Gordon (Eds.), *Handbook of adult and continuing education* (pp. 167–175). Thousand Oaks: Sage.

Gay, G., & Hembrook, H. (2004). *Activity centered design: An ecological approach to designing smart tools and usable systems*. Cambridge, MA: MIT Press.

Govindarajan, V., & Trimble, C. (2013). *Beyond the idea: How to execute innovation in any organization*. New York, NY: Saint Martin's Press.

Gregory, H., Van Orden, O., Jordan, L., Portnoy, G. A., Welsh, E., Betkowski, J., . . . DiClemente, C. C. (2012). New directions in capacity building: Incorporating cultural competence into the interactive systems framework. *American Journal of Community Psychology, 50*(3–4), 321–333.

Hardee, K., Feranil, I., Boezwinkle, J., & Clark, B. (2004). A framework for analyzing the components of family planning, reproductive health, maternal health, and HIV/AIDS policies. *Policy Working Papers Series, 11*, 1–38.

Harold, D. M., & Fedor, D. B. (2008). *Change the way you lead change: Leadership strategies that really work*. Stanford, CA: Stanford University Press.

Horner, R. H., Sugai, G., & Fixsen, D. L. (2017). Implementing effective educational practices at scales of social importance. *Clinical child and family psychology review, 20*(1), 25–35.

Hund, A. (2016). ADDIE curriculum model. In S. Danver (Ed.), *The Sage encyclopedia of online education* (pp. 61–61). Thousand Oaks: CA: Sage.

Mariotti, F. (2012). Exploring interorganizational learning: A review of the literature and future directions. *Knowledge and Process Management, 19*(4), 215–221.

May, C. (2013). Towards a general theory of implementation. *Implementation Science, 8,* Article 18.

Nastasi, B. K., & Hitchcock, J. H. (2016). *Mixed methods research and culture-specific interventions: Program design and evaluation.* Thousand Oaks, CA: Sage.

Nastasi, B. K., Moore, R. B., & Varjas, K. M. (2004). *School-based mental health services: Creating comprehensive and culturally specific programs.* Washington, DC: American Psychological Association.

National Center for Education Statistics. (n.d.). *Data tools.* Retrieved from https://nces.ed.gov/datatools/

Plested, B. A., Edwards, R. W., & Jumper-Thurman, P. (2006). *Community readiness: A handbook for successful change.* Fort Collins, CO: Tri-Ethnic Center for Prevention Research.

Shadish, W. R., Cook, T. D., & Campbell, D. T. (2002). *Experimental and quasi-experimental designs for generalized causal inference.* Boston, MA: Houghton-Mifflin.

Tusting, K. (2012). Learning accountability literacies in educational workplaces: Situated learning and processes of commodification. *Language and Education, 26*(2), 121–138.

U.S. Department of Labor. (2016). Career pathways toolkit: An enhanced guide and workbook for system development. Retrieved from https://careerpathways.workforcegps.org/resources/2016/10/20/10/11/Enhanced_Career_Pathways_Toolkit

U.S. Department of Labor. (n.d). Bureau of Labor Statistics, databases, tables & calculators by subject. Retrieved from https://www.bls.gov/data/

United Nations Development Program. (2008). Capacity assessment methodology: users guide. Retrieved from http://www.undp.org/content/dam/aplaws/publication/en/publications/capacity-development/undp-capacity-assessment-methodology/UNDP%20Capacity%20Assessment%20Users%20Guide.pdf

Wandersman, A., Duffy, J., Flaspohler, P., Noonan, R., Lubell, K., Stillman, L., . . . Saul, J. (2008). Bridging the gap between prevention research and practice: The interactive systems framework for dissemination and implementation. *American Journal of Community Psychology, 41*(3-4), 171–181.

Workforce Investment and Opportunity Act. (2014). Pub. L. No. 113-128, 128 Stat 1425.

PART THREE

ASSESSMENT AND EVALUATION PRACTICES FOR ADULTS IN HIGHER EDUCATION

9

MOVING BEYOND
POSITIVISM

Integrating Transformative Perspectives in Health Professions Education and Evaluation

Wendy M. Green

I began working in the field of health professions education in 2011 when I joined a team that was developing a year-long fellowship in global health. Although I am an expert in adult education, it was my first experience working with medical doctors and nurses as we codeveloped the curricular materials. Once the curriculum was completed and implemented, I moved into a monitoring and evaluation role to understand program effectiveness and how it might be improved. The evaluation process provided insight into a variety of aspects of the program including how the learners received the information, how they viewed the instructors, and whether they felt the program was worthwhile. The program directors guided the evaluation process, relying heavily on quantitative methods that included competency-based checklists. There was minimal reflection on participants' transformational moments, which I had anecdotally uncovered, or the application of the skills in their apprenticeships, workplaces, or communities. Personally, I believed these areas were important and merited additional investigation, but these questions were not prioritized in the evaluation process.

I currently teach in a master of education in the health professions education program and work with a variety of health professionals, including medical doctors, nurses, nutritionists, program coordinators, and technicians. My students are future educators in the health care field and will be creating, implementing, and evaluating their programs. In this cohort-based model, I teach Introduction to Adult Learning and Development, Teaching

Methods for Adult Learners, and Program Planning and Program Evaluation for Adult Learners. Over the past four years, I have come to understand that many of my students view the world through a positivist lens that has been developed through earlier educational experiences, training, and their work experiences. As I have adopted a transformative paradigm in my research, teaching, and evaluation practice, I have come to understand we have differences in perspectives that influence how we approach our work. Learners enter the classroom with a particular understanding of the world that influences how they see knowledge, what strategies they use for research, how they develop educational programming, and how they evaluate programs. Consider the question, "How does one incorporate a transformative paradigm into evaluation?" I believe this begins with the education of health care professionals.

A positivist framework has assumptions about knowledge and truth and how both are understood. Working from this perspective, evaluators would argue there is one objective reality that is observable and measurable. The evaluator is an expert in their field, an unbiased observer who employs scientifically rigorous data collection tools. The evaluation is designed in a way that allows comparison with similar programs (Guba & Lincoln, 1994). For those who employ a transformative paradigm, programming and evaluation are linked to a critical, emancipatory framework that focuses on the development of people to understand and critique broader systems like health care (Chiavaroli, 2017). For a transformative perspective to be fully implemented in evaluation, health care professionals would have to adopt a critical perspective of the system they work in and understand how their programming is situated in a larger system of change. They would have to investigate how their choices reflect their values, biases, and training. It is essential for program evaluators to develop an understanding that paradigms influence how we approach educational and evaluation activities (Patton, 2017). Making these paradigms explicit is the first step in understanding how they influence educational and evaluation practice (Guba & Lincoln, 1994).

Health professions educators are tasked with creating and implementing robust educational programming that may include helping medical professionals engage in patient-centered education, patient care, or interprofessionalism. Shifting the focus to the development of effective, patient-centered, community-informed care would be better served by health care professionals who see the value in community engagement and community perspectives and who are able to acknowledge that different ways of knowing exist. These concepts are embedded in a transformative paradigm. As our approaches to teaching, learning, and evaluation are often embedded in our foundational beliefs, it is important to explain these belief systems so that evaluators understand what guides their choices. Developing future health care professionals who employ transformative paradigms in their programs and evaluations may shift the perspectives of and approaches to education in health education broadly. By recognizing that health care professionals are socialized as well as educated in positivist-oriented systems, educators can begin the process of emphasizing how different paradigmatic approaches to education and evaluation exist and how these paradigms influence practice. As an educator of health professions educators who will plan, implement, and evaluate educational programs in the health care field, I can provide learning experiences that create a space for understanding these perspectives.

A Call for a Transformative Perspective in Health Professions Education

Health professions education has been defined as "prelicensure programming that prepares individuals to function as professionals in one of the health professions, such as medicine or nursing" and "master's degree, doctoral degree, or certificate programs that prepared professionals who are already licensed to be educators" (Daley & Cervero, 2017, p. 229). Cervero and Daley (2018) illustrated a need to incorporate foundational adult learning and continuing education principles in the field of health professions education. Incorporating specific approaches to educational methods, evaluation, research, and scholarship would require a reexamination of the philosophies that undergird health professions education. This reflects Frenk et al.'s (2010) call for a third generation of health profession education grounded in a transformative perspective, which would begin to close the gaps between population and patient needs and correct the outmoded professional competencies that result from outdated curricula and pedagogy. In the first generation of health professions education, the focus was on a science-based curricula where the dominant pedagogy was didactic in nature and assessment was test oriented. The second generation introduced problem-based learning and began a movement away from the sole use of didactics as the instructional methodology. The third and current generation of health professions education focuses on interprofessional education and the need to understand contextual factors in the health care arena. Although patient centeredness and team-based approaches are deemed essential to practice, they have not been strongly reflected in the earlier generations of health professions curricula. Frenk et al. (2010) argued for additional areas of development that include centering different ways of knowing in medicine and the inclusion of a social justice focus. Others argued for the development of a critical consciousness embedded in a social justice framework to expand the health care profession-als' abilities to interact effectively with patients, particularly across racial and ethnic difference (Kumagai & Lypson, 2009).

Frenk et al. (2010) argued that

> all health professionals in all countries should be educated to mobilize knowl-edge and to engage in critical reasoning and ethical conduct so that they are competent to participate in patient and population centered health systems as members of locally responsible and globally connected fields. (p. 1924)

Populations coproduce an understanding for need-based care and help iden-tify programming that is deemed essential. As a result, stakeholder groups require expansion to include educators, students, professional bodies, uni-versities, nongovernmental and international agencies, donors, and foun-dations. Engagement at the community level and with local policy makers is needed to address the challenges associated with "aging, shifting patient demographics, cultural diversity, chronic disease, care-seeking behavior, and heightened public expectations" (p. 1938). Shifts in the curriculum can emphasize the concept of socially responsible professionalism as well as a belief that access to health care is a human right. This recentering requires recognition of a person's dignity and respect for their cultural background. Working in conjunction with hospitals and community-based programs, employing a systems-based approach, in addition to technological innova-tion, can result in more effective deployment of cost-effective preventative and treatment strategies.

Frenk et al. (2010) proposed several reforms, three of which are relevant to this chapter. Proposed Reform 6 argued for the alignment of national efforts through cooperative planning in the education and health sectors by an expanded group of stakeholders. This can be accomplished by expand-ing "academic learning sites" in communities while developing a "culture of critical inquiry and public reasoning" (p. 1952). Proposed Reform 7 stressed the need to integrate of stakeholders into the joint planning process to cre-ate a streamlined process of understanding national contexts so priorities and policies can be developed that meet the health needs of the population. Finally, Proposed Reform 8 argued for the

> expansion from academic centers to academic systems, extending the tra-ditional discover-care-education continuum in schools and hospitals into primary care settings and communities, strengthened through external col-laboration as a part of more responsible and dynamic professional educa-tion systems. (p. 1952)

Grounding educational activities in a transformative perspective would require shifting educational approaches from a focus on didactics, memorization, and exams to instructional methods that are reflective and contextualized while integrating global and localized knowledges.

Frenk et al. (2010) drew on Freire (1970) to support the integration of a transformative perspective in health professions education; however, they failed to connect it with the key concept that education is an avenue for self-determination for those from marginalized groups. Adopting a critical perspective would also require an examination of the larger systems to understand where they support or fail to support marginalized groups. Frenk and colleagues called for developing relationships with communities and health care populations; however, they did not center these groups in their discussion. Although there is a focus on centering of population and patient needs in evaluation and health care, Frenk and colleagues did not include these groups in an expanded stakeholders' list. Frenk and colleagues argued that health professions education should connect to communities but failed to examine the ways these relationships could be developed to foster equity and prevent further marginalization. Ultimately, a transformative paradigm linked to a critical, emancipatory framework argues for people to be able to understand and critique broader systems like health care (Chiavaroli, 2017). For a transformative perspective to be fully implemented, health care professionals would have to adopt a critical perspective of the system they work in, examine how it meets or fails to meet the needs of the population served, how it replicates inequity, and how it continues to marginalize underrepresented groups locally and globally. To adopt a true Freirean model of transformational learning, we must go further. We must develop an understanding of how our paradigms influence educational and evaluation activities, and attached to these paradigms are assumptions, values, and perspectives (Patton, 2017). An explanation of different paradigms would allow health professions educators to understand how their worldviews guide their thinking as it relates to their educational and evaluation practice (Guba & Lincoln, 1994).

Three Paradigms

In this section, I describe three dominant paradigms that influence the development, implementation, and evaluation of educational programs: positivist, constructivist, and transformative. This is not an exhaustive discussion of these paradigms, but it provides a framework for the remainder of the chapter. Although the three paradigms are discussed separately, I follow Lincoln,

Lynham, and Guba's (2011) assertion that there are no specific boundaries in the paradigms and that often the boundaries are fluid and subject to change.

Positivist Paradigm

The positivist paradigm is grounded in the idea of rationality (Chiavaroli, 2017) and the belief that there is a set of established verified facts and laws (Lincoln et al., 2011). Research, education, and evaluation practice grounded in this paradigm operate from the perspective that the world can be understood through value-neutral activities that include observation and experimentation and uses particular methodologies to answer questions. Chiavaroli (2017) said that "medical practice is explicated epistemologically as 'scientific'—defined by reasoning that is logico-deductive, universalizing, generalizable, predictable, and empirical" (p. 18). Medical knowledge is grounded in bioscientific frameworks, and *medical practice* is defined as the "objective application of the most advanced medical sciences to patient care" (Kuper & D'Eon, 2011, p. 37).

When positivist approaches ground evaluation processes, the evaluator is viewed as objective and value neutral with the ability to collect, analyze, and report data in an unbiased way. Ontologically, there is one reality that can be observed and understood when appropriate data are collected and analyzed (Frye & Hemmer, 2012; Lincoln et al., 2011). Evaluation questions are decided by content area experts who identify specific stakeholder groups for input (Fitzpatrick, Sanders, & Worthen, 2011). Program recipients are viewed acontexually; their perspectives are not foregrounded, and they are not integrated into the process of designing the evaluation (Lincoln et al., 2011). Questions regarding the construction of knowledge are not considered. The scientific method informs the selection of evaluation design and data collection tools and relies heavily on quantitative methods (Fitzpatrick et al., 2011). Replicability and generalization of evaluation metrics is essential for comparison across sites. Positivism lends itself to focusing on expert-led, outcomes-only-based evaluations and does not delve into how context influences programming or how grounding in other paradigms might provide a different type of insight. Specific examples of positivist embedded evaluation are evident in outcomes-based areas such as graduate medical education where there is a focus on expertise.

Outcomes-based evaluation is defined by the Accreditation Council of Graduate Medical Education "as evidence showing the degree to which program purposes are or are not being attained including achievement of appropriate skills and competencies of students" (Musick, 2006, p. 761). Although the field of graduate medical education does not currently implement a standardized program evaluation process and lacks a specific theoretical orientation, threads in the evaluation questions and methods imply its reliance on positivism. First, *program evaluation* is embedded in accreditation standards, institutional needs, specific projects, or research and is defined as the "systematic collection and analysis of information related to the design, implementation, and outcomes of a program, for the sole purpose of monitoring and improving the quality and effectiveness of the program" (Frye & Hemmer, 2012, p. 289). Second, methods employed include performance ratings, exams, attendance sheets, rotation objectives checklists, surveys, and clinical skill examinations. Holmboe, Sherbino, Long, Swing, and Frank (2010) advocated for the incorporation of qualitative data but in the form of syntheses of evaluation sessions and argued this provides an important data point. Others have acknowledged outcomes-based evaluation is top down and involves minimal use of data collection tools that are focused on the perspectives of the participants (Musick, 2006). Still others stressed the need for uniform learner assessments that can be compared across sites, arguing for standardized assessment tools that have proven validity and can be used in all programs in specific countries because too much variability in evaluation systems has hurt the field of medical education (Holmboe et al., 2010). Frye and Hemmer (2012) asserted that the fluid nature of programming should be addressed through evaluations that inform program development and revision; however, standardization remains a goal, and there is a need to develop standardized metrics that can be compared across sites.

The data collected in this framework provide insight into how programs operate, but the heavy reliance on quantitative data may only point out issues without providing information that help evaluators deeply understand and mitigate problem areas. For example, if learners do not acquire the required knowledge, it is difficult to pinpoint whether the materials, the learning environment, or the assessment tool requires adjustment. When participants are incorporated into these models they are viewed as a data source in the areas of learning performance data, test results, focus groups, and participant interviews. These models do not incorporate participants in the planning process as potential sources of information as they are not given the opportunity to provide insight into program development.

Constructivist Paradigm

The constructivist paradigm shifts from a purely objective, acontextual perspective and incorporates the specific context in which the program takes place. The nature of knowledge shifts from an objective understanding to an acknowledgment of lived realities and constructed knowledge grounded in these lived realities (Pouliot, 2007). In a constructivist paradigm, multiple truths and socially constructed realities are acknowledged as knowledge situated in relativism, meaning they are "local and specific constructed and co-constructed realities" (Lincoln et al., 2011, p. 109). Knowledge is created through a process of sense making and negotiation and is coconstructed through interactions. The processes of meaning-making are centered as they ultimately lead to action or inaction and can be shifted when necessary (Lincoln et al., 2011).

In this paradigm, program implementation and evaluation are influenced by context and local understanding. Program planners and evaluators acknowledge that their values influence their work; make explicit these value systems; and try to understand how their perspectives influence the program goals, methods, and outcomes. They recognize that lived experiences are viewed through individual lenses, and in the constructivist paradigm, lived experiences must be understood. Program participants are viewed as important sources of knowledge and information and are brought into the program planning and evaluation design process. Meaning is negotiated among stakeholder groups, which include participants and evaluators, until consensus is reached (Lincoln et al., 2011).

Examples of program evaluations that are embedded in a constructivist paradigm include responsive and participatory approaches. Responsive evaluation takes into account that local contexts, local knowledge, and individual interpretations are essential in understanding the effectiveness or ineffectiveness of a program (Fitzpatrick et al., 2011). Participatory approaches focus on the integration of program participants as key stakeholders and are brought into the planning process. Collaboration is an important element of the participatory approach, and success is more likely when program managers and evaluators show a propensity for learning and working in groups and are in alignment with the tenets of this approach (Smits, Champagne, & Farand, 2012).

Utilization-focused approaches may also fall into the constructivist category based on assumptions about the design process. Although Patton (2011) advocated for the inclusion of the primary users and consideration of their needs and perspectives on the program, ultimately he argued that the utilization-focused evaluation can be implemented from a variety of paradigmatic perspectives that can shift over time (e.g., Haylock & Miller, 2016). However, evaluators using the utilization-focused evaluation should be clear regarding the perspective they are working from and explain the affordances and constraints of each approach. Vassar, Wheeler, Davison, and Franklin (2010) provided an additional example of utilization-focused evaluation as a context-specific approach requiring the incorporation and active involvement of stakeholders in the design and goal-setting processes. Active involvement of an enlarged stakeholder group encourages inclusion and participation of those who are committed to the program and the evaluation process, thus increasing the likelihood of a more robust process (Fitzpatrick et al., 2011). Methods are expanded to include qualitative data in the form of interviews or focus groups, ethnography, and participant observation (Pouliot, 2007; Sandars & Sarojini Hart, 2015).

The constructivist paradigm broadens the ways evaluators see program planning and evaluation. Acknowledgement of local knowledge and experiences allows the idea that person and place influence how a program is implemented and received. The incorporation of an expanded stakeholder group that includes participants' perspectives can provide the evaluator with more nuanced information to make a more collaborative and meaningful evaluation of the program. Critiques of a constructivist approach include a lack of standardization in the evaluation tools and metrics. It is harder to collect and analyze qualitative data in relation to quantitative data and often requires team members who have expertise in the area. Qualitative data are specific to the particular context and it is difficult to compare across settings. Perhaps most important from a positivist perspective, qualitative evaluation and research are not viewed as empirically rigorous, thus making it more difficult to argue for program efficacy if the evaluation is not viewed as scientifically rigorous by stakeholder groups.

Transformative Paradigm

The transformative paradigm incorporates a focus on social justice and critical perspectives in the educational, planning, implementation, and evaluation processes. Ontologically in this paradigm, a variety of realities are formed from the social location and power differentials across groups (Lincoln et al., 2011; Mertens, 2016). A transformative paradigm draws on Freirean ideas, is emancipatory and participative in nature, and focuses on ameliorating oppression and discrimination (Freire, 1970). This paradigm has multiple lenses for understanding socially constructed realities (Mertens, 1999). Complex issues, like gender-based violence that are embedded in cultural norms and practices or certain health outcomes that cannot be understood without expanding the questions that are asked and the types of data that are collected, may be better understood through a transformative paradigm (Mertens, 2016). Research has emphasized the "search for truth, objectivity, credibility, and validity, while warning against the dangers associated with the appearance of advocacy, political motivation, and ontological nihilism" (Mertens, 1999, pp. 1–2). The adoption of perceived neutrality may lead to a lack of acknowledgment of issues, such as social injustice and oppression that influence an individual's or a groups' experiences (Mertens, 1999).

The integration of these perspectives can result in a better understanding of community contexts, ways programs are designed to foster change, and the ways they unexpectedly foster or fail to foster change. Taking this approach to program evaluation shifts how problems are framed and the questions that are asked. Mertens (2001) argued that "putting forth the effort that is necessary to understand the community of interest is the key to enhancing the impact of evaluation work towards a goal of a more just society" (p. 368). The program participant's position moves from recipient to collaborator, and their experiences and expectations are central to the evaluation process. The participants are not framed as the objects or recipients of a program but as individuals who have agency and a voice in the process (Mertens, 2016).

Transformative evaluation processes push evaluators to address discrimination, oppressive systems, and power differentials and to adopt the role of facilitator versus evaluator (Mertens, 1999, 2016). It bridges the relationships among program evaluators, program participants, and the communities where these programs take place (Walker, 2015). It helps the evaluator to understand and incorporate the views of program participants (Mertens, 1999, 2016). The focus of transformative evaluation is to empower marginalized groups, set agendas and outcomes for community-based programming, build capacity, and create change (Walker, 2015).

Several considerations in facilitating effective transformative evaluations include diversity, maintaining multiple partiality, and reconsidering programmatic outcomes. Diversity in the evaluation team is essential, and community members are equal partners. The evaluator must engage with the community in a way that acknowledges its history and issues of trust so that the relationship between the two groups is strengthened (Jackson et al., 2018). Additionally, the evaluator must strive to maintain multiple partiality, meaning they are open to all stakeholder ideas and allow multiple perspectives (Baur, Abma, & Widdershoven, 2010). By viewing program participants as active partners, the design of the intervention can be made more inclusive and participatory in nature rather than stemming from a deficit perspective in which the individual is viewed as the problem (Mertens, 2001). This approach focuses on community assets and allows "forward planning and the well-being of the community, rather than the specific workings and outcomes of a program" (Jackson et al., 2018, p. 112). It also leads to a reconsideration of programmatic outcomes. In this paradigm, evaluators acknowledge that the choice of indicators, design, timing, and outcomes are made by a smaller stakeholder group under the guise of objectivity, whereas there is implicit subjectivity in these decisions. Mertens

(2001) highlighted the need to develop evaluation "performance indicators that are meaningful, culturally appropriate, and encompassing of a caring ethic" (p. 371). Therefore, expanding the stakeholder group is an important aspect of incorporating additional voices into the process (Baur et al., 2010). As the stakeholder group expands to include a wider array of people, outcomes are broadened to include the community's interpretation of the intervention and any additional benefits they view as important.

Rather than viewing methods as a value-neutral proposition, in the transformative paradigm methods are informed by ethics, political orientation, and pedagogy (Gadotti, 2017). The transformative paradigm emphasizes participatory and responsive evaluation frameworks to incorporate the perspectives of all stakeholders and promote action and change (Janzen et al., 2017). This is accomplished through interviews, focus groups, surveys, and collecting demographic data (Jackson et al., 2018). Narrative inquiries, including autobiographical narratives, allow participants to share experiences (Walker, 2015). Storytelling enables the exploration of experiences and ideas and facilitates learning through hermeneutic dialogue, which is an opportunity for stakeholders to learn from each other (Baur et al., 2010). Also, the transformative paradigm underscores participatory and collaborative development of needs assessments and data collection (Jackson et al., 2018). This allows evaluators to understand the community's assets and needs and to engage in a process of negotiation on the purpose of the evaluation, thus allowing all stakeholders to work toward a common goal (Janzen et al., 2017). As Smith (2013) argued, data collection tools should be culturally relevant and culturally responsive and designed with the input of community members because those who design the tools hold the power. Furthermore, data are presented to participants and community members at appropriate education levels and languages to ensure comprehension of the results.

Discussion

Frenk et al. (2010) called for the integration of transformative perspectives into health professions education. Drawing on Freire, they argued that critical consciousness embedded in a transformative framework is essential to address gaps between the field of medical education and community- and population-based needs. They believe this is the first step in developing a cadre of leaders who can employ a transformative stance as they manage complex systems.

Each of the perspectives presented in this chapter inform health professions education, program planning, and evaluation in health care. Moving toward a transformative lens would shift how we engage in each of these areas. I teach program evaluation in a health professions education program, and I have the opportunity to provide experiences to learners that allow them to develop a broader lens on educational practice and program evaluation. There are a number of ways this can be accomplished. I can ensure that I implement a variety of pedagogical and assessment strategies and connect my practice to the adult learning and continuing education literature (Cervero & Daley, 2018). In my program planning and evaluation courses, I stress the need to incorporate the perspectives of potential participants and for learners to understand that context matters in relation to program development and the evaluation. The population or community would be viewed as a source of essential knowledge and ways of knowing (Smith, 2013).

Specifically in relation to evaluation, I would want to ensure that learners were aware they operate from particular paradigms. Learners would be asked to explain their paradigms to understand how they influence their evaluations. For example, evaluation goals are significantly different if viewed from a positivist or a transformative lens. In addition, from a transformative perspective, the individuals involved in setting evaluation goals would come from an expanded stakeholder group. Program evaluators would be encouraged to acknowledge that their decisions reflect their values and perspectives and should be able to explain how their perspective influences program design and evaluation questions. In a transformative paradigm, inclusion of community members in the planning and design process as partners creates a broadened view of how issues are interpreted, addressed, and evaluated, thus allowing a deeper understanding of how resource allocation influences power structures in program planning and evaluation processes. The inclusion of community perspectives makes it more likely that community strengths are recognized, and the questions are reframed to reflect these strengths rather than solely focusing on perceived weaknesses. This could potentially expand the types of methodologies that are employed while recognizing that power resides in individuals who select these methods (Smith, 2013). Adopting a transformative perspective allows evaluators to engage in capacity building with the communities where they work to promote equitable participation and to create an environment where all can fully participate (Janzen et al., 2017; Mertens, 2001).

Health professions educators are charged with the task of providing educational programming across a variety of settings that include other medical professionals as well as potentially patient-based or community-based programming. They may be responsible for creating educational activities designed to help medical professionals engage in patient-centered education, patient care, or interprofessionalism. The development of effective, patient-centered, community-informed care would be better served by health care professionals who see the value in community engagement and community perspectives and acknowledge different ways of knowing. Lincoln et al. (2011) emphasized the issue with value-free programming: "While scientists firmly believe that as long as they are not conscious of any bias or political agenda they are neutral and objective . . . in fact they are only unconscious" (p. 184). Transformative perspectives urge individuals to consider that uncritically accepting one's own paradigm involves the unconscious acceptance of assumptions in that paradigm (Guba & Lincoln, 1994) and a failure to recognize that, ultimately, knowledge is context dependent and changeable (Lincoln et al., 2011; Smith, 2013). Future health care professionals who employ a transformative paradigm in their programs and evaluations may have the propensity to change how we view education in health care more broadly. If we recognize that health care professionals are socialized as well as educated in positivist-oriented systems, educators can begin the process of explaining that different paradigmatic approaches to education and evaluation exist, and they influence our practice.

References

Baur, V. E., Abma, T. A., & Widdershoven, G. A. M. (2010). Participation of marginalized groups in evaluation: Mission impossible? *Evaluation and Program Planning, 33*(3), 238–245.

Cervero, R. M., & Daley, B. J. (2018). The need and curricula for health professions education graduate programs. *New Directions for Adult and Continuing Education, 2018*(157), 7–16.

Chiavaroli, N. (2017). Knowing how we know: An epistemological rationale for the medical humanities. *Medical Education, 51*(1), 13–21.

Daley, B. J., & Cervero, R. M. (2017). Advancing health professions education. In S. C. O. Conceição, L. G. Martin, & A. B. Knox (Eds.), *Mapping the field of adult and continuing education: An international compendium* (pp. 229–230). Sterling, VA: Stylus.

Fitzpatrick, J. L., Sanders, J. R., & Worthen, B. R. (2011). *Program evaluation: Alternative approaches and practical guidelines*. New York, NY: Pearson.

Freire, P. (1970). *Pedagogy of the oppressed*. New York, NY: Continuum.

Frenk, J., Chen, L., Bhutta, Z. A., Cohen, J., Crisp, N., Evans, T., . . .Zurayk, H., & Kistnasamy, B. (2010). Health professionals for a new century: Transforming education to strengthen health systems in an interdependent world. *The Lancet, 376*, 1923–1958.

Frye, A. W., & Hemmer, P. A. (2012). Program evaluation models and related theories: AMEE guide no. 67. *Medical Teacher, 34*(5), e288–e299.

Gadotti, M. (2017). The global impact of Freire's pedagogy. *New directions for evaluation, 2017*(155), 17–30.

Guba, E. G., & Lincoln, Y. S. (1994). Competing paradigms in qualitative research. In N. K. Denzin & Y. S. Lincoln (Eds.), *The Sage handbook of qualitative research* (pp. 105–117). Thousand Oaks, CA: Sage.

Haylock, L., & Miller, C. (2016). Merging developmental and feminist evaluation to monitor and evaluate transformative social change. *American Journal of Evaluation, 37*(1), 63–79.

Holmboe, E. S., Sherbino, J., Long, D. M., Swing, S. R., Frank, J. R., & International CBME Collaborators. (2010). The role of assessment in competency-based medical education. *Medical Teacher, 32*(8), 676–682.

Jackson, K. M., Pukys, S., Castro, A., Hermosura, L., Mendez, J., Vohra-Gupta, S., . . .Morales, G. (2018). Using the transformative paradigm to conduct a mixed methods needs assessment of a marginalized community: Methodological lessons and implications. *Evaluation and Program Planning, 66*, 111–119.

Janzen, R., Ochocka, J., Turner, L., Cook, T., Franklin, M., & Deichert, D. (2017). Building a community-based culture of evaluation. *Evaluation and Program Planning, 65*, 163–170.

Kumagai, A. K., & Lypson, M. L. (2009). Beyond cultural competence: Critical consciousness, social justice, and multicultural education. *Academic Medicine, 84*(6), 782–787.

Kuper, A., & D'Eon, M. (2011). Rethinking the basis of medical knowledge. *Medical Education, 45*(1), 36–43.

Lincoln, Y. S., Lynham, S. A., & Guba, E. G. (2011). Paradigmatic controversies, contradictions, and emerging confluences, revisited. In N. K. Denzin & Y. S. Lincoln (Eds.), *The Sage handbook of qualitative research* (Vols. Vol. 4, pp. 97–128). Thousand Oaks, CA: Sage.

Mertens, D. M. (1999). Inclusive evaluation: Implications of transformative theory for evaluation. *American Journal of Evaluation, 20*(1), 1–14.

Mertens, D. M. (2001). Inclusivity and transformation: Evaluation in 2010. *American Journal of Evaluation, 22*(3), 367–374.

Mertens, D. M. (2016). Assumptions at the philosophical and programmatic levels in evaluation. *Evaluation and Program Planning, 59*, 102–108.

Musick, D. W. (2006). A conceptual model for program evaluation in graduate medical education. *Academic Medicine, 81*(8), 759–765.

Patton, M. Q. (2011). *Essentials of utilization-focused evaluation.* Thousand Oaks, CA: Sage.

Patton, M. Q. (2017). Pedagogical principles of evaluation: Interpreting Freire. *New Directions for Evaluation, 2017*(155), 49–77.

Pouliot, V. (2007). "Sobjectivism": Toward a Constructivist Methodology. *International Studies Quarterly, 51*(2), 359–384.

Sandars, J., & Sarojini Hart, C. (2015). The capability approach for medical education: AMEE guide no. 97. *Medical Teacher, 37*(6), 510–520.

Smith, L. T. (2013). *Decolonizing methodologies: Research and indigenous peoples.* New York, NY: Zed Books.

Smits, P. A., Champagne, F., & Farand, L. (2012). Beyond resistance: Exploring health managers' propensity for participatory evaluation in a developing country. *Evaluation and Program Planning, 35*(2), 256–268.

Vassar, M., Wheeler, D. L., Davison, M., & Franklin, J. (2010). Program evaluation in medical education: An overview of the utilization-focused approach. *Journal of Educational Evaluation for Health Professions, 7,* 1.

Walker, E. M. (2015). Evaluation considerations for community-based gender-informed health interventions. *Evaluation and Program Planning, 51,* 4–7.

10

ASSESSMENT AND EVALUATION PRACTICES IN ADULT DISTANCE EDUCATION

Simone C.O. Conceição

E arly discussions of assessment of online education involved comparisons to face-to-face education (Bernard et al., 2004; Saba, 2000); however, the field has matured, and those in the field have developed assessment practices for online education itself. The latest data on higher education enrollments in the United States indicate that distance education has continued to grow since 2012 (Seaman, Allen, & Seaman, 2018). This steady growth of enrollment, even surpassing the growth of brick-and-mortar institutions, is evidence that the quality of online education is an important aspect of program policy and curricular offerings that higher education administrators must take into account to predict success.

Assessment and evaluation in adult and distance education can be viewed from different perspectives, and the terms are often used interchangeably. In this chapter, *student learning assessment* refers to learner performance during an online course. Evaluation involves a systematic process for collecting, analyzing, and presenting information about an adult education program's activities, characteristics, and outcomes. Evaluation makes judgments about a program's effectiveness, efficiency, and appeal to inform future adult education program decisions (Patton, 1987). With the emergence of digital technologies, there are a variety of ways to assess the online learning of adult students, evaluate courses and programs, and determine the value of online education. The purpose of this chapter is to provide the current status of practices in online learning assessment and evaluation of online programs in adult education. The chapter concludes with quality assurance in online education through a review of benchmarks; standards from accrediting bodies; and national, state, and institutional policies.

Student Learning Assessment Strategies and Practices

Assessing online learning is formative and uses strategies from the beginning of a course until the course is complete. A student learning assessment in adult education can focus on a process or a product or a learners' demonstration of a task. It can take place before the course starts as a needs assessment strategy to collect learner information about prior knowledge, during the course as a formative strategy to determine if adult learners are acquiring knowledge and to verify where improvement in that learning is needed, and at the end of the course as a way to determine if learners met the outcomes of a course. Learning assessments are connected to course learning outcomes and should be taken into consideration during the online course design to create an impactful learning experience for the learners. Learning assessment strategies before the course begins, during the course, or at the end of the course can provide a detailed representation of a learners progress and achievement.

Assessment Strategies Before the Course Begins

Assessment strategies before the course begins can be used to identify learners' knowledge of the subject matter, their technology competency, and their readiness to learn in an online environment. These strategies tend to be part of orientation activities during the week before the course begins or during the first week of the course using survey software tools. These strategies are often not connected to a grade unless the instructor assigns bonus points as an incentive for students to participate. This type of information can be valuable to predict adult learners' needs during the course (Lehman & Conceição, 2014).

Learning analytics in the institution's learning management system (LMS) can provide timely information about adult learners' pattern of technology access and usage as they initially enter the online course. The analytics can predict learner behavior in the technology-based environment. An adult learner's lack of participation during the first weeks of the course can create a domino effect and lead to failure or course withdrawal. By monitoring learner progress through the LMS learning analytics, faculty can keep in touch with learners through personal e-mail messages and alert them of the consequences of nonparticipation in the course.

Instructors' communication with adult learners can begin before the class starts using logs in the news feature or with direct e-mails. Using the news feature of the LMS to send announcements, reminders, or course clarifications can help learners stay on track. The same communication in the news feature can be sent by e-mail to alert learners about what is going to happen in the course and as a reminder for them to access the LMS. Social media can also be used with the same purpose; however, with short messages to announce activities or reminders about course time lines, adult learners may have more immediate access to this type of communication as social media can be set up as a widget on a smartphone.

Introductory discussion forums in the online course can allow adult learners to introduce themselves to one another through sharing of personal information, help create a sense of presence, promote the development of trust among class members, and create a course community. For the instructor, information shared in these forums can be inserted into a database to create learners' individual profiles. Table 10.1 provides examples of assessment strategies and the type of information to be collected before the online course begins.

TABLE 10.1
Assessment Strategies and Information to Collect Before an
Online Course Begins

Assessment Strategy	Information to Collect
Communication log	This is information collected by direct e-mail with instructor. Keeping information accessible on a dedicated folder in the e-mail system can help monitor misunderstandings.
LMS learning analytics	This provides a user progress report, such as the number of postings, access frequency, postings authored, or postings read.
Introductory forum	This is for learners' personal information about job, family, and hobbies. The LMS resembles a social media site with photos and potential use of emoticons, which makes the discussion more personal.
Social media	This is for short posts with a specific purpose such as announcements or reminders.
Survey tool	This is to collect individuals' information about their interests in the course, technology competency, and their future use of what they learned from the course.

Assessment Strategies During the Course

Assessment strategies during the course may or may not be graded. Graded assessment strategies can be individual or group based. Individual assessment gives adult learners direct advice on their performance in the course. Group-based assessment is usually used when learners participate in team activities that involve them in common tasks (Lehman & Conceição, 2014). Nongraded assessment strategies focus on learner feedback about the course.

Graded Assessment Strategies

Instructors new to the online environment tend to recreate face-to-face assessment strategies and practices when designing their online courses. Bailey, Hendricks, and Applewhite (2015) found that learners prefer less traditional types of assessments online. Instructors are more comfortable using quizzes, group projects, and papers; however, these traditional assessment strategies lack active learner engagement. In their study, learners rated video, Twitter summaries, and interviews as enjoyable assessments followed by interviews and field experience.

Rogerson-Revell (2015) used a constructive alignment approach for online activities as a way to introduce flexible and innovative approaches to learning assessments. She used voice-based discussion boards, podcasts, wikis, and blogs to implement group-based reflective activities, which helped provide a thorough formative assessment and encourage collaborative learning and engagement with course content. This type of online activity does not provide formal assessment; it provides feedback on the learning process and prepares adult learners for the final module or unit assessment.

Lock and Johnson (2015) proposed an intentional design model that includes formative and summative strategies during the course with the purpose of fostering knowledge construction. This model involves three interconnected components: self, peer, and instructor assessment strategies. These formative assessment strategies engage the adult learner through different activities: (a) blogs students write so that they can review their work in succession (self-assessment) and reading in progression, which allows learners to reflect on their learning progress and process; (b) learners review each other's postings in the online course and provide feedback (peer assessment); and (c) during the process the instructor also provides feedback to individual learners (instructor assessment). Summative assessment is conducted at the end of a module or unit to compare learning against a standard or benchmark. These assessment strategies are carefully aligned with course learning outcomes. Table 10.2 shows examples of graded assessment strategies in the online course.

TABLE 10.2
Graded Assessment Strategies During an Online Course

Strategy	Description and Use
Book reflection	After reading a book, learners post comments in the general discussion area reflecting on the questions posted by the instructor through review and comments on the responses of others. Reflection questions focus on concepts in the book, how the books impact practice, and future use of concepts or strategies in the book. Instructor assessment focuses on learners' contributions, accuracy and originality of insights, and critical analysis.
Field experience	Field experiences involve a specific number of hours of fieldwork outside the scope of a regular job. Instructor reviews the work log of hours and a written reflection.
Group projects	Learners work together in their assigned groups to complete tasks and submit one finished product representative of the group. Assessment may be peer based or group based or both. Peer assessment involves group members evaluating each other (including self-assessment) based on leadership and logistical, intellectual, and creative contributions. Group-based assessment involves the instructor's review of the product developed by the group based on design, quality, and presentation.
Interviews	Interviews involve sharing transcripts of the interviews along with summative reflection of the experience interviewing someone else. This activity is usually based on a defined interview protocol and a rubric for the reflection.
Online discussions	Discussions involve interactions with the entire class or in assigned groups through original posts to a discussion board and replies to others' posts. Using a rubric, discussions may be assessed in groups or individually. They best serve students if they are contained in a module or unit, organized by topics.
Role-playing	Role-playing can be part of different course activities. Learners may role-play a conversation explaining the information from a course reading or create a video of a mock presentation.
Social media	A social media activity may involve developing a short (tweetlike) summary of an article or a book chapter based on a specific rubric.
Video	After watching a documentary, learners post a reaction to the video in the online discussion through a written analysis based on a critical thinking rubric.

Instructor feedback plays an important role in graded assessments. Feedback keeps adult learners aware of their performance and progress during the course and gives them a sense of accomplishment. Instructor feedback helps adult learners know how they are performing in the course and can help them stay motivated. One of the common complaints of online learners is the lack of regular, consistent, and prompt feedback from instructors (Lehman & Conceição, 2014). Lack of feedback can cause learner anxiety, lack of self-confidence, and dissatisfaction. Regular and ongoing feedback throughout the online course tells the learners their work is recognized and helps them feel part of the course. Consistent feedback can boost learner self-confidence and provides a sense of the course pace. Prompt feedback involves the timing of the instructor's response to a question, clarification of assignments, and follow-up on the learner's performance. When following up, direct feedback to the individual learner is warranted. If there is a pattern of misunderstanding or the assignment is group based, group feedback is appropriate.

The type and format of the feedback has an impact on learners' motivation and the support they are receiving. Praise, encouragement, recognition for insightful learning, constructive criticism, and rewards can affect learner performance and motivation to stay in the course. Praise and encouragement build confidence. Recognition of learners' progress helps keep them aware of their learning growth and development. Constructive criticism can affect learners' performance and self-esteem. In a text-based environment, the feedback language should have a positive tone. Rewards or bonus points can serve as motivators for adult learners' satisfaction in an online course (Lehman & Conceição, 2014). Regular, consistent, and prompt feedback from the instructor posted in the LMS grade book within 7 or 10 days gives adult learners a sense of progress and accomplishment. Table 10.3 provides types of and reasons for instructor feedback.

TABLE 10.3
Types of and Reasons for Instructor Feedback

Type of Feedback	Reasons
Regular and ongoing feedback	Recognizes learners' work and helps them feel part of the course
Consistent feedback	Encourages learner self-confidence and provides a sense of the course's pace
Prompt feedback	Quick response to a question, clarification of assignments, and follow-up on learner's performance avoids learners' anxiety

Nongraded Assessment Strategies

Vonderwell and Boboc (2013) provide examples of nongraded assessment strategies, which include online journals, reflection papers, minute papers, hook questions, things to keep in mind, a questions wall, and checking in with students. These strategies help learners during the learning process but also help instructors understand adult learners' needs and anticipate issues. Vonderwell and Boboc suggest considering how much time adult learners need to devote to completing these assessments, how frequently they should be conducted during an online course, and if these assessments should be part of the grading rubric. The length of the course should determine the frequency of the assessment.

Online journals (or self-reflection) can evaluate learning and progress. They can be completed with other course activities as part of the assignment (Vonderwell & Boboc, 2013). For example, participating in a self-reflection after completing a concept map activity can provide clues about the ease or challenge of the activity, the changes to the learning process, areas that need clarification, or connections among the different activities in a module or unit.

A reflection paper can also serve as an assessment and a learning component. It may be completed at the end of an asynchronous or synchronous discussion for analysis and reflection of the discussion content (Vonderwell & Boboc, 2013). This can be in the form of a discussion summary on group members' posts and learning and can build on the subsequent discussion and learning materials. Often if an activity is not graded, learners may not participate. Thus, including points for completing the activity may motivate adult learners to participate, and the instructor can get valuable information about learners' perceptions and course progress.

The one-minute paper (or critical incident) collects information on adult learners' progress and understanding. This strategy can help to improve communication and learner engagement. Instructors can ask adult learners to answer a few questions related to the most important thing learned in the course during a module or unit and if there are any questions related to the module or unit. It is often done anonymously in the form of open-ended questions to check learners' perceptions and feelings about the course, concerns, course progress, and needs (Conceição & Lehman, 2011).

Things to Keep in Mind or Hook Questions is a discussion area in which adult learners can post brief messages before a synchronous session in the form of short summaries of a reading to prepare learners for the topic of the discussion and help them focus on the content (Vonderwell & Boboc, 2013).

Questions Wall (or Logistics) is the title of a specific discussion forum that features questions from adult learners and the instructor as an open space to discuss technical or logistical topics related to course content or assignments (Conceição & Schmidt, 2010; Vonderwell & Boboc, 2013).

Checking in with students (or virtual office hours) can be offered as synchronous chat sessions with the instructor, individually or in small groups, to informally clarify course issues, reinforce weak areas in the course, correct writing style, demonstrate software programs, and review course requirements and sample assignments. It is also an opportunity for the instructor to provide informal feedback on learner assignments.

Noncontent-related forums, often called Help Desk, Q&A, or Sharing Resources, are used by adult learners to pose questions to the instructor or other classmates that are not directly related to course content. Questions are often on course mechanics, pertaining to course work (e.g., expectations and time line), course navigation, or technology issues. These forums are not directly related to course content, but they do help adult learners clarify issues, which is beneficial as the course progresses (Conceição & Schmidt, 2010).

LMS course statistics document the number of adult learners who visited a specific content area and the average time spent viewing content. This information can capture specific statistics for individual topics and can provide evidence of learner participation or nonparticipation throughout the online course and serve as points of awareness of learner progress. Table 10.4

TABLE 10.4
Nongraded Assessment Strategies During the Online Course

Strategy	When to Use
Virtual office hours or checking in with students	Once a week
Noncontent-related forums	Ongoing
One-minute paper or critical incidents	Midway through the online course
Online journals or self-reflection	After completion of a course activity
Questions Wall or Logistics	Ongoing during the online course
Reflection paper	End of an asynchronous or synchronous discussion
Things to Keep in Mind or Hook Questions	Before a synchronous session
LMS course statistics	Ongoing

provides examples of the previously discussed nongraded assessments strategies and when to use them.

Assessment Strategies at the End of the Course

For many adult learners, it is challenging to persist in an online course. The lack of physical presence, the flexible sense of time, and the lack of close proximity to the online environment can cause feelings of isolation and disconnection and obstacles to learning. Staying motivated throughout an online course requires intentional designon the part of the instructor (Conceição & Lehman, 2011; Lehman & Conceição, 2014). Assessment strategies have the power to help adult learners stay focused, maintain enthusiasm, and show accountability to complete course tasks. Assessment strategies are the means to achieve course goals through incentives and rewards. The end of the course can also be impactful in the learning experience.

Instructors often assign one final paper or a team project at the end of a course. However, focusing solely on final performance assignments may create a sense of an unfinished learning experience. Generally, the end of an online course can be overwhelming as adult learners may have the aha moment when they feel they are able to apply theory to practice; it is when all courses are coming to completion. Adult learners need to decompress and process the learning experience, which can be done through noncontent-based debriefing activities in a discussion area in the LMS that focuses on reflecting on the course process through sharing feelings and experiences. Course closure can leave a positive feeling about the online learning experience.

Online Program Evaluation Approaches

Evaluation is an essential aspect of an online program because it tells the story and provides certification of the course's quality, which is a way to determine if a program is unique and appealing. Evaluation validates the online program and documents the effectiveness of the content, design of the online environment, learning technologies, support services, and delivery aspects. In this section, approaches for evaluating online programs are discussed along with examples and applications.

Formative and Summative Evaluation Approaches

Formative evaluation is ongoing and conducted during a program cycle; it examines the processes of an online course, offers timely feedback about online program services, and helps with program adjustments as the program occurs to help achieve its goals. Common types of formative evaluation include needs assessment, structured conceptualization, and process-based or implementation evaluation (Pell Institute, 2010). Needs assessment determines the needs or gaps between current conditions and desired conditions or wants. Structured conceptualization assists in defining the program, the target population, and the possible outcomes. Process-based or implementation evaluation examines the process of delivering the online program as intended based on strengths and weaknesses.

Summative evaluation happens at the end of a program cycle and measures program effectiveness by focusing on whether program objectives were met, improving and modifying program structure, the impact of the program, and the resources needed to address program limitations (Pell Institute, 2010). Summative evaluation can determine whether the online program should continue as it stands, be discontinued, or be improved for future offerings. Common types of summative evaluation include goal-based evaluation, outcome evaluation, impact evaluation, and cost-effectiveness and cost-benefit analysis (Pell Institute, 2010). Goal-based evaluation determines if the intended outcome of an adult education program is achieved based on the original program plan. Outcome evaluation determines the benefits of a program to its clients by considering the progress in the outcomes that the program intends to achieve. Impact evaluation measures the effects of the program. Cost-effectiveness and cost-benefit analysis address the costs of a program and its values. Evaluation may focus on comparing the use of an online technology and its support or the design development effectiveness by comparing gains and losses.

McCutcheon, Lohan, Traynor, and Martin (2015) used outcome measures to determine the effectiveness of the use of online or blended learning to teach clinical skills in nurse education. The evaluation showed that both methods had similar benefits for learners' clinical skill knowledge, indicating that there was no difference in terms of effectiveness. Results provided implications for the future direction of nurse education.

Meyer and Murrell (2014) used outcome measures and procedures to evaluate faculty development satisfaction in the online teaching experience. This evaluation was conducted at the national level among 39 institutions. The evaluation informed faculty satisfaction, assessment of usefulness, and assessment of the relevance of training. Evaluation results showed that 90% of the institutions used a measure of faculty satisfaction and usefulness of professional development; however, there was an absence of information regarding learner outcomes or changes in teaching methodology. Results indicated a need to include other variables to understand the different perceptions of faculty roles, student learning, and relevant pedagogy in different disciplines.

Categories of Measures for Program Evaluation

Woodley and Kirkwood (1986) proposed six categories of measures for program evaluation: activity, efficiency, outcomes, program aims, policy, and organizations. They emphasize that not all measures are used for each program activity; they must match program needs. Table 10.5 provides a summary of the six categories, measures, and methods used for this evaluation approach. This approach was used to evaluate Open University of Great Britain.

TABLE 10.5
Categories of Measures for Program Evaluation

Category	Measures	Methods
Activity	Counts the number of events, people, and objects	Administrative records: courses produced, learners served, and learners turned away
Efficiency	Measures of activities	Administrative records: number of learners who successfully completed the program, average learner's workload, learners enrolled in additional courses, course cost, tuition generated
Outcomes	Adequate learning	Course grades, interviews to identify learners' perceptions about program, use of course materials
Program Aims	What and whom program intends to teach	Survey of learners
Policy	Market research	Survey of prospective learners and employers to determine demand for program, tuition cost, and program success
Organizations	Monitors the process of course development and program delivery (institutional organization and procedures)	On-site visits, interviews, and journals by key institutional leaders

Note. Adapted from Woodley and Kirkwood (1986).

TABLE 10.6
Kirkpatrick and Kirkpatricks' Four Levels

Level	Type	Description
Level 1	Reaction	How learners in an online program react to the online program: favorable, engaging, and relevant
Level 2	Learning	The extent to which learners change attitudes, improve knowledge, and/or increase skills after participating in the online program
Level 3	Behavior	The extent to which learners changed behavior because they took the online course and are able to apply learning on the job
Level 4	Impact	The extent to which targeted outcomes occurred because learners attended the online course

Note. Adapted from Kirkpatrick and Kirkpatrick (2006).

Kirkpatrick and Kirkpatrick's Four Levels

Kirkpatrick and Kirkpatrick's (2006) four levels model is often used to evaluate programs in general and is characterized by sequential strategies. According to Kirkpatrick and Kirkpatrick, each level must be used in sequence to provide valuable information. Table 10.6 provides a summary of the four levels and how they can be used when evaluating an online program in adult education.

Online program evaluation using adult learner's satisfaction (reaction) of course design can provide implications for learning outcomes. Lee's (2014) study of effective online learning showed student satisfaction was associated with clear guidelines on assignments, precise rubrics, and constructive feedback, as well as instructor's knowledge of materials.

Jaggars and Xu (2016) found that the quality of online course (interpersonal) interactions positively and significantly relates to learner grades (learning). Frequent and effective learner-instruction interaction in the online environment resulted in student commitment to the course and stronger academic performance. This study showed the importance of the instructor's presence through regular postings, student solicitation of participation and inclusion of learner feedback, and rapid response to learners' inquiries. These behaviors from the instructor showed a sense of caring, and in return learners felt encouraged to commit to the online course and provided implications for increased learner skills.

Program Evaluation Approach

This approach for program evaluation, proposed by Fortune and Keith (1992), Sweeney (1995), and Sorensen (1996), has five components: accountability, effectiveness, impact, organizational context, and unanticipated consequences (AEIOU). This approach uses quantitative and qualitative methods and has two purposes: to provide formative information to the staff about the program and to provide summative information about the value of the program and its activities. For each component, a series of

TABLE 10.7

AEIOU Context, and Unanticipated Consequences Program Evaluation

Component	*Focus*	*Methods*
Accountability	Completion of a specific activity; counts the number of people, things, and activities	Collect administrative records such as program goals, objectives, and activities; staff interview
Effectiveness	Participant attitudes and knowledge determined by grades, achievement test, and attitude inventories	Adult learner course evaluations determine reactions to program; adult learner and instructor survey, focus groups, and participants' journals
Impact	Changes resulting from program activities through longitudinal data by following adult learners' progress from course to course	Standardized tests, record data, surveys, interviews, focus groups, and direct observations
Organizational context	Contextual and environmental factors that contribute or detract from the program's ability to conduct activities	Interviews with instructors and adult learners, focus groups with individuals affected by the program, and document analysis; adult learner journal; direct participation by the evaluator
Unanticipated consequences	Ex post facto data	Interviews, focus groups, journals, and surveys on narrative format; evaluator has active and continuous involvement with program participants

key questions are asked. Table 10.7 provides a summary of the five components, focus, and methods to collect data using this approach. This approach has been employed by the Iowa Distance Education Alliance as a flexible framework for effective program evaluation and provides formative data to stakeholders regarding the implementation of the program and summative data about the program value (Manternach & Maushak, 1997).

Quality Assurance in Online Education

As online education has become a popular mode of delivery for institutions of higher education, one of the major concerns is quality assurance. Quality is often measured based on benchmarks, standards of accrediting bodies, or national, state, and institutional policies.

Benchmarks for Online Education

With the rapid growth of distance education, in the mid-1990s administrators of higher education institutions saw the need to establish benchmarks as a way to incorporate them into their policies and practices. In 2000 the National Education Association and Blackboard were commissioned by the Institute for Higher Education and Policy to conduct a case study with active distance learning programs at 6 institutions to identify factors that could assess quality online education. The final outcome of the study resulted in 24 benchmarks for quality in 7 categories: institutional support, course development, teaching/learning, course structure, faculty support, student support, and evaluation and assessment (Phipps & Merisotis, 2000).

In the early years of the first decade of the twenty-first century, the Sloan Consortium created the Quality Scorecard for the Administration of Online Education Programs, which provided a quality framework for institutions to evaluate administrative practices (Moore & Shelton, 2014). This framework was used as a benchmark to compare scores with an aggregated score of all institutions that completed the instrument, which included five quality indicators: access, learning effectiveness, scale (cost-effectiveness and commitment), faculty satisfaction, and student satisfaction. According to Moore and Shelton (2014), when results of the quality scorecard were made widely available, they "provide [the] opportunity to advance toward the goal of making education accessible to anyone who is qualified and motivated to learn" (pp. 48–49).

In 2003, Quality Matters emerged as a process and a tool used by institutions to improve online learning course quality. It is based on a rubric of course design standards and conducted through a peer-review process. It started as part of the Fund for the Improvement of Postsecondary Education grant from the U.S. Department of Education until the grant ended in 2006, and then it became self-sustaining. Today, Quality Matters is recognized internationally as a leader in quality assurance for online education (Quality Matters, 2018).

Several higher education institutions have used Quality Matters as their framework for online learning for different purposes. Lowenthal and Hodges (2015) used Quality Matters to examine the quality of massive, open, online courses. Gibson and Dunning (2012) used Quality Matters to conduct a peer-reviewed evaluation of a public administration program focusing on course design. Barczyk, Buckenmeyer, Feldman, and Hixon (2011) used Quality Matters to evaluate the Distance Education Mentoring Program at Purdue University Calumet with the purpose of improving the development of online courses through faculty mentoring on instructional design principles.

Accrediting Commissions

Accrediting commissions establish educational, ethical, and business standards for their members, who in turn use them as procedures and guidelines for evaluating programs and accredit institutions that qualify (Moore & Kearsley, 2012). One example is a set of guidelines created by the Council of Regional Accrediting Commissions for the evaluation of online learning (Higher Learning Commission, 2009). These guidelines assist institutions in planning distance education and provide an assessment framework for institutions.

Regional accreditation commissions' standards have addressed five areas of institutional activity relevant to distance education: institutional context and commitment, curriculum and instruction, faculty support, student support, and evaluation and assessment (Stella & Gnanam, 2004). The commissions' intent to create standards was to guarantee that online learning programs are subject to the same level and scope of examination used by traditional brick-and-mortar higher education settings.

Another example is the American Council on Education's guiding principles for distance learning that focus on learning support and outcomes such as learning design, learner support, organizational commitment, and learning outcomes and technology (Stella & Gnanam, 2004).

National, State, Regional, or Institutional Policies

National, state, regional, or institutional policies provide administrators with a set of guidelines they can use to plan and run programs, obtain resources, hire faculty, or purchase new technology. At the national level, the Higher Education Act of 1965 has gone through several changes since the introduction of distance education (Amendments to the Higher Education Act of 1965, 1998). Over the years, eligibility for student aid was expanded, and the use of innovative technologies have been encouraged. Changes focused on developing measures to maintain the integrity of courses and programs.

At the state level, many states adopted the State Authorization Reciprocity Agreement (SARA), which established voluntary standards for interstate offerings of distance education courses and programs at the postsecondary level (Anderson, 2018).

Between 2014 and 2017, several states in the United States introduced legislation related to competency-based education, which provided advantages to place-bound and adult learners such as military personnel and veterans. This policy permits institutions to grant credit after the successful completion of a standardized examination developed by the institution, a portfolio assessment, or any other method that validates the competencies (Anderson, 2018).

At the institutional level, policies address faculty compensation, workload, intellectual property rights, and rewards (Moore & Kearsley, 2012). Policies may vary from institution to institution; they depend on the type of institution (public or private, for profit or nonprofit), size of institution, institutional priorities related to research and teaching, and support resources. Online education is still not recognized as part of the tenure and promotion process by some institutions.

Conclusion

Online education still has the stigma of a lower standard of education. Concerns about the quality of online education have been similar to those of conventional education; however, online education has undergone more scrutiny. Therefore, the evaluation of adult education programs plays an even more important role for an organization. Using appropriate learning assessment strategies, evaluation approaches, and benchmarks can ensure quality, accountability, and transparency. The ultimate goal is to satisfy a more informed consumer of online education and create an impactful experience for adult learners.

References

Amendments to the Higher Education Act of 1965. (1998). P.L. 105–244. Retrieved from https://www2.ed.gov/policy/highered/leg/hea98/index.html

Anderson, L. (2018). Competency-based education: Recent policy trends. *Journal of Competency-Based Education, 3*(1), e01057.

Bailey, S., Hendricks, S., & Applewhite, S. (2015). Student perspectives of assessment strategies in online courses. *Journal of Interactive Online Learning, 13,* 112–125.

Barczyk, C., Buckenmeyer, J., Feldman, L., & Hixon, E. (2011). Assessment of a university-based distance education mentoring program from a quality management perspective. *Mentoring & Tutoring: Partnership in Learning, 19*(1), 5–24.

Bernard, R. M., Abrami, P. C., Lou, Y., Borokhovski, E., Wade, A., Wozney, L., . . .Huang, B. (2004). How does distance education compare with classroom instruction? A meta-analysis of the empirical literature. *Review of Educational Research, 74*(3), 379–439.

Conceição, S. C. O., & Lehman, R. M. (2011). *Managing online instructor workload: Strategies for finding balance and success.* San Francisco, CA: Jossey-Bass.

Conceição, S. C. O., & Schmidt, S. (2010). How non-content-related forums influence social presence in the online learning environment. *Indian Journal of Open Learning, 19*(2), 73–85.

Fortune, J., & Keith, P. (1992). *Program evaluation for Buchanan County Even Start.* Blacksburg: Virginia Polytechnic Institute and State University.

Gibson, P. A., & Dunning, P. T. (2012). Creating quality online course design through a peer-reviewed assessment. *Journal of Public Affairs Education, 18*(1), 209–228.

Higher Learning Commission. (2009). *Guidelines for the evaluation of distance education (on-line learning).* Retrieved from http://download.hlcommission.org/C-RAC_Distance_Ed_Guidelines_7_31_2009.pdf

Jaggars, S. S., & Xu, D. (2016). How do online course design features influence student performance? *Computers & Education, 95,* 270–284.

Kirkpatrick, D. L., & Kirkpatrick, J. D. (2006). *Evaluating training programs: The four levels.* San Francisco, CA: Berrett-Koehler.

Lee, J. (2014). An exploratory study of effective online learning: Assessing satisfaction levels of graduate students of mathematics education associated with human and design factors of an online course. *The International Review of Research in Open and Distributed Learning, 15*(1), 111–132.

Lehman, R. M., & Conceição, S. C. O. (2014). *Motivating and retaining online students: Research-based strategies that work.* San Francisco, CA: Jossey-Bass.

Lock, J., & Johnson, C. (2015). Triangulating assessment of online collaborative learning. *Quarterly Review of Distance Education, 16*(4), 61–70.

Lowenthal, P., & Hodges, C. (2015). In search of quality: Using Quality Matters to analyze the quality of massive, open, online courses (MOOCs). *The International Review of Research in Open and Distributed Learning, 16*(5), 671–680.

Manternach, L., & Maushak, N. (1997). Iowa Distance Education Alliance. Evaluation report. *Retrieved from ERIC database. (ED416818)*.

McCutcheon, K., Lohan, M., Traynor, M., & Martin, D. (2015). A systematic review evaluating the impact of online or blended learning vs. face-to-face learning of clinical skills in undergraduate nurse education. *Journal of Advanced Nursing*, *71*(2), 255–270.

Meyer, K. A., & Murrell, V. S. (2014). A national survey of faculty development evaluation outcome measures and procedures. *Online Learning, 18*(3), 1–18.

Moore, J. C., & Shelton, K. (2014). The Sloan Consortium pillars and quality score-card. In K. Shattuck (Ed.), *Assuring quality in online education: Practices and processes at the teaching, resource, and program levels* (pp. 40–49). Sterling, VA: Stylus.

Moore, M. G., & Kearsley, G. (2012). *Distance education: A systems view of online learning*. Independence, KY: Cengage Learning.

Patton, M. Q. (1987). *How to use qualitative methods in evaluation*. Newbury Park, CA: Sage.

Pell Institute. (2010). Evaluation approaches & types. Retrieved from http://toolkit.pellinstitute.org/evaluation-101/evaluation-approaches-types/printpage/

Phipps, R., & Merisotis, J. (2000). *Quality on the Line: Benchmarks for success in Internet-based distance education*. Washington, DC: Institute for Higher Education Policy.

Quality Matters. (2018). Why QM? A grassroots beginning. Retrieved from https://www.qualitymatters.org/why-quality-matters/about-qm

Rogerson-Revell, P. (2015). Constructively aligning technologies with learning and assessment in a distance education master's programme. *Distance Education, 36*(1), 129–147.

Saba, F. (2000). Research in distance education: A status report. *The International Review of Research in Open and Distributed Learning, 1*(1), 1–9.

Seaman, J. E., Allen, I. E., & Seaman, J. (2018). *Grade increase: Tracking distance education in the United States*: Babson Survey Research Group. Retrieved from https://onlinelearningsurvey.com/reports/gradeincrease.pdf

Sorensen, C. (1996). *Final evaluation report: Iowa Distance Education Alliance*. Ames, IA: Research Institute for Studies in Education.

Stella, A., & Gnanam, A. (2004). Quality assurance in distance education: The challenges to be addressed. *Higher Education, 47*(2), 143–160.

Sweeney, J. (1995). *Vision 2020: Evaluation report*. Ames, IA: Research Institute for Studies in Education.

Vonderwell, S. K., & Boboc, M. (2013). Promoting formative assessment in online teaching and learning. *TechTrends, 57*(4), 22–27.

Woodley, A., & Kirkwood, A. (1986). *Evaluation in distance learning*. ERIC database. (ED304122).

ASSESSMENT AND EVALUATION PRACTICES FOR ADULT STUDENTS IN HIGHER EDUCATION

Jovita M. Ross-Gordon and Royce Ann Collins

T his chapter considers practices, policy issues, and possibilities for advocacy by adult education professionals related to assessment and evaluation practices for adult students in higher education programs. It begins with a discussion of practices related to assessment of student learning. The next section focuses on program evaluation and accountability of adult-focused programs in institutional and accountability systems still largely structured around traditional notions of higher education. Finally, the conclusion poses questions regarding the roles adult educators may play in efforts to affect public and institutional policy on behalf of adult learners in postsecondary settings.

Assessment of Student Learning

Topics considered in this section include (a) assessment of prior college-level learning, (b) other uses of portfolio-based assessment, (c) authentic assessment, and (d) competency-based education (CBE).

Assessment of Prior College-Level Learning

For many adult learners in higher education, assessment begins with efforts to acquire credit for prior learning through various modes of prior learning assessment (PLA), one of the key features of adult higher education that has helped increase access for adults (Klein-Collins, 2010; Maehl, 2000; Michelson & Mandell, 2004; Ross-Gordon, 2011). Travers (2012) traced the origins of PLA, beginning with the establishment of the College Entrance Exam Board in the 1930s and the creation of the Advanced Placement (AP) program in 1955 and College Level Examination Program in 1967. In the 1970s further developments advanced interest in PLA, including the formation of the Commission on Non-Traditional Study; the formation of the Council for the Advancement of Experiential Learning (CAEL); and the emergence of colleges, universities, and divisions focused on adult learners. PLA has evolved to include four primary modes of assessment of students' prior collegiate-level learning acquired through work or other life experiences: (a) standardized exams such as the College Level Examination Program, (b) institutionally created challenge exams, (c) student-developed portfolios, and (d) credit recommendations based on previously evaluated training programs in the military or business and industry.

Klein-Collins and Hain (2009) reported on the growing acceptance of the various modes of PLA as indicated by increases in the institutional use of PLA, particularly portfolio-based PLA. They noted that although only 50% of institutions reported offering portfolio-based assessment of student learning in a 1991 study by CAEL, 66% did so by the time of a 2006 CAEL survey (Klein-Collins & Hain, 2009). In addition, 87% of institutions accepted CLEP exam credits, and 70% offered credit for training evaluated by the American Council on Education (Klein-Collins & Hain, 2009). The latest CAEL study of PLA includes findings from longitudinal research based on more than 62,000 students at 48 institutions (Klein-Collins, 2010). This study collected data on rates of degree completion, time to completion, and persistence, comparing data from PLA learners to those of similar students who did not use PLA. Findings indicated that PLA students had higher degree completion rates, regardless of institutional size; grade point average; student age, gender, race or ethnicity; or student financial aid status. Among those who had not yet graduated, PLA students also persisted at a higher level, with 56% of PLA students earning 80% or more of credits toward the degree, versus 22% of credits for non-PLA students (Klein-Collins, 2010). In a CAEL brief focused on study findings for underserved students, Klein-Collins (2011) noted that "Hispanic and black, non-Hispanic students who earn PLA credits had higher graduation rates and required less time to earn their degrees, compared to their peers without PLA credit" (p. 4), adding that Hispanic PLA students earned the bachelor's degree at almost 8 times the rate of non-PLA students.

Hayward and Williams (2015) examined differences in graduation rates between PLA users and nonusers among students attending four community colleges. A significant difference was found between the four-year graduation rates of non-PLA students (11.8%) and PLA students (28.4%). Differences in graduation rates held across race, ethnicity, and gender; notably, Hispanic PLA learners graduated at a rate of almost five times that of non-PLA learners in the same race or ethnicity category (36.6% vs. 7.4%; Hayward & Williams, 2015). This study suggests that PLA offers substantial benefits for community college learners—a context where PLA is currently underused.

Several theses and dissertations using qualitative methods have focused on learner outcomes associated with completing PLA through the portfolio method. These outcomes have included (a) enhanced self-esteem and self-confidence (Jimenez, 2015), (b) perspective transformation (Lamoreaux, 2005), (c) greater awareness of personal learning style (Blinkhorn, 1999), and (c) enhanced learning through reflection (Jimenez, 2015).

Other Uses of Portfolio-Based Assessment

Kruger, Holtzman, and Dagavarian (2013) reviewed various uses of student portfolios beyond PLA, including developmental portfolios, individual class portfolios, credentialing portfolios, and comprehensive education portfolios (CEP). They suggested that the greatest potential of the CEP may be in career development. They also suggested that career-focused CEP provides learners with an opportunity to reflect on their career and present themselves "as . . . accomplished individual[s] who [are] career-ready or prepared for a new career or the next stage in an existing career" (Kruger et al., 2013, p. 48).

Matas and Allan (2004) described the use of a class-based portfolio with beginning adult learners enrolled in an Australian Labor Relations course at Griffith University. An essay assignment was modified to a requirement for three short-answer submissions as part of a learning portfolio, with students receiving online feedback from the instructor and a peer. Although a number of first-round submissions were rated as failing, by the third round no submissions were rated as failing. Students also reporting learning to analyze essay criteria more critically as a result of providing feedback to peers. In the end, students in the online and portfolio group performed as well as the group assessed by traditional means in terms of overall course means.

Curtis and Wu (2012) reported on the use of a developmental ePortfolio in a newly designed master of healthcare administration program in the context of the growing use of ePortfolios in higher education for assessment, evaluation, and accreditation with the aim to enhance transparency in learning and assessment. They focused on four features of transparency for adult learning programs. Two features were framed in terms of transparency in learning. First was relevance, that is, were learners provided information on the relevance of the content knowledge and methods? Second was visibility, or was learning visible to learners and educators? The other two features, relating to transparency of assessment, were accessibility, meaning learners had access to the review results and to the assessment process and evaluators had access to products and the learning process, and scalability, meaning that "the assessment model must scale to the demands of the current education environment to conduct evaluations at different levels: individual, programmatic, and institutional" (p. 67).

Authentic Assessment

Scholars interested in improvement of instruction in higher education have called for greater use of authentic modes of assessment. Berg (2006) pointed to changes occurring in K–12 education as an impetus for placing greater emphasis on student learning in higher education, including use of authentic forms of assessment to measure student learning outcomes. Referring to increasing external pressures for accountability in higher education, Berg stated, "I would rather work with my colleagues to develop good assessment techniques than to have the legislature tell me what to do" (p. 15). In this light, Ashford-Rowe, Herrington, and Brown's (2014) study sought to determine critical elements of an authentic learning activity, to include those elements in a framework design, and to use that framework to guide the design, development, and application of authentic assessment for a learning module of the Australian army's course, Evaluating Educational Multimedia. Based on a review of the literature and conversations with education practitioners and experts, they created questions to serve as a heuristic framework for the design and development of an authentic assessment. The final list of questions, which were revised following program implementation and feedback from students, is

1. To what extent does the assessment activity challenge the student?
2. Is a performance, or product, required as a final assessment outcome?
3. Does the assessment activity require that transfer of learning has occurred, by means of demonstration of skill?
4. Does the assessment activity require that metacognition is demonstrated?
5. Does the assessment require a product or performance that could be recognized as authentic by a client or stakeholder? (accuracy)
6. Is fidelity required in the assessment environment? And the assessment tools (actual or simulated)?
7. Does the assessment activity require discussion and feedback?

8. Does the assessment activity require that students collaborate? (Ashford-Rowe et al., 2014, pp. 219–220)

Hay, Tan, and Whaites (2010) contextualized their discussion of authentic assessment in the changing demographics in higher education, questioning whether traditional modes of assessment are well suited to the deep cognitive processes typically used by adult learners with work experience. In a study comparing A-level (traditional) dental science students with hygiene and therapy students enrolled in the Dental School at King's College London, they examined differences in performance by the two groups of students on a traditional multiple-choice question exam and on a concept-mapping activity designed to assess meaningful learning and factual knowledge acquisition in a course on dental radiological science. Notably, the hygiene and therapy students as a group were older than the A-level students (80% were older than 21, and 89% of A-level students were under 21) and were more likely to have prior clinical experience as dental nurses. As hypothesized, the A-level students outperformed the hygiene and therapy students on the multiple-choice exam. Interestingly, although the A-level students also scored more of the factual knowledge targets in their end-of-course concept maps, the concept maps of hygiene and therapy students demonstrated greater complexity and understanding of dental radiography "in a broader personal and professional context" (Hay et al., 2010, p. 558). Hay and colleagues (2010) pointed to potential implications of assessment approaches as cognitive barriers for adult learning, a topic rarely addressed in the literature on adult learners in higher education.

CBE

Klein-Collins (2013) described CBE programs focusing on what students know and can do rather than on learning activities. She attributed their origins to the changing demographics in higher education once the Higher Education Act of 1965 expanded access to adults, prompting the development of adult-focused institutions and programs such as those at Alverno College, De Paul University School for New Learning, Empire State College, and Thomas Edison State College (Klein-Collins, 2013; Maehl, 2000). Today, this emphasis on demonstration of performance can be seen in CBE programs such as the computer-aided manufacturing program at Texas State Technical College in which assessment is based on a go or no-go standard borrowed from the military. Learners move on to the next task only after they have demonstrated satisfactory performance on the current one (Geigerich, 2017).

Current Approaches to CBE

Klein-Collins (2012), identified as the chief researcher for CAEL, distinguished between course-based models, such as those used at Alverno College, Delaware County Community college, and Rio Salado College, and innovative models, which disrupt the traditional curriculum structure, such as those at DePaul University's School of New Learning, where learners demonstrate competencies in three domains through a variety of means including PLA, course work, independent study, and transfer courses.

Learning modules rather than traditional courses serve as the foundational element in the integrated, competency-based 3-year bachelor's degree model described by Bradley, Seidman, and Painchaud (2012). In this model, unlocking the traditional course structure supports a focus on the assessment of learning outcomes identified as crucial for program graduates. Curricular restructuring allows institutions to identify institutional and program level competencies deemed crucial for graduates, redesigning the curriculum by remapping existing courses into learning modules that can be completed in 3 years (6 semesters), which saves time and money without sacrificing the accomplishment of learning outcomes. Bradley and colleagues said 2 institutions were fully implementing this model—Southern New Hampshire and University of Charleston—and listed 35 institutions offering 3-year competency-based degree programs based on the model.

In describing another category of CBE programs, Klein-Collins (2012) noted that programs using direct assessment rely entirely on direct assessment of learning for awarding credit:

> While students taking courses, or studying on their own might accumulate credit hours along the way, it is not the sequence of courses or the number of credit hours that results in a degree or certificate. Rather, to graduate and earn a credential, students must demonstrate through competency-based assessments what they know and can do. (p. 5)

Students enrolled in programs of this type often pay subscriber fees for a set period of time, during which they are allowed to complete assessments at their own pace rather than paying tuition to attend courses during a fixed time interval. Western Governors University, where undergraduate students have no required courses but complete assessments based on learning acquired, is mentioned as one of the best-known institutions relying on direct assessment.

Issues Related to Competency-Based Degree Programs

Wellman and Ehrlich (2003, September 26) have suggested that the credit hour is the most pervasive performance measure in higher education and the vehicle for translating many complex activities—student learning, faculty workloads and productivity, enrollments, graduate rates, time to degree, cost per student—into quantifiable units. (p. B16)

This conflation of seat time with learning time in higher education poses one of the biggest challenges to programs that rely substantially on competency-based assessment of student learning rather than the delineation of credit hours (Bradley et al., 2012; Fiddler, Marienau, & Whitaker, 2006; Klein-Collins, 2012).

One implication of not equating CBE assessment of learning to credit hours is the difficulty that may arise in transferring hours earned to a different institution. One major attempt to address this problem is the effort led by Lumina Foundation to develop the Degree Qualifications Profile (DQP), a common but adaptable set of identified learning proficiencies for associate's, bachelor's and master's degree levels. Through the development and beta testing of the profile with more than 400 colleges in 45 states, learning proficiencies were identified in 5 categories: specialized knowledge, broad and integrative knowledge (akin to general education requirements), intellectual skills (including traditional cognitive skills and nontraditional ones), applied and collaborative learning, and civic and global learning. Adelman, Ewell, Gaston, and Schneider (2014) suggested that for adult learners attempting to earn credit for prior learning or to transfer credits from other institutions, "the DQP provides a framework useful for aligning degree requirements across institutions" (p. 8) and that the "DQP is as applicable to learning assessed outside the framework of courses as it is to traditional, course-based degree programs" (p. 5).

Another issue related to the ubiquity of the credit hour is the strongly established link between credit hours earned and financial aid, affecting individual learners and institutions. Current financial aid policies, at federal and state levels and for many institutionally administered scholarship programs, are based on students earning a minimum number of credit hours per semester equivalent to part-time enrollment status if not full-time status (Kazis et al., 2007; Klein-Collins, 2012; Wellman & Ehrlich, 2003, September 26). Such policies disqualify adult students who complete programs that do not equate competencies achieved to credit hours from many forms of financial aid. Similarly, student credit hours completed serve as the basis for determination of institutional qualification for administering federal financial aid. Thus, institutions are incentivized to either bundle learning modules in terms of traditional credit hours or, as in the case of Western Governor's University, to devise a process for converting competency units into credit hours (Klein-Collins, 2012).

Program Evaluation

Program evaluation or review is "the application of systematic methods to address questions about program operations and results" (Newcomer, Hatry, & Wholey, 2010, p. 5). Program review incorporates not only assessment of student learning but also policies and procedures that affect the degree program's development. The objective of any program review in higher education is to examine the degree program from all perspectives (students, faculty, administrators, graduates, and employers). It should also examine policies, procedures, and curriculum. Data collected includes the assessment of learning outcomes; surveys to students, faculty, graduates, and employers; admission rates and graduate rates; and the currency of the curriculum.

Higher education institutions are responsible for the quality of their academic programs. The regional accreditation agencies maintain that institutions should practice regular program reviews every three to five years. The purpose of a program review is program improvement through the lens of quality, currency, value, and effective use of resources (Arns & Poland, 1980; Murry & Hall, 1998).

Publications concerning academic program review processes proliferated during the late 1970s and into the 1980s and 1990s (Mets, 1995). By the 1980s most academic programs were engaged in program reviews (Barak & Breier, 1990; Conrad & Wilson, 1985). The literature further discusses the difficulty in defining and measuring quality (Conrad & Wilson, 1985; Scott, 1980). Although institutions are required to conduct program evaluations by external agencies, the quality of the review varies based on the experience of administrators and faculty who understand program evaluation criteria (Arns & Poland, 1980; Murry & Hall, 1998). The 1980s and 1990s saw deeper scrutiny of adult degree programs because they challenged the long-held standard of the Carnegie Unit for a credit hour (Carnegie Foundation for the Advancement of Teaching, 2014). Degree-completion programs moved to alternative delivery formats, which included meeting on weekends and evenings. These programs required less contact time with the instructor and, applying adult education practices, increased student responsibility for learning (Wlodkowski, 2003). An alternative delivery face-to-face program may provide 20 to 24 contact hours with the instructor for a 3-credit-hour course versus 45 contact hours with the instructor in the Carnegie model for equivalent credit. The programs were criticized for lacking academic rigor (Wolfe, 1998). This scrutiny still exists today. Program reviews are used by faculty and administrators of higher education programs for adult learners to substantiate their academic rigor and learning outcomes (Culver, 1993; Hoyt & Allred, 2008; Johnson, Collins, & Millburn, 2014).

Dissertation research has expanded the conversation about program evaluation the most; however, few focus on the adult learner. Topics range from best practices in academic program review (Feikema, 2016) to reviewing undergraduate programs at regional campuses. Goetsch (2015) and Feikema (2016) research focused on the process of academic program evaluation and needed data. Their results demonstrated commonality in data points for academic program review: student outcomes (graduate and employment rates); student data (admission and enrollment trends, numbers, demographics, retention rates); student satisfaction; assessment of student learning outcomes; program curriculum (syllabi); faculty teaching and composition, as well as scholarship and community outreach; effectiveness of teaching methods; occupational and employer trends (demand for program and required skills); and external agency recommendations (external and discipline experts and potential accreditation reviews). Other items included by Goetsch (2015) focused on the program's strengths and weaknesses, needs assessment, budget, resources, and other revenue funding (grants, scholarships). The purpose of a program review is continuous academic, programmatic, and administrative improvement. Program reviews should be conducted by the school or college involved; collect input from faculty, staff, and administration; and result in an action plan. Although program reviews should be included in budgeting decisions, they should not be the only factor, and although these items are important and contribute to the overall picture of the academic program, few institutions initiate a thorough comprehensive review.

Despite the growth of adult programs, there is a paucity of published research or conference presentations on the topic of a program review targeting adults in higher education. Although presentations are given on the topic of program review at regional accrediting agencies' annual conferences, none were found in the past 10 years that focused on degree programs targeting adults in higher education. Except for regional accreditation agencies' annual conferences, the topic of program review or evaluation rarely appears on any organization's conference programs or proceedings, and no presentations on this topic were found within the past 10 years at the annual conferences of Association of Continuing Higher Education, American Association of Adult and Continuing Education, Adult Education Research Conference, and University Professional and Continuing Education Association.

Published research focused on the results of program reviews is limited; however, aspects of the program evaluation, for the most part using indirect measures, have been published. Culver (1993) reported on the program review at Radford University where he surveyed alumni and students from the adult degree-completion program. Both groups had a very positive view of the adult degree program. The alumni rated the effect of the program on their work and personal life as very positive. Nanna (2001) provided an overview of the outcomes assessment process for degree-completion programs stating that these programs have been "criticized for not providing documentation to support their effectiveness" (p. 20). Cantwell, Archer, and Bourke (2001) compared the academic achievement of the "mature-aged" (p. 221) with traditional-age learners in Australia and found that older students performed better than younger students in academic achievement. Hoyt and Allred (2008) surveyed alumni of a degree-completion program, and from the student's perspectives, the program prepared them very well academically for their future employment. From a degree-completion program review, Johnson et al. (2014) reported on the positive alumni feedback and how it had helped in their career pursuits. The analysis of the curriculum included course objectives, textbooks and course materials, and learning outcomes assessment plan and data. Although most publications do not report on the next step, after a series of meetings with faculty and staff, Johnson and colleagues (2014) found that the faculty and staff had developed new courses for the program to address the weaknesses that emerged from the program evaluation.

With the help of organizations focused on adults in higher education, more research should be published on evaluations of programs targeting the adult learner. Institutional researchers need to take the evidence produced from a program review and show the public the strengths and weaknesses of the program targeting adult learners. All institution administrators are feeling the pressures of transparency and accountability but especially those whose institutions offer adult degree programs using alternative delivery models.

Accountability

Although accountability in higher education has changed over the years, quality assurance has always been a focus in U.S. higher education. State and federal agencies, national and regional accreditation, and other organizations are among the external agencies that set a variety of policies and procedures that continually shape and restrain higher education institutions (Carifio, 2012). Adult degree-completion programs have always garnered increased focus by accreditation agency peer reviewers and the U.S. Department of Education. Rood's (2011) research indicated that even employers were biased and perceived the quality of a degree earned through an accelerated format to be less than that of a traditional format. With the current financial aid regulations, many adult learners qualified for federal financial aid loans or grants as the responsibility for those monies moved from private sector banks to the Department of Education (Eaton, 2012). Although the Department of Education cannot make decisions on academic quality, its control over Title IV of the Higher Education Act of 1965 on financial aid funding has allowed it to have greater authority over institutions and to exert pressure on accreditation agencies.

For regional accrediting bodies, the traditional role of accreditation is increasingly overshadowed by regulatory practices imposed by the government. Since 1992 accreditation agencies must be approved by the Department of Education through the National Advisory Council on Integrity and Quality Initiatives to maintain federal recognition (Eaton, 2012). This committee has expanded the role of federal authority and judgement of accreditation standards, requirements and processes of institutional review.

Effective in 2011, the Department of Education program integrity regulations were mandatory for all higher education institutions (Program Integrity Issues, 2010). These regulations included gainful employment tracking and reporting, definition of the credit hour, and state authorization for online course delivery, to name a few new compliance matters.

The federal credit hour definition made a significant impact on institutions with adult degree-completion programs, stating that a single credit hour was essentially 15 hours of direct faculty instruction with a minimum of at least 30 hours of student work outside class, following the standard Carnegie unit, or "at least an equivalent amount of work for other academic activities as established by the institution including laboratory work, internships, practium, studio work, and other academic work leading to the award of credit hours" (Program Integrity Issues, 2010, p. 66946).

Therefore, if higher education institutions were authorized to use federal financial aid funds, they were required to define a credit hour as they used it to award credit hours to students. Many institutions gravitated or defaulted to the age-old standard of the Carnegie unit (Carnegie Foundation for the Advancement of Teaching, 2014). This caused major difficulty for the adult degree-completion programs, which were using a more innovative approach, as directed by learning outcomes, to demonstrate equivalent learning as the standard semester. This additional requirement deeply affected any higher education institution with a degree program targeting adult learners that focused on learning outcomes instead of the strict Carnegie unit. Although many in higher education accept this as the norm, the history of the Carnegie unit shows that it was not set up to measure learning. It was created for the Carnegie Foundation in 1906 to distribute retirement pensions to college teachers (Shedd, 2003). For decades, the traditional credit hour definition has been a barrier for innovative institutions (e.g., Western Governors, Empire State College, Evergreen State College, Alverno College), which center their approaches on learning outcomes.

Associations concentrating on the adult learner in higher education also supported the validity and academic rigor of alternative delivery formats for adult learners and began to address these new compliance issues. To provide consistent quality criteria for institutions with adult degree-completion programs, the Council for Accelerated Programs created quality standards for higher education programs targeting the adult learner to help them address these new demands for compliance and accountability. The vision was to build collaboration, research, and communication among accelerated programs internationally. From this research and collaboration, the council created best practices and eventually the Quality Standards for Accelerated Programs in Higher Education (Council for Accelerated Programs, 2011).

The quality standards were created to assist institutions in understanding how to serve adult learners and to demonstrate the quality of the degree programs targeting adult learners. Many of these degree programs use alternative scheduling formats. Thus, addressing the credit hour definition was extremely important to the survival of these programs. The standards focus on nine areas: program mission and integrity; leadership and administration; educational offerings (definition of credit hour); assessment and program evaluation; faculty appraisal, support, and appreciation; student support services; planning and resources; facilities and auxiliary services; and program marketing and recruitment. Each quality area was carefully addressed through research. In addition, instructional equivalencies (quality learning activities where the instructor's direct presence is not necessary but similar to an activity conducted in a traditional semester course; e.g., viewing a three-hour documentary film outside class time with guided questions) were documented to assist institutions in demonstrating the "equivalent amount of academic activities" (Program Integrity Issues, 2010, p. 66946).

Furthermore, the Office of Postsecondary Education, Department of Education (2010) requires regional accrediting agencies to gather data on institutional compliance with the program integrity rules. For instance, the Higher Learning Commission (2019) requires institutions to document the credit hour for all types of courses, formats, and modality, which is then verified by peer reviewers. The assignment of credit hours and clock hours focuses solely on the credit hour documentation and compliance with federal regulations. All higher education institutions are required to post on their website how they define the credit hour. Peer reviewers have the responsibility to document if institutions meet federal compliance regulations and if the institution needs monitoring on this issue. All delivery formats must be able to meet the institution's published credit hour definition: "Institutions that provide instruction through online, alternative, compressed or other formats should also have policies that address how learning is determined, organized and evaluated, and how the institution determines instructional equivalencies" (Higher Learning Commission, 2019, p. 3). Monitoring federal compliance is required of any federally recognized accrediting agency (Higher Learning Commission, 2019).

Innovative institutions and nontraditional delivery models need to monitor and document academic rigor, just as traditional educational models do. However, quality assurance issues should not detract from the initiative of learning.

Conclusion

Postsecondary education and specifically degree programs for adult learners must adopt a culture of evidence to provide accountability. The avenue to advocate for adult learners in higher education and the quality of the academic rigor is through learning outcomes assessment and program review. Access and convenience are the demands of the adult learners seeking higher education. Online and alternative delivery models are the new demands to meet the growing need for an educated workforce. Adult education has always been a force for innovation and this marginalized population in higher education. Institutions and accreditation agencies are being called to the task by outside entities. Therefore, innovative higher education programs for the adult learner must document the academic effects of their program through the assessment of learning and program evaluation.

References

Adelman, C., Ewell, P., Gaston, P., & Schneider, C. G. (2014). Degree qualifications profile. Retrieved from https://www.luminafoundation.org/publications

Arns, R. G., & Poland, W. (1980). Changing the university through program review. *The Journal of Higher Education, 51*(3), 268–294.

Ashford-Rowe, K., Herrington, J., & Brown, C. (2014). Establishing the critical elements that determine authentic assessment. *Assessment & Evaluation in Higher Education, 39*(2), 205–222.

Barak, R. J., & Breier, B. E. (1990). *Successful program review; A practical guide to evaluating programs in academic settings.* San Francisco, CA: Jossey-Bass.

Berg, S. L. (2006). Two sides of the same coin: Authentic assessment. *Community College Enterprise, 12*(2), 7–21.

Blinkhorn, K. W. (1999). *Prior learning assessment: An investigation of nonsponsored learning for college credits* (Doctoral dissertation). Available from ProQuest Dissertations and Theses database. (UMI No. NQ41010).

Bradley, M. J., Seidman, R. H., & Painchaud, S. R. (2012). *Saving higher education: The integrated, competency-based three-year bachelor's degree program.* San Francisco, CA: Jossey-Bass.

Cantwell, R., Archer, J., & Bourke, S. (2001). A comparison of the academic experiences and achievement of university students entering by traditional and nontraditional means. *Assessment & Evaluation in Higher Education, 26*(3), 221–234.

Carifio, J. (2012). The program assessment and improvement cycle today: A new and simple taxonomy of general types and levels of program evaluation. *Creative Education, 03*(06), 951–958.

Carnegie Foundation for the Advancement of Teaching. (2014). What is the Carnegie unit? Retrieved from https://www.carnegiefoundation.org/faqs/carnegie-unit/

Conrad, C. F., & Wilson, R. F. (1985). Academic program reviews: Institutional approaches, expectations, and controversies. *ASHE-ERIC Higher Education Report, 5.*

Council for Accelerated Programs. (2011). *Quality standards for accelerated programs in higher education.* Denver, CO: Author.

Culver, S. M. (1993). A survey of adult degree program alumni and current students at one university. *The Journal of Continuing Higher Education, 41*(2), 23–44.

Curtis, R. S., & Wu, W. (2012). Learning and assessment: The application of ePortfolios. *Journal of Higher Education Theory and Practice, 12*(3), 66–74.

Eaton, J. (2012). The future of accreditation. *Planning for Higher Education, 40*(3), 8–15.

Feikema, J. L. (2016). *Best practices for academic program review in large post-secondary institutions: A modified Delphi approach* (Doctoral dissertation). Available from ProQuest Dissertations and Theses database. (UMI No. 10107002).

Fiddler, M., Marienau, C., & Whitaker, U. (2006). *Assessing learning: Standards, principles, and procedures* (2nd ed.). Dubuque, IA: Kendall Hunt.

Geigerich, S (2017). Real-life learning programs are helping redefine the post-secondary landscape. *Focus Magazine*, September, 1. Retrieved from https://www.luminafoundation.org/resources/focus-magazine-summer-2017-real-life-learning

Goetsch, L. J. (2015). *Meaningful program review for regional campus undergraduate programs within a public research university: An action research study* (Doctoral dissertation). Available from ProQuest Dissertations and Theses database. (UMI No. 3681155).

Hay, D. B., Tan, P. L., & Whaites, E. (2010). Non-traditional learners in higher education: Comparison of a traditional MCQ examination with concept mapping to assess learning in a dental radiological science course. *Assessment & Evaluation in Higher Education, 35*(5), 577–595.

Hayward, M. S., & Williams, M. R. (2015). Adult learner graduation rates at four U.S. community colleges by prior learning assessment status and method. *Community College Journal of Research and Practice, 39*(1), 44–55.

Higher Education Act. (1965). 20 U.S.C. § 1001 et seq.

Higher Learning Commission. (2019). Federal compliance program. Retrieved from https://www.hlcommission.org/Accreditation/federal-compliance-program.html

Hoyt, J. E., & Allred, E. (2008). Educational and employment outcomes of a degree completion program. *The Journal of Continuing Higher Education, 56*(2), 26–33.

Jimenez, B. A. (2015). *A phenomenological study of adult learners' experiences with the portfolio form of prior learning assessment* (Doctoral dissertation). Available from ProQuest Dissertations and Theses database. (UMI No. 3725334).

Johnson, C., Collins, P., & Millburn, J. (2014). What do they know? Assessing learning outcomes in an adult degree completion program. In C. J. Boden & K. P. King (Eds.), *Developing and sustaining adult learners* (pp. 379–394). Charlotte, NC: Information Age.

Klein-Collins, B., & Hain, P. (2009). Prior learning assessment: How institutions use portfolio assessments. *The Journal of Continuing Higher Education, 57*(3), 187–189.

Klein-Collins, R. (2010). Fueling the race to postsecondary success: A 48-institution study of prior learning assessment and adult student outcomes. Retrieved from http://www.cael.org/pdfs/PLA_Fueling-the-Race

Klein-Collins, R. (2011). Underserved students who earn credit through Prior Learning Assessment (PLA) have higher degree completion rates and shorter time-to-degree. Retrieved from http://www.cael.org/pdfs/126_pla_research_brief_1_underserved04-2011

Klein-Collins, R. (2012). *Council for Adult and Experiential Learning. Competency-based degree programs in the U.S: Postsecondary credentials for measurable student learning and performance*. Retrieved from https://www.cael.org/cbe-publications

Klein-Collins, R. (2013). Sharpening our focus on learning: The rise of competency-based approaches to degree completion. Retrieved from https://www.cael.org/cbe-publications

Kazis, R., Callahan, A., Davidson, C., McLeod, A., Bosworth, B., Choitz, V., & Hoops, J. (2007). *Adult learners in higher education: Barriers to success and strategies to improve results* (Report No. Occasional Paper No. 2007-03). Washington, DC: U.S. Department of Labor, Employment, and Training Administration.

Kruger, E. J., Holtzman, D. M., & Dagavarian, D. A. (2013). Comprehensive education portfolio with a career focus. *The Journal of Continuing Higher Education, 61*(1), 46–53.

Lamoreaux, A. J. (2005). *Adult learners' experience of change related to prior learning assessment* (Doctoral dissertation). Available from ProQuest Dissertations and Theses database. (UMI No. 3180108).

Maehl, W. H. (2000). *Lifelong learning at its best: Innovative programs in adult credit programs*. San Francisco, CA: Jossey-Bass.

Matas, C. P., & Allan, C. (2004). Using learning portfolios to develop generic skills with on-line adult students. *Australian Journal of Adult Learning, 44*(1), 6–26.

Mets, L. A. (1995). Lessons learned from program review experiences. *New Directions for Institutional Research, 1995*(86), 81–92.

Michelson, E., & Mandell, A. (2004). *Portfolio development and the assessment of prior learning: Perspectives, models and practices.* Sterling, VA: Stylus.

Murry, J. W., & Hall, B. L. (1998). A systematic approach to designing and evaluating effective adult degree completion programs. *The Journal of Continuing Higher Education, 46*(2), 19–26.

Nanna, M. J. (2001). The rising tide of outcomes assessment in adult higher education: Implications for nontraditional and accelerated programs. *The Journal of Continuing Higher Education, 49*(1), 19–28.

Newcomer, K., Hatry, H., & Wholey, J. (2010). Planning and designing useful evaluations. In J. S. Wholey, H. P. Hatry, & K. E. Newcomer (Eds.), *Handbook of practical program evaluation* (pp. 5–29). San Francisco, CA: Jossey-Bass.

Office of Postsecondary Education, Department of Education. (2010). Program Integrity Issues 34 CFR (Parts 600, 602, 603, 668, 682, 685, 686, 690, and 691). *Federal Register, 75*(209). [Docket ID ED–2010–OPE–0004].

Program Integrity Issues. (2010). Federal register 34 cfr (parts 600, 602, 603, 668,682, 685, 686, 690, and 691). Office of Postsecondary Education, Department of Education. [Docket ID ED–2010–OPE–0004].

Rood, R. (2011). Traditional versus accelerated degree program graduates: A survey of employer preferences. *The Journal of Continuing Higher Education, 59*(3), 122–134.

Ross-Gordon, J. M. (2011). Research on adult learners: Supporting the needs of a student population that is no longer nontraditional. *Peer Review, 13*(1), 26–29.

Scott, R. A. (1980). Quality: Program review's missing link. *College Board Review, 118*(18–21), 30.

Shedd, J. M. (2003). The history of the student credit hour. *New Directions for Higher Education, 2003*(122), 5–12.

Travers, N. L. (2012). What is next after 40 years? Part 1: Prior learning assessment: 1970–2011. *The Journal of Continuing Higher Education, 60*(1), 43–47.

Wellman, J. V., & Ehrlich, T. (2003, September 26). Re-examining the sacrosanct credit hour. *Chronicle of Higher Education, 50*, B16.

Wlodkowski, R. J. (2003). Accelerated learning in colleges and universities. *New Directions for Adult and Continuing Education, 2003*(97), 5–16.

Wolfe, A. (1998). How a for-profit university can be invaluable to the traditional liberal arts. *Chronicle of Higher Education, 45*(15), B4–B5.

12

ASSESSMENT PRACTICES IN HIGHER EDUCATION WITH IMPLICATIONS FOR GRADUATE ADULT EDUCATION

Mary V. Alfred and Patrice B. French

Assessment, evaluation, and accountability have been emerging priorities in higher education since the 1980s (Kuh, Ikenberry, Jankowski, & Cain, 2014), particularly as colleges and universities received criticism from state and federal governments regarding the need for greater accountability and transparency for determining student achievement (Middaugh, 2009). The question of assessment became highly publicized with the U.S. National Commission on Excellence in Education (1983). This report stressed the need for improvement in the quality of education, primarily in undergraduate education, which was the focus of assessment at the time. Since then, considerable efforts and investments have been made to articulate and document the outcome of student learning and program effectiveness.

Although attention on documenting assessment has increased, concerns about the quality of postsecondary education remain high on the national agenda. Many have credited the U.S. Department of Education (2006) Secretary of Higher Education's Commission on the Future of Higher Education report for the increasing demand for evidence of learning quality and, hence, increased assessment activities in higher education. Then U.S. Secretary of Education Margaret Spellings commissioned the report to assess and document the state of U.S. higher education. Despite achievements in higher education, she said that "many unfilled promises remained at the start of the twenty-first century" (U.S. Department of Education, 2006, p. ix). The commission's report noted a lack of clear and accessible data on students' progress through the pipeline and called for higher education to be more transparent and accountable for student learning. Moreover, the commission recommended colleges and universities embrace a culture of continuous innovation and quality improvement and emphasized the development of new approaches, curricula, and technologies to improve learning.

Although the Association of American Colleges & Universities (2006) endorsed the commission's report, it pointed out some major flaws with the findings and recommendations, arguing that the report focused almost exclusively on workforce preparation while ignoring the "longstanding and distinctively American goal of preparing students for engaged citizenship" (p. 2). Moreover, the AAC&U said that the role of faculty in the future of higher education was completely ignored. This absence is a troubling observation as the quality and accountability the commission members called for rest with the faculty for execution and demonstration. Another concern raised with the report was the heavy reliance on "a small set of standardized tests to measure outcomes of a college experience. . . . They can perhaps signal a problem but tests themselves do not point to where the problem exists" (p. 3).

Despite the concerns raised by the AAC&U and others about the report findings, colleges and universities are required to develop assessment plans to measure student performance and determine the effectiveness of the curriculum in meeting learning outcomes (Skinner & Feder, 2007; Stassen, 2012). According to Stassen (2012), "Following the Spellings Commission Report in 2006, higher education associations moved quickly to develop accountability systems that would demonstrate responsiveness to external requests for information" (p. 137). Examples include the Voluntary Systems of Accountability, established by the American Association of State Colleges and Universities; the Voluntary Framework of Accountability, which is the community college version of an accountability system; and the University College Accountability Network, established by private colleges and universities (Stassen, 2012). Therefore, colleges and universities have internal accountability systems in place, often administered by the department or office of institutional research and effectiveness. In addition, external accountability systems in place are driven by independent regional accrediting bodies (Kuh et al., 2014).

Although higher education institutions have implemented various assessment and accountability systems, many individuals and state and federal governing bodies continue to question whether they are meeting the mission of providing quality education to the nation's citizens. In other words, assessment and evaluation results from higher education do not clearly demonstrate the value of the education enterprise. According to Astin and Antonio (2012):

> Our assessment efforts are handicapped in part because we are not really clear about what we are trying to accomplish and, in part, because we perpetuate questionable practices out of sheer habit, or convenience, or to fulfill purposes that are unrelated, or at best, tangential to the basic mission of our colleges and universities. (p. 1)

There is general agreement that despite their efforts, higher education institutions have not effectively used assessment activities to communicate their value to their stakeholders. Moreover, assessment and accountability priorities overwhelmingly focus on undergraduate education with less emphasis on graduate education outcomes. Hence, discussions of the realities and pressures of accountability and assessment priorities on graduate programs, particularly those of adult education, are warranted.

Graduate Programs and Accountability Requirements

Although much of the focus is on undergraduate education, master's and doctoral programs are expected to produce evidence of student learning and program effectiveness (Middaugh, 2009; Orzoff, Peinovich, & Riedel, 2008). Many graduate programs are concerned with national rankings, research productivity, grant funding availability, and access to qualified students and scholars (Orzoff et al., 2008). Moreover, graduate programs must often comply with accreditation requirements, standardize assessment processes, and produce program time-to-degree completion rates when those accountability metrics are not specifically created to address their unique needs (Orzoff et al., 2008). The long-term focus on undergraduate program assessment causes graduate assessment to lag, triggering higher education institutions to prioritize assessment and accountability measures to fill the gap.

The Council of Graduate Schools (formerly known as the U.S. Council of Graduate Schools; 2011) released a framework for colleges and universities to guide "developing, or evaluating their program review activities, and [as] a useful reference to anyone involved in the review of graduate programs" (Palm et al., 1990, p. 7). The first edition addressed issues that affect successful program review—locus of control, differences between master's and doctoral programs, accreditation reviews, relationship between academic and professional programs, and structural components of a program review (Palm et al., 1990). The latest edition of the publication expands on guidance to graduate programs and institutions by developing successful program reviews, conducting meaningful outcomes assessments, and integrating assessment into program reviews (Baker, Carter, Larick, & King, 2011). To build an assessment infrastructure for graduate education, it is important for program administrators to view assessment practices from a holistic perspective, including institutional accreditation review, departmental-level program review, and course and curricula-based assessment.

Assessment Infrastructure for Graduate Education

Undergirding the culture of assessment are institutional accreditation and programmatic reviews that require colleges and universities to examine and provide evidence of student achievement and institutional performance. Accreditation provides a foundation for various accountability efforts through review of institutions and programs to ensure that standards for academic quality are in place and that institutions are living up to their commitments to students and society (Wiley, 2009). Moreover, many federal funding programs require institutions to be accredited, a designation that symbolizes quality and competitive value for the institution. As Skinner and Feder (2007) state,

> Under the Higher Education Act (HEA), institutions of higher education must be accredited by an agency or association recognized by the secretary of the U.S. Department of Education (ED) to participate in HEA Title IV federal student aid programs. While this process is voluntary, failure to obtain accreditation could have a dramatic effect on an institution's student enrollment, as only students attending accredited institutions are eligible to receive federal student aid (e.g., Pell grants and student loans). (p. 1)

Under this process, eligible institutions apply for accreditation and are reviewed by professional teams of expert examiners from peer institutions "to verify assertions and data in institutional self-studies, to determine whether all accreditation standards have been met or exceeded, and to suggest areas for further improvement when appropriate" (Wiley, 2009, p. 2). According to Wiley (2009), the following areas guide assessment practices in graduate education at the program and institutional levels:

- Time to degree (especially time to PhD in the social sciences and humanities)
- Retention and graduation rates

- Adviser-advisee relationship (especially PhD advisers and viable remedies in the event of personality or other conflicts or disputes)
- Degree definitions, degree inflation, and degree proliferation (defining the product)
- Pipeline issues

Congress has assigned the role of overseeing and evaluating the quality and academic sufficiency of instructional programs in institutions to accrediting agencies, commonly referred to as accreditors (U.S. Department of Education, 2018). Accreditors are classified as either institutional or programmatic. These are independent membership-based organizations that use peer review to ensure member institutions meet certain standards of academic quality and rigor: "Accreditors ensure that students have access to qualified instructors, an adequate curriculum, and necessary support services to enable them to meet their personal, academic, intellectual, and career goals" (U.S. Department of Education, 2018, p. 1). Additionally, according to the Council for Higher Education Accreditation (2006), assessment activities serve to verify academic quality, evaluate value for the cost, measure efficiency and effectiveness of public and private resources usage, protect students from fraudulent and questionable practices, and provide transparent information to the public.

It is important to note that the graduate program review is different from an accreditation review. While the accreditation review focuses broadly on the institution, the program review focuses on individual programs in the institution's schools and colleges. In Texas, for example, the Texas Higher Education Coordinating Board (THECB) maintains an online system that tracks the review schedule for all graduate programs in each state institution of higher education. Programs are reviewed every seven years beginning with a comprehensive self-assessment, followed by a review of discipline- and program-specific experts invited from institutions outside the state to serve on the review panels. For instance, if a department has four programs, each program must have outside faculty experts from the discipline on the review panel.

We draw from Texas to illuminate an example of the program review process. To guide planning and performance activities in graduate programs, the THECB requires higher education institutions to define their graduate programs as either professional or research and make that information clearly visible and available to consumers. For example, an adult education PhD program is considered a research program, and a doctorate in veterinary medicine is a professional graduate program. The 18 characteristics of Texas public doctoral programs, as defined by the THECB, guide all research and professional doctoral program reviews in Texas's higher education

Figure 12.1. Characteristics of Texas public doctoral programs.

Number of degrees per year
Graduation rates
Average time to degree
Employment profile of graduates
Admissions criteria (most recent year)
Core faculty qualifications (in disciplinary area)
Core faculty activities (research and publications)
Core faculty external funding
Faculty diversity
Ratio of students to core faculty
Last program accreditation

Additional indicators for research doctoral programs include the following
(past three years):

Percentage of full-time students
Average institutional support to students
Percentage of full-time students with institutional financial support
Faculty teaching load
Student publications and presentations

The following are required for professional doctoral programs:

Average tuition and fees to complete the degree
Number and percentage of those who pass licensure exam

Note. From Texas Higher Education Coordinating Board (2017).

institutions (see Figure 12.1). The latest three years of data are considered in the evaluation.

In addition to the list in Figure 12.1, the graduate program review (including master's degree programs) takes into account issues such as program curriculum and duration in comparison to programs at peer institutions, program alignment with institutional goals, facilities and equipment to support program delivery, financial and other resources, and program administration. It is clear from the indicators and characteristics in Figure 12.1, a graduate program review is not simply an evaluation of what students have learned but a comprehensive assessment of the program and its many intersecting features that include students, faculty, resources, administration, institutional infrastructure, and capacity. However, burrowing down to the student-level assessment provides stakeholders with an additional set of data for more of a micro view of the quality and effectiveness of the institution's colleges, schools, and programs in comparison to its peer institutions. Hence, the admissions process is the first opportunity for student assessment in graduate education.

Graduate Admissions: Initial Phase in Graduate Assessment

Assessment for graduate students begins with the admissions process. These activities often include a grading system that identifies class rankings and grade point average (GPA) over the course of the student's postsecondary enrollment. Also, admissions considerations often include large-scale testing programs like the Graduate Record Examination (GRE), all of which use quantitative scores to determine ranking and eligibility. Although admissions committees consider other factors in graduate admissions decisions, many rely heavily on quantitative measures like GPAs and test scores to enroll the best and brightest students who are likely to succeed and elevate the program, college, and institution's profile (Astin & Antonio, 2012). Colleges and universities are motivated to use rigorous assessment criteria in the admissions process because of the presumption that selective admissions signify academic excellence, suggesting that the higher the admissions scores, the greater the quality and value of the institution (Astin & Antonio, 2012).

Indeed, the higher the admission scores and the more selective the admissions, the higher the institutions are ranked by national associations such as the *U.S. News and World Report.* According to Marginson (2011), "Ranking exercises are arrangements whereby institutions are ordered in a hierarchy to identify and separate the best, the excellent institutions from the rest" (p. 25). The higher ranking provides an appearance of quality, which then suggests more applications for entry to a program. The high number of applications results in stiff competition for admissions and, consequently, a low admissions ratio. For example, if 50 students apply to a graduate program, and only 10 are admitted because of the high bar in terms of admission scores or resource allocation, 20% of students admitted positively affects the program's national rankings, whereas a higher number of admitted students would negatively affect it. Therefore, the more selective the institution, the more excellent it is presumed to be (Astin & Antonio, 2012).

Drawing from our experiences at the College of Education at a major research university, most of the programs at one point published GRE scores as one of the criteria for consideration for admission. Yet, applicants with low scores were sometimes admitted, and admissions results in some cases were above 50% for doctoral applicants. Noting the stagnation and, sometimes, decline in the college's and programs' national rankings, the dean charged department heads with developing a strategic plan for doctoral admissions. He asked that departments justify the requirement for the GRE as a condition for admission when it was not being used uniformly in making decisions and to provide a rationale for admitting students to doctoral programs with such low scores. Additionally, department heads were asked to justify the high number of students admitted to programs who had no intentions of going into the professoriate—a stated goal for the college's PhD programs.

In this scenario, the college had a strategic goal of preparing faculty for research institutions, a positive indicator in national rankings. However, the admissions practices in some programs were not aligned with the institution's goals for its doctoral program, Therefore, to the leadership, program quality, as defined by national rankings, was compromised with the high rate of admissions, particularly those with average or low GRE scores. Astin and Antonio (2012) refer to this as "reputational conception" in that we view our excellence or quality in terms of what others think of us, and that "to be highly selective is to be highly ranked or academically excellent" (p. 10). Overall, the student assessment that is required as part of the admissions process is primarily used to promote the reputational conceptions of excellence.

Equity, Excellence, and Admissions Assessment

Those in higher education who embrace a social justice philosophy continue to encounter tension in adhering to a culture of assessment that may not be flexible enough to expand access beyond the highly ranked students who are selected based on quantitative measures. They are caught in a quandary of adhering to institutional goals and values while they struggle with their personal philosophy of creating access for groups of individuals who remain underrepresented in important spaces in education and society. As Astin and Antonio (2012) note, the resistance to assessment in higher education, particularly in admissions, from those who advocate for social justice can be easily understood, given the following facts: (a) African American, Hispanic, and poor students are substantially underrepresented in U.S. higher education, particularly in the more elite research universities; (b) higher education relies heavily on GPA and scores on standardized national exams to guide admissions decisions; and (c) African Americans, Hispanics, and poor students generally score lower than the other groups. Hence, the continuing reliance on these measures makes it difficult for educationally disadvantaged groups to have equal or proportionate access to higher education opportunities.

Those concerned with social justice and equal access value other assessment measures beyond numerical GPAs and scores on normative standardized tests. However, this social justice orientation, while generally supported by some institutional leaders, results in tension between equity and excellence as they are often considered to be on opposite sides of the spectrum. To be *excellent* (as defined by national rankings), there is the presumption that we must abandon diversity and equity as those who often do not meet established criteria are generally racial and economic minorities.

To address this conflict, Astin and Antonio (2012) propose a talent development approach rather than an educational excellence approach: "The talent development philosophy suggests any student, given sufficient motivation and sufficient time and resources could, in theory, reach any desired level of competence" (p. 225). However, they caution that one should be mindful of situations when selective admissions are necessary and that the talent development approach should be used in combination with the educational excellence approach. This combination is particularly important because there is ample evidence from the literature to suggest that standardized test scores (e.g., the GRE) predict little about academic performance. Hence, the decision by many adult education graduate programs to use a multitiered approach that includes GPA, test scores, writing sample, evidence of program fit, prior work experience, and the panel interview (among others) makes room for diversity and the talent development approach that Astin and Antonio (2012) recommend. Beyond admissions assessment practices, multiple approaches are in place to support institution and program reviews mandated by internal and external stakeholders.

Assessment Methods in Graduate Education

Assessment approaches vary widely, the most common of which include national student surveys, alumni surveys, locally developed surveys, general knowledge and skills measures, rubrics, employer surveys, external performance assessments, and portfolios (Kuh et al., 2014). Most institutions categorize assessment methods in two ways: direct assessment and indirect assessment (Elbeck & Bacon, 2015). Elbeck and Bacon define *direct assessment* as a process that "Direct assessment involves scoring learners' task performance in which the performance is believed to be contingent on achieving a learning goal" (p. 279). The validity of direct assessment measures can be established with scoring by multiple raters with high interrater reliability, using rubrics, aligning assessment with course and program goals, and using an adequate sample size. Elbeck and Bacon define *indirect assessment* as "measuring variable[s] assumed to be related to learning that do not involve scoring task performance or demonstration" (p. 282), often involving perceptions and feelings about learning. In many cases, programs are encouraged to use direct assessment methods as they more clearly demonstrate evidence of learning and performance. However, Elbeck and Bacon agree that direct and indirect assessment methods, when employed in accurate and valid ways, contribute to measuring student learning. Although assessment in higher education has traditionally been an activity at the undergraduate level, there is an increasing demand for more accountability and assessment of learning at the graduate level.

Evaluation of Graduate Student Performance

As stated earlier, assessment guidance is provided mostly for undergraduate education. However, master's and doctoral programs may require assessment methods different from those used at the undergraduate level. Institutional effectiveness offices in colleges and universities are now requiring more graduate programs, particularly those at the doctoral level, to demonstrate how student performance is evaluated. Academic leaders and those in assessment-related roles recognize that student academic performance varies widely by program and faculty. Therefore, it is incumbent on the program to articulate what and how discriminating criteria are used. This requirement lies in the need for more context on how programs evaluate student learning fairly and consistently.

Master's programs, for example, vary widely in degree purpose, as some are practitioner focused, and others are thesis programs. For practitioner-based master's programs, assessment methods commonly include internship evaluations, external accreditation exams, written course assignments, case studies, capstone courses, and portfolios. Thesis-based master's programs may include similar assessment methods as practitioner-focused programs and will often include a research or thesis component (Baker et al., 2011; Middaugh, 2009). In either case, assessment of learning outcomes should be guided by measurable curricular goals aligned with a "current body of knowledge in the field to ensure that when students graduate they can find employment and make a contribution to the field" (Carter, 2014, p. 168). Hence, Carter (2014) advocates for learning assessments to be driven by curricular goals that demonstrate how learning contributes to meaningful employment and professionalization in the field of study.

In the case of doctoral programs, Carter (2014) suggests that the goal of doctoral programs is to train students in research and publication with a secondary goal of preparing them to become faculty members. Therefore, assessment of doctoral student learning should be guided by these broad goals that assess faculty, students, and the curriculum. Carter then advocates for a formative and summative approach to assessment that measures program outcomes such as faculty productivity, characteristics of admitted students, learning outcomes, and other variables required by accrediting bodies. However, the most common assessment methods among doctoral programs include preliminary or qualifying exams, a successful dissertation proposal and defense, manuscripts published in peer-reviewed journals, and papers presented at peer-reviewed research conferences. Although these methods are commonly found in most doctoral programs, much variance exists on how proficiency is determined and demonstrated. For example, simply stating that a student successfully defended their dissertation by committee approval is not enough. Instead, many doctoral programs are highly encouraged to use a rubric, checklist, or other metric that demonstrates the context of how a student's work is evaluated.

Therefore, assessment experts advocate for programs to adopt rubrics and portfolios to demonstrate student learning and program effectiveness. Because of the need for transparency using rubrics and other identifiable measures, many assessment practitioners deem methods such as conference presentations and published articles ineffective as student learning demonstrations. Moreover, assessment practitioners argue that unless faculty witness the conference presentation or have evaluated the proposal before submission, the presentation or proposal is not enough to measure student learning. The same argument is made for manuscripts accepted for publication. Faculty often counter this argument, stating the students' manuscript acceptance and conference proposals to peer-reviewed bodies demonstrate the students' ability to write effectively in an academic manner and contribute to the knowledge of their field.

In response to these arguments, Orzoff et al. (2008) proposed strategies for effective graduate assessment including (a) use of rubrics for theses and dissertations, (b) use of student portfolios, and (c) program reviews or external studies. They recommend creating program-, department-, or institution-produced thesis and dissertation rubrics because these provide students and faculty with clear expectations about performance and can be used to communicate approaches and results more easily to external stakeholders. However, they acknowledge challenges to using rubrics, for example, resistance from faculty, particularly at the doctoral level, because of concerns about standardizing a unique learning activity and experience. Other challenges in using rubrics involve a perceived insult to faculty knowledge and expertise, thereby impeding one's academic freedom. Despite the challenges, rubric usage has increased in popularity and now is an acceptable assessment standard in graduate education (Kuh et al., 2014).

In addition, Orzoff et al. (2008) recommend graduate assessment activities include portfolios to demonstrate "authentic assessment of students' ability to produce products actually used in their profession" (p. 15). Portfolios provide advantages because the artifacts used by students are often forms of assessment embedded in course work and program milestones. Practical challenges to using portfolios include managing the volume of materials and access to software to organize and analyze content. Using portfolios could be a time-intensive process without the proper technology. Hence, faculty may be less inclined to use portfolios as an assessment method.

Finally, a growing number of graduate programs are using individual reviews to communicate student performance and program outcomes to external stakeholders during and after the completion of the degree program (Orzoff et al., 2008). One example is the external review of the dissertation by an experienced faculty from a peer institution. Regardless of the assessment method, Baker et al. (2011) emphasize that "formal review and outcomes assessment be seen as parts of the same whole, with a common goal of improving the quality of graduate education" (p. 168). Graduate programs will continue to adopt and implement assessment processes that best align with their unique learning goals. In the case of adult education programs, the Commission of Professors of Adult Education (Commission of Professors of Adult Education, 2014) standards can serve as a framework to guide the planning, implementation, and assessment of programs in the field.

Commission of Professors of Adult Education Standards: Potential Guide to Assessment and Accountability

In 1986 the American Association for Adult and Continuing Education's Commission of Professors of Adult Education (CPAE) produced its first standards for graduate programs in adult education (DelGesso, 1995) and later revised them in 2008 and 2014. The first standards were developed "from a perceived need from within the adult education professoriate to provide a framework— especially in the absence of any accrediting agency for adult education—for what the curriculum of doctoral education should look like" (Sonstrom, Rachal, & Mohn, 2013, p. 149). The Commission of Professors of Adult Education (CPAE) did not require adult education programs to comply with the standards but recommend it as a guide for developing and administering quality programs. As stated in the rationale of the latest version, "It is intended to meet the demand for providing graduate education for those interested in understanding, fostering and articulating the ways in which adults learn and can be helped to learn in a wide range of settings" (CPAE, 2014, p. 4). It is important to differentiate the CPAE standards as voluntarily and internally driven by the members of the association from politically driven standards like those resulting from the Secretary of Higher Education's Commission on the Future of Higher Education (U.S. Department of Education, 2006) report mentioned earlier.

Although the standards were internally motivated and do not mandate compliance, there is evidence that program leaders and other adult education faculty draw from the suggested guidelines in planning, administering, and evaluating adult education programs. DelGesso (1995) was among the first to conduct an audit of graduate education programs' adherence to the 1986 CPAE Standards and found that more than two thirds of doctoral programs (71.9%) implemented uniform program requirements as outlined in the guidelines. As DelGesso noted, "it appears the CPAE standards have had an influence on the programs in that the doctoral programs share a measurable, positive level of conformity to each other and to the standards" (p. 3). DelGesso also found some items that were not closely followed, particularly in the areas of independent study, program administration, and dissertation committee chairs. He concluded with the following recommendations: (a) a periodic CPAE review of standards to maintain timeliness; (b) the CPAE review its role and obligation to adult education community, specifically in adult educator preparation; (c) representation of each institution offering adult education graduate degrees in the CPAE; (d) a review of graduate curricula to determine adherence and to identify changes, trends, and adult educator preparation; (e) an examination of the specialization in graduate programs; (f) an examination of an independent study component; (g) assurance that doctoral programs adhere to CPAE guidelines on dissertations as so much literature in the adult education field comes from dissertations; and (h) a reexamination of noncompliance and application of corrective measures. It is important to note that DelGesso's study was conducted after the original CPAE standards were developed in 1986 and before two revisions in 2008 and 2014.

Sonstrom et al. (2013) followed DelGesso's (1995) work by conducting a website analysis to evaluate 37 adult education doctoral programs for adherence to the CPAE's (2008) standards, finding a 65.8% mean compliance with the standards. However, results indicated that 5 of the standards had less than 40% compliance, most often because of a lack of specificity to adult education in the curriculum. Sonstrom and colleagues suggested that program administrators might be uninformed about the standards, complacent about the curriculum, and lack adequate personnel as other possible reasons for low compliance. Nonetheless, they noted their study had limited evidence of programs' curricula, and results should be received cautiously as internal assessment processes by program faculty and students are best used to determine compliance with the standards.

Since Sonstrom, Rachal, and Mohn's (2013) study, the CPAE (2014) published a revised version of its standards. After reviewing all three versions, we found a lack of specific assessment criteria to demonstrate students' learning and program effectiveness. Moreover, there are no consequences for failing to comply with the standards because it was meant to be an optional guide and not a mandate for adult education programs. To create effective adult education graduate programs and maintain some consistency across programs, it is important for programs to align with the standards. For example, faculty serving as external program reviewers often report using the standards to guide their review. Hence, the standards as a guiding framework add more credibility to these activities. Additionally, the CPAE should consider developing specific competencies at the master's and doctoral levels to guide expectations of student learning outcomes and program effectiveness.

Discussions and Conclusion

Assessment is a multilayered activity that calls for transparency and accountability at many levels including the (a) individual student, (b) course, (c) program, and (d) institution (Miller & Leskes, 2005). Central to each level of assessment is the generation of data for informed decisions about student learning and institutional effectiveness. Another major purpose of assessment is to provide transparency in communicating the value of the educational enterprise to essential stakeholders. To that end, assessment at all levels must be clearly understood by faculty, staff, and administrators to avoid the complacency that is often found on college campuses on these activities (Astin & Antonio, 2012). Therefore, an important consideration is to make assessment a strategic priority of the institution with well-trained individuals to direct and be involved in assessment activities.

Although the goal is to ensure student learning and institutional effectiveness through engaged assessment, many processes consciously and unconsciously disregard concern for faculty obligations, program pedagogy, and curricula (Stassen, 2012). In our institution, for example, we found some programs with only one faculty member who was responsible for collecting data, interpreting findings, and identifying assessment improvements. Delegating this role to one faculty member reduces the effectiveness in examining student learning from multiple angles, comprehensively reviewing the program's current learning status, and implementing meaningful improvement. Astin and Antonio (2012) note this is a common practice in higher education and refer to this approach as the independent assessor model. They argue that this is the worst possible model for the effective use of assessment results as it places the assessor and practitioners in an adversarial relationship, with the assessor claiming to be the expert and practitioners as uninformed, hostile, and defensive (Astin & Antonio, 2012). Instead, they recommend the collegial model whereby faculty and staff have significant involvement in the various phases of the process, thus resulting in more useful and plausible data for informed decision-making at all levels.

Drawing on graduate programs of adult education, there is an opportunity for a more structured approach to individual, course, and program assessment using the Commission of Professors of Adult Education (2014) standards. There is already an infrastructure in place to guide much of the planning and administration of adult education, and research has found utility in various components of the standards across programs. Adding an assessment component to the framework would allow greater consistency in the demonstration of student learning and program effectiveness.

References

Association of American Colleges & Universities. (2006). Statement on Spellings Commission report. Retrieved from https://aacu.org/about/statements/2006/spellings

Astin, A. W., & Antonio, A. L. (2012). *Assessment for excellence: The philosophy and practice of assessment and evaluation in higher education* (2nd ed). New York, NY: Rowman & Littlefield.

Baker, M. J., Carter, M. P., Larick, D. K., & King, M. F. (2011). *Assessment and review of graduate programs* (D. D. Denecke Ed., 3rd ed.). Washington, DC: Council of Graduate Schools. Retrieved from http://cgsnet.org/assessment-and-review-graduate-programs-0.

Carter, S. D. (2014). Doctoral programs outcomes assessment: An approach to assessing program inputs, learning objectives, and postgraduation outcomes. *Journal of Assessment and Institutional Effectiveness, 4*(2), 160–179.

Commission of Professors of Adult Education. (2014). Standards for graduate programs in adult education. Retrieved from https://cdn.ymaws.com/www.aaace.org/resource/resmgr/Engage/Commissions/CPAE/cpae_2014_standards_update.pdf

Commission of Professors of Adult Education. (2008). Standards for graduateprograms in adult education. Retrieved from https://cdn.ymaws.com/www.aaace.org/resource/resmgr/commissions/cpae/cpae_standards_2008.pdf

Council of Graduate Schools. (2011). *Assessment and review of graduate programs* (3rd ed.). Washington, DC: Author.

Council for Higher Education Accreditation. (2006). Accreditation professional interest and the public interest: Conflict or convergence? *Inside Accreditation, 2*(6). Retrieved from http://www.chea.org/4DCGI/cms/review.html?Action=CMS_Document&DocID=240&MenuKey=main

DelGesso, D. D. (1995). *American adult education doctoral programs in comparison to the commission of professors of adult education standards for graduate programs in adult education (Report No. CE 069-851)*. Retrieved from ERIC database.

Elbeck, M., & Bacon, D. (2015). Toward universal definitions for direct and indirect assessment. *Journal of Education for Business, 90*(5), 278–283.

Kuh, G. D., Ikenberry, S. O., Jankowski, N., & Cain, T. R. (2014). *Using evidence of student learning to improve higher education*(1st ed.). New York, NY: Wiley.

Marginson, S. (2011). The new world order in higher education: Research rankings, outcomes measures and institutional classification. In R. Rostan & M. Vaira (Eds.), *Questioning excellence in higher education: Policies, experiences and challenges in national and comparaative perspectives* (pp. 3–20). Rotterdam, The Netherlands: Sense.

Middaugh, M. F. (2009). *Planning and assessment in higher education*(1st ed.). San Francisco, CA: Jossey-Bass.

Miller, R., & Leskes, A. (2005). Levels of assessment: From the student to the institution. Retrieved from https://aacu.org/sites/default/files/files/publications/LevelsOfAssessment.pdf

Orzoff, J. H., Peinovich, P. E., & Riedel, E. (2008). Graduate programs: The Wild West of outcomes assessment. *Assessment Update: Progress, Trends and Practices in Higher Education, 20*(3), 1–16.

Palm, R., Baker, M. J., Goldenberg, R. E., Hiiemae, K., Powell, R. E., & Yeates, M. (1990). *Academic review of graduate programs: A policy statement.* Retrieved from ERIC database. (ED331421).

Skinner, R. R., & Feder, J. (2007). *CRS report to congress: Accreditation and reauthorization of the Higher Education Act.* Washington, DC: Congressional Research Service.

Sonstrom, W. J., Rachal, J. R., & Mohn, R. S. (2013). The Commission of Professors of Adult Education 2008 standards as evidenced in the curricula of doctoral education in North America. *Adult Education Quarterly, 63*(2), 147–164.

Stassen, M. L. A. (2012). Accountable for what? *Journal of Assessment and Institutional Effectiveness, 2*(2), 137–142.

Texas Higher Education Coordinating Board. (2017). Characteristics of doctoral programs. Retrieved from http://reportcenter.thecb.state.tx.us/agency-publication/miscellaneous/aqw-characteristics-of-doctoral-programs-3-14-2017/

U.S. Department of Education. (2006). A test of leadership: Charting the future of U.S. higher education. Retrieved from https://www2.ed.gov/about/bdscomm/list/hiedfuture/reports/pre-pub-report.pdf

U.S. Department of Education. (2018). Rethinking higher education accreditation reform. Retrieved from https://www2.ed.gov/admins/finaid/accred/rethinking-higher-education-accreditation-reform.pdf

U.S. National Commission on Excellence in Education. (1983). *A nation at risk: The imperative for educational reform: A report to the nation and the secretary of education.* Retrieved from https://www.edreform.com/wp-content/uploads/2013/02/A_Nation_At_Risk_1983.pdf

Wiley, J. D. (2009). Quality, accreditation, and graduate education: What does the future hold? Retrieved from https://www.chea.org/quality-accreditation-and-graduate-education-what-does-future-hold

13

PREPARING HIGHER EDUCATION FACULTY TO CONDUCT QUALITY ASSESSMENT OF STUDENT LEARNING

Natalie Bolton and E. Paulette Isaac-Savage

Adult education stakeholders are demanding accountability through the use of direct measures that involve asking students to demonstrate what they have learned rather than using self-reported indirect measures. However, faculty are rarely trained and prepared to develop high-quality assessments or determine if the assessments they are using are high quality (Stiggins, 2014). Therefore, investing time training and preparing faculty to conduct quality assessment of student learning is needed in higher education institutions. Guetterman and Mitchell (2016) have proposed that creating a supportive campus environment is a prerequisite for quality assessment. Grunwald and Peterson (2003) found that significant predictors of faculty satisfaction with institutional support for student assessment included institution-wide activities, faculty instructional impacts, and educational uses of student assessment.

Regulatory, accreditation, and funding agencies require higher education programs to demonstrate that their students have mastered program outcomes. Therefore, program faculty and their students should have a clear understanding of their program outcomes and how they can be strategically met throughout a program. This chapter discusses assessment practices that best allow students in higher education programs to know they have mastered course and program outcomes in addition to describing instructional decisions faculty should make for students to learn to what degree they have mastered course and program outcomes. This chapter begins by describing quality assessment practices and strategies in higher education, incorporates results of a faculty survey about campuswide and department-specific assessment, and concludes with comments about faculty development needs to support effective assessment practices.

Quality Assessment Practices

Galbraith and Jones (2010) and Stiggins (2014) defined *assessment* as the process of measuring student achievement and using results to inform instructional decisions. This definition may offer more promise for promoting learner success than any other instructional practice instructors have at their disposal (Stiggins, 2014). However, Stiggins (2014) also argued that assessment must be used differently from the way it has been used in the past to improve student performance. Improved student performance occurs with high-quality instruction; however, to be extremely effective, instruction must work in continuous close harmony with good assessment practices. Ideally, instruction and assessment need to occur almost simultaneously, whereas at present, only instruction is continuous with assessment often attached somewhere at the end of it (Stiggins, 2014). Faculty must learn to become competent assessors and use classroom assessment methods to increase student confidence, engage students in managing their own learning, and foster higher levels of achievement than students even thought was possible.

Chappuis, Stiggins, Chappuis, and Arter (2011) offer five keys to quality assessment: purpose, targets, design, communication, and student involvement. Similar to the five keys, Bearman et al. (2016) describe an assessment design decision framework of six categories (purpose of assessment, context of assessment, learner outcomes, tasks, feedback processes, and interactions) of assessment considerations, which together present a learning-centered approach to assessment design. Faculty need to ensure their course and program assessments embed these five keys or six characteristics to achieve quality assessments.

Assessment Purpose

Prior to administering an assessment, faculty need to clearly communicate to students about whether an assessment is being used for diagnostic, formative, or summative purposes. Students should be informed what the key assessments are throughout a course and their program and how results from the assessments will be used. In many cases, programs will share an assessment plan with students. The assessment plan will note key course and program assessments aligned with program outcomes. Development of assessment plans should involve collaboration among faculty and agreement on desired program outcomes and relevant assessments. This is often a requirement of many accreditation body expectations and potentially challenges faculty autonomy (Andrade, 2011). Vanderbilt University (2010), the University of Virginia (2017a), and Lowery (2015) from the University of Wisconsin-Madison have published examples of program assessment plans and mapping program outcomes resources.

Learner Outcomes/Learning Targets

Learner outcomes, or learning targets, focus on identifying and clearly articulating what students will do in courses and programs. Outcomes need to be written so they can be mastered in the given time, and resources should be available to support course or program outcomes. Assessments must align with outcomes. Outcomes or targets that are unclear or fuzzy make it extremely difficult to write clear assessment items, tasks, and scoring guides. Additionally, each outcome or learning target should be sampled, providing the student and instructor with enough information to inform them if each relevant outcome/learning target is being mastered by students. If an assessment "is to be instructionally helpful then it needs to suggest to the instructor what comes next in the student's learning" (Stiggins, 2014, p. 71). Examples of how to write learning outcomes are provided by the University of Hawai'i–Manoa (2017) and Potter and Kustra (2012).

Assessment Design

Bearman et al. (2017) define *assessment design* as all the processes that take place to develop specific assessment tasks for a particular course or unit, including selection, timing, development of rubrics, and redevelopment of a task in response to student performance. When designing an assessment, there are four methods to choose from including selected responses (multiple choice, true or false, matching, fill in the blank), written responses (short or extended), performance assessment tasks, or personal communications. Some of these methods work better than others to assess learning outcomes or targets. For example, the selected response method can only be used to assess learning outcomes or targets that require students to recall information, provide a conceptual understanding of a topic, or demonstrate procedural knowledge. More complex learning outcomes and targets focused on reasoning proficiency or performance skills must be assessed using written response assessments, performance assessment tasks, or personal communication tasks. Chappuis et al. (2011) developed a learning outcome or target and assessment method chart to easily assist assessment designers regarding the best assessment method to use based on learner outcome or target type.

Many online resources are available related to assessment design (Carnegie Mellon Eberly Center, 2015; University of Adelaide, 2015; University of Washington Center for Teaching and Learning, 2017). Additionally, Brame (2013), Clay (2001), Holder (2012), Pittock (2014), and University of Virginia (2017b) have published resources specific to designing assessments by method (multiple choice, performance tasks, and rubrics).

Communication

Feedback is one of the most powerful tools influencing student achievement of learning outcomes (Hattie, 2008). Effective communication related to students' progress in mastering learning targets needs to occur on an ongoing basis. Boud (2000) noted that one of the most forgotten aspects of effective formative assessment is for students to be able to use feedback to produce improved work:

> Unless students are able to use feedback to produce improved work, through for example redoing the same assignment, neither they nor those giving feedback will know it has been effective. This is one of the most often forgotten aspects of formative assessment. (p. 158)

Characteristics of effective feedback to improve learning include (a) referring to the learning targets, pointing out what the student is doing well on, still needs to improve on, or next steps; (b) providing tangible and transparent feedback related to the learning targets; (c) providing actionable information that is concrete, specific, and useful; (d) providing information to the student that is easy to understand and is not overwhelming; (e) offering timely feedback and the sooner the better; (f) providing ongoing feedback or formative assessment so the student has opportunities to act on the feedback to achieve the learning targets; and (g) providing consistent feedback that is stable, accurate, and trustworthy (Wiggins, 2012). Numerous resources related to effective feedback have been published (Carless, 2015; Killian, 2017; Sambell, 2011; University College Dublin, n.d.; Wiggins, 2012).

Student Involvement

Students must play a critical role in assessment for them to own their learning and instructors must continuously provide these opportunities. Student-involved assessment can motivate productive action on the part of learners (Stiggins, 2014). To support student productive action, Chappuis (2009) identified seven strategies for using assessment to promote learning, also known as formative assessment strategies. Chappuis's (2009) seven strategies integrated findings of a study on the impact of formative assessment conducted by Black and Wiliam (1998) and guidelines presented by Sadler (1989) of what students need to know and be able to do to monitor their work during the actual production of work.

Chappuis (2009) turned Sadler's (1989) guidelines during learning in the classroom into the following student questions with suggestions on how an instructor can answer them:

- Where am I going?
  - Provide students with a clear understanding and vision of the learning targets at the beginning of the learning.
  - Provide examples or models of student work at different performance levels to promote deeper understanding of the learning targets.
- Where am I now?
  - Offer students regular access to descriptive feedback aligned with learning targets focused on specific qualities of their work and inform them on ways to improve.
  - Teach students to self-assess so they can monitor their own academic development and set goals by learning targets to determine what comes next in their learning.
- How can I close the gap?
  - Design lessons focused on learning targets aligned with student needs.
  - Teach students to do a focused revision of their work.
  - Teach students to track, communicate, and reflect on their work.

A more detailed description of each strategy follows. Strategies 1 and 2 assist students to know where they are going with their learning.

Strategy 1: Learning Targets

Sharing a clear understanding of the learning target with students allows them to know where they currently are with the learning and where they are headed. Knowing this information builds student confidence and allows them to feel in control of their learning because they know in advance the requirements of what to demonstrate. Programs that have required standards or student learning outcomes can associate these with learning targets. The standards or student learning outcomes should be shared with students and connected to instructional activities, readings, resources, and assessment tasks. Students should regularly be engaged in using the learning targets throughout a lesson. Feedback in performance of assessments should also be aligned to performance on the standards or student learning outcomes.

Strategy 2: Models of Student Work

Models of student work at different performance levels aligned with the learning targets provide even further guidance to students and clear expectations of what performance of the learning target needs to look like. Models exemplifying different performance levels help clarify misconceptions or errors students might have with understanding a learning target and shows students the needed steps to master a learning target. Students can use the models for noting the differences between performance levels. Using models during instruction assists in building students' confidence and understanding prior to completing a task.

Strategy 3: Student Access to Descriptive Feedback

Students need ongoing feedback as they are working on a learning target that lets them know the aspects of the target they are doing well on (success feedback) and the aspects they still need to work on to improve their performance (next step or intervention feedback).

According to Boud (2000),

> assessment activities should leave students better equipped to tackle their next challenge, or minimally, no worse off than they would otherwise be. Part of being equipped for the next task is having sufficient confidence that it can be approached with some chance of success. (p. 161)

In the context of learning targets and student performance on tasks, success feedback can highlight and identify what was done correctly, describe the quality that is present in the work, and point out the effective use of a strategy or process. The next step or intervention feedback can identify a needed correction, describe a feature of quality needing work, point out a problem with a strategy or process, offer a reminder, make a specific suggestion, or ask a question. Students should have ample opportunity to practice during this time without being penalized by a grade. Learning goals that have been accomplished are a sign to the faculty of when it is appropriate to grade the task.

Strategy 4: Teach Students to Self-Assess

Providing students with time to self-assess, set goals regarding their strengths, and identify flaws in their work is motivating. If students have an understanding of the learning targets associated with the task, know what proficiency looks like and how to get there, and receive initial risk-free descriptive feedback about their performance on the task, then students are better prepared and motivated to generate their own feedback and determine what should come next in their learning. Strong academic self-efficacy may result from this strategy, and it can serve as a very powerful step for struggling learners (Stiggins, 2014).

Strategies 5 through 7 assist students in closing any gaps they may have with their learning. Strategies 5 and 6 are often integrated when implemented.

Strategy 5: Design Lessons Focused on Learning Targets

Common planning practices often include designing and implementing learning activities, administering an assessment, and providing students with a grade. Instead, when designing lessons, the instructor should be implementing a feedback loop and using data from prior assessments (diagnostic, formative, or summative) to assist with planning. Instructional activities need to align with student learning needs. Consider the following questions when planning instructional activities: (a) What are the most common misunderstandings I can anticipate when teaching this lesson, (b) How will I know if those misunderstandings are manifesting, and (c) What actions will I take in response if they do manifest themselves (Schimmer, 2018)? To some degree, the instructor is acting as a coach during this strategy by providing specific guided practice on individual skills and needs to help master broader learning outcomes.

Strategy 6: Teach Students to Do a Focused Revision of Their Work

Related to the feedback loop discussed in Strategy 5, students need time to practice learning targets and improve their performance. Providing opportunities for students to respond to descriptive feedback allows students to own their learning and the improvement of their work. Additionally, providing opportunities for students to refine their work to meet learning outcomes builds student confidence. Boud (2000) noted that finding a balance between new learning opportunities and having time for students to confidently achieve learning outcomes by completing the feedback loop enough times is a challenge. Faculty must embed formative assessment into their teaching practices for these learning opportunities to occur.

Strategy 7: Teach Students to Track, Communicate, and Reflect on Their Work
Similar to Strategy 4, Strategy 7 is a destination instructors want students to reach. Providing opportunities throughout a course or program for students to track, reflect, and share their learning builds students' learning skills. The focus is placed more on what a student has accomplished related to learning outcomes over time rather than waiting until the end of a course for the instructor to give students a grade. If students know the course or program learning outcomes, have a vision of developing proficiency on those outcomes, and receive constructive feedback on their performance related to those outcomes, they most likely will become a key partner with the instructor who is able to communicate how students have performed in the course or program.

The seven strategies of assessment for learning are only effective if the instructor whole-heartedly believes that (a) students can master any learning target or outcome that does not change, (b) students are motivated to keep trying if they are able to monitor their progress and develop as a learner over time, and (c) students who track and communicate about their learning develop confidence, engagement, and achievement (Stiggins, 2014). A learning partnership develops between the instructor and students when students track and control their own learning. Students develop responsibility for owning their learning, allowing teachers to focus more on targeted instruction based on assessment evidence. Additionally, "instructors who have more time for assessment, course improvement, and experimentation may improve student success and retention" (Scott & Danley-Scott, 2015, p. 43).

Although formative assessment is stressed here, summative assessment is also important. Instructors must make periodic judgments during a course and communicate to learners how well they are doing. This often takes the form of a midterm or final grade. However, it does not have to be limited to these two periods. Summative and formative assessment applications are important, but they are significantly different. Course instructors should embed both applications by finding a balance between the two. Summative assessment has historically been the norm. Valuing and placing importance on formative assessment should become a norm too.

Faculty Professional Development and Assessment Literacy

To assist in establishing a supportive assessment literacy environment, evaluating faculty assessment practices will provide useful information to higher education institution administrators who desire to improve their assessment culture and practices. The following case study demonstrates the results of a campus-wide survey implemented to support one institution's improvement initiatives.

Evaluating Faculty Assessment Practices: A Case Study

Aligned with the five keys to quality assessment: purpose, targets, design, communication, and student involvement from Chappuis et al. (2011), a needs assessment survey was administered to 1,306 faculty at a public midwestern urban university in spring of 2016 to evaluate faculty acumen in implementing assessment practices. The needs assessment survey was conducted in collaboration with the associate provost of academic affairs and the Senate Committee on the Assessment of Educational Outcomes to (a) provide baseline data to the Office of Academic Affairs regarding faculty course assessment practices and (b) assist the campus' Center for Teaching and Learning in developing assessment workshops for faculty related to faculty course assessment strengths and needs.

Survey Background

Part One of the survey was adapted from Chappuis et al. (2011) and consisted of 25 Likert-type scale items and 5 open-ended items related to course assessment practices. Part Two of the survey focused on department or program assessment practices and faculty demographics. The Part Two survey questions were adapted from a survey administered to University of Oklahoma faculty on assessment practices and consisted of 7 Likert-type scale items and 6 selected-response demographic items. All Likert-type scales for both parts of the survey had 5 levels with the anchors *strongly disagree* to *strongly agree*; *I don't know* was also a response choice for all Likert-type scale items.

Survey Reliability

Typically, Part One of the survey was completed by K–12 teachers so a principal component factor analysis was conducted to determine reliability for its use with higher education faculty. The overall scale reliability for Part One of the survey was $\alpha = .941$ (24 items), indicating high reliability. The principal component factor analysis with orthogonal rotation (varimax) revealed 5 components, which were very similar to the 5 keys of quality assessment from Chappuis et al. (2011). The Senate Committee on the Assessment of Educational Outcomes labeled the 5 components as beginning assessment practices or purposes ($\alpha = .844$, 7 items), assessment design ($\alpha = .892$, 7 items), student focus (α = .779, 5 items), using assessment information (α = .737, 4 items), and assessment design and method (only 1 item).

Case Study Survey Results

Nineteen percent of faculty anonymously completed the assessment practices survey, proportionally corresponding to the faculty population by college and position (see Table 13.1 and Table 13.2). Most respondents (35%) reported being in their current position 10 or more years, followed by 30% of respondents who reported being in their current position 2 to 5 years. A majority of respondents taught face-to-face undergraduate or face-to-face graduate courses. Face-to-face courses included 0% to 29% online content.

Part One: Course Assessment Practices Results

The greatest strengths identified by faculty related to course and classroom assessment practices occurred in the beginning assessment practices and student focus subscales. A majority of faculty strongly agreed with four of the seven beginning assessment practices as their strengths including selecting outcomes for the instructor's courses with an eye toward retention of knowledge or skill beyond the semester; designing courses with formative (i.e.,

TABLE 13.1
Assessment Practices Survey Responses by College

Answer	n	%
College of Arts and Sciences	109	44
College of Education	56	23
College of Business Administration	38	15
College of Nursing	14	6
School of Fine and Performing Arts	12	5
Pierre Laclede Honors College	5	2
School of Social Work	5	2
College of Optometry	2	1
No report	7	2
Total	248	100

TABLE 13.2
Assessment Practices Survey Responses by Position

Reported Current Position	n	%
Professor	28	12.33
Associate professor	47	20.70
Assistant professor	20	8.81
Nontenure-track professor	13	5.73
Nontenure-track associate professor	20	8.81
Nontenure-track assistant professor	14	6.17
Instructor or lecturer	19	8.37
Part-time instructor	41	18.06
Graduate assistant	10	4.41
Other (Please specify)	15	6.61
Total	227	100

observations, reflective journals, questioning, conferencing) and summative feedback (i.e., exam, project, lab) assessments; offering students feedback during their learning aligned with course learning outcomes; and aligning course learning outcomes to assessments and the instructor's instruction. A majority of faculty strongly agreed with two of the six student focus practices including writing outcomes using student-friendly language (e.g., avoiding jargon) and offering students feedback during their learning aligned with course learning outcomes.

Areas of greatest need aligned with the literature (Stiggins, 2014) and the subscale assessment design. At least 25% of faculty strongly disagreed or disagreed that they create course assessment plans to map the content of their course assessments or use program assessment plans to map the content of their course assessments.

The open-ended survey questions were qualitatively analyzed and revealed a need for (a) more information and resources relating to assessment standards that are department specific and (b) a glossary of universal assessment terms. Additionally, faculty requested formal instruction and training regarding collaboration, mentorship, and better use of technology with assessments.

Part Two: Department Assessment Practices Results

Faculty reported the strongest agreement with monitoring student outcomes by program, being required to monitor what students were learning, and monitoring student outcomes by course. Faculty reported that they somewhat agreed that their department demonstrated a great deal of consensus on its approaches to student learning and collecting information about employer needs for specific skills and knowledge among program graduates. Items that faculty reported the least agreement with included coordinating student assessment activities annually with campus administrators and that a department had influence on the assessment techniques used in a course.

Although the survey results provided beneficial information to campus leadership regarding faculty perception of course and department assessment practices, there were limitations to the study results. The survey was administered before, during, and right after the university spring break. The sample size potentially could have been larger if it had been administered during a different window of time that did not incorporate a break. Qualitative feedback also indicated that consistent use of assessment language across campus and participant understanding of questions might have affected the results. Some of the immediate next steps based on the survey results included reporting the results in accreditation evidence related to assessment of programs and student learning outcomes, collaborating with the campus Center for Teaching and Learning on developing workshops to target faculty members' highest needs and needs not identified as areas of strength, and embedding assessment literacy practices in the work of departments and programs.

Faculty Development Needs: Where Do We Go Next?

Assessment in general involves identifying appropriate standards and criteria and making judgments about quality. Boud (2000) argues that this is as necessary to lifelong learning as it is in any formal education experience. If assessment can be viewed as essential to lifelong learning, then it has to move into the hands of the learners and away from just being owned only by the assessor. Methods and techniques must be taught and used by faculty to support this enhanced vision of assessment. As the case study from one institution showed, faculty agreed that there was a need for (a) more information and resources relating to assessment standards that are department specific and (b) for formal instruction and training including collaboration, mentorship, and better technology use with assessments.

Additionally, institutions of higher education must emphasize using student assessment for internal institutional academic improvement. More research should be conducted in this area to see how institutions can support faculty with student assessment. Grunwald and Peterson (2003) reported that faculty are more supportive of an institution's approach to student assessment when there are

- institution-wide plans, policies, and administrative offices to guide student assessment efforts and methods implemented to monitor and report the various institutional benefits and impacts of assessment;
- task forces, faculty committees, forums, and seminars on student assessment, and when more attention is given to using student assessment for educational decisions and promoting faculty interest in teaching and instructional methods;
- opportunities to educate faculty about and involving them with the external influences on student assessment (accreditation, state policy, etc.), providing faculty with professional development opportunities to learn about student assessment, and distributing evidence of the benefits of student assessment; and
- methods used to increase faculty involvement with classroom student assessment through promoting the benefits and, with caution, using it for faculty reward and promotion decisions.

High-quality assessment is essential to student learning. An effective assessment system is an important investment for building confident and independent learners. If we desire to maximize student learning to demonstrate mastery of student learning outcomes, we must pay greater attention to improving course and program assessment. Faculty participation is a key component of an effective campuswide assessment system for building successful learning and meeting accreditation requirements. Universities must value faculty contributions to assessment work and provide effective faculty development and practical support to implement and maintain high-quality assessment practices.

References

Andrade, M. S. (2011). Managing change—Engaging faculty in assessment opportunities. *Innovative Higher Education, 36*(4), 217–233.

Bearman, M., Dawson, P., Boud, D., Bennett, S., Hall, M., & Molloy, E. (2016). Support for assessment practice: Developing the assessment design decisions framework. *Teaching in Higher Education, 21*(5), 545–556.

Bearman, M., Dawson, P., Bennett, S., Hall, M., Molloy, E., Boud, D., & Joughin, G. (2017). How university teachers design assessments: A cross-disciplinary study. *Higher Education, 74*(1), 49–64.

Black, P., & Wiliam, D. (1998). Inside the black box. *Phi Delta Kappan, 80*, 139–148.

Boud, D. (2000). Sustainable assessment: Rethinking assessment for the learning society. *Studies in Continuing Education, 22*(2), 151–167.

Brame, C. (2013). Writing good multiple choice test questions. Retrieved from https://cft.vanderbilt.edu/guides-sub-pages/writing-good-multiple-choice-test-questions

Carless, D. (2015). Student feedback: Can do better—here is how. Retrieved from https://www.timeshighereducation.com/opinion/student-feedback-can-do-better-heres-how

Carnegie Mellon Eberly Center. (2015). How to assess students' learning and performance. Retrieved from https://www.cmu.edu/teaching/assessment/assesslearning/index.html

Chappuis, J. (2009). *Seven strategies of assessment for learning.* Portland, OR: Pearson Assessment Training Institute.

Chappuis, J., Stiggins, R. J., Chappuis, S., & Arter, J. A. (2011). *Classroom assessment for student learning: Doing it right—using it well.* New York, NY: Pearson.

Clay, B. (2001). Is this a trick question? A short guide to writing effective test questions. Retrieved from https://www.k-state.edu/ksde/alp/resources/Handout-Module6.pdf

Galbraith, M. W., & Jones, M. S. (2010). Assessment and evaluation. In C. E. Kasworm, A. D. Rose, & J. M. Ross-Gordon (Eds.), *Handbook of adult and continuing education* (pp. 165–175). Thousand Oaks, CA: Sage.

Grunwald, H., & Peterson, M. W. (2003). Factors that promote faculty involvement in and satisfaction with institutional and classroom student assessment. *Research in Higher Education, 44*(2), 173–204.

Guetterman, T. C., & Mitchell, N. (2016). The role of leadership and culture in creating meaningful assessment: A mixed methods case study. *Innovative Higher Education, 41*(1), 43–57.

Hattie, J. (2008). *Visible learning: A synthesis of over 800 meta-analyses relating to achievement.* Abingdon, Oxfordshire, UK: Routledge.

Holder, L. (2012). How to design assessment that promotes the learning process. Retrieved from https://elearningindustry.com/design-assessments-promote-learning-process

Killian, S. (2017). How to give effective feedback to students: The advance guide. Retrieved from https://www.evidencebasedteaching.org.au/wp-content/uploads/How-To-Give-Feedback-To-Students-The-Advanced-Guide-2nd-Edition-Web.pdf

Lowery, R. (2015). Example assessment plan template: Undergraduate academic degree programs. Retrieved from https://assessmentwiscweb.wisc.edu/wp-content/uploads/sites/92/2017/02/Quickguide_-_Assessment_Plan_081915.pdf

Pittock, S. P. (2014). Designing writing assignments. Retrieved from https://teachingcommons.stanford.edu/teaching-talk/designing-writing-assignments

Potter, M. K., & Kustra, E. (2012). *A primer on learning outcomes and the SOLO taxonomy.*. Retrieved from http://www.uwindsor.ca/ctl/sites/uwindsor.ca.ctl/files/primer-on-learning-outcomes.pdf

Sadler, D. R. (1989). Formative assessment and the design of instructional systems. *Instructional Science, 18*(2), 119–144.

Sambell, K. (2011). Rethinking feedback in higher education: An assessment for learning perspectives. Retrieved from https://www.plymouth.ac.uk/uploads/ production/document/path/2/2729/RethinkingFeedbackInHigherEducation .pdf

Schimmer, T. [Tom Schimmer @TomSchimmer]. (2018, January 23). 3 things to consider when lesson planning: (1) What are the most common misunderstandings I anticipate when teaching this lesson, (2) How will I know if those misunderstandings are manifesting, & (3) What action will I take in response if they do? #atAssess #sblchat [Tweet]. Retrieved from https://twitter.com/TomSchimmer/ status/955816082199101440

Scott, G., & Danley-Scott, J. (2015). Two loops that need closing: Contingent faculty perceptions of outcomes assessment. *The Journal of General Education, 64*(1), 30–55.

Stiggins, R. (2014). *Revolutionize assessment: Empower students, inspire learning.* Thousand Oaks, CA: Corwin Press.

University College Dublin. (n.d.). UCD teaching and learning: Giving effective feedback. Retrieved from http://www.ucd.ie/teaching/resources/teachingtoolkit/ givingeffectivefeedback/

University of Adelaide. (2015). Learning & teaching: Key ideas for designing assessments. Retrieved from https://www.adelaide.edu.au/learning/teaching/assessment/ designing-assessment.html

University of Hawai'i–Manoa. (2017). Assessment how-to. Retrieved from https:// manoa.hawaii.edu/assessment/howto/outcomes.htm

University of Virginia. (2017a). Curriculum mapping. Retrieved from http://ias . virginia.edu/assessment/outcomes/tools/curriculum-mapping

University of Virginia. (2017b). Rubrics. Retrieved from http://ias.virginia.edu/ assessment/outcomes/tools/rubrics

University of Washington Center for Teaching and Learning. (2017). Constructing tests. Retrieved from http://www.washington.edu/teaching/constructing-tests/

Vanderbilt University. (2010). Sample assessment plans and templates. Retrieved from https://virg.vanderbilt.edu/sacs/./TS%20Assessment%20Plan.doc

Wiggins, G. (2012). Seven keys to effective feedback. *Educational Leadership, 70*(1), 10–16.

PART FOUR

CONCLUSION

14

USING ASSESSMENT AND EVALUATION TO ADVOCATE FOR ADULT EDUCATION PROGRAMS

Lilian H. Hill

The introductory chapters in Part One of this book provide background information about assessment, evaluation, and accountability relevant to adult education, and the chapters in Parts Two and Three discuss applications of assessment and evaluation practices in settings relevant to adult education programs, adult learners in higher education, and the community. Despite the lack of current literature on assessment and evaluation in adult education, the chapters in this book demonstrate that meaningful assessment and evaluation activities are taking place in varied adult education settings.

Are Assessment and Evaluation Practices in Adult Education Unique?

Many of the assessment and evaluation tools, techniques, and processes described in this book are not unique to adult education settings. However, assessment and evaluation practices are not neutral or dispassionate; they integrate the assumptions and values of their creators. In chapter 9, Wendy M. Green cites Smith (2013) to indicate that, "Those who design the tools hold the power" (p. 159, this volume). Therefore, it is important for adult education to control or at least significantly contribute to the assessment and evaluation processes being used. Assessment and evaluation practices should be responsive to our beliefs about adult learning; however, no single indicator provides sufficient information about the multidimensional nature of adult learning.

Assessment and evaluation should be attentive to learners' goals and their sociocultural environments to capture complex skills in context. Assessment and evaluation methods can be judged by the degree to which they challenge students, promote learning transfer, require metacognition and self-reflection, involve discussion and feedback, and teach the knowledge or skills that adult learners want to attain. Assessment and evaluation processes should support lifelong learning and respect adult learners' knowledge and experiences.

Adult learners can be vested stakeholders in assessment and evaluation processes. Predetermined evaluations do not allow learner input or support self-direction in learning. According to Su (2015),

> Conventional assessment practices, which assume highly prescribed knowledge and develop convergent one-dimensional learning, fail to account for the complexity of adult learning and insufficiently demonstrate how lifelong learners can apply their agency to meet the challenges of uncertain, rapidly changing futures. (p. 78)

Assessment and evaluation should support learners' self-efficacy, self-direction, critical thinking, and personal development. Boud (2010) indicated that "students themselves need to develop the capacity to make judgements about both their own work and that of others in order to become effective continuing learners and practitioners" (para. 4).

In the *Handbook of Adult and Continuing Education*, Galbraith and Jones (2001) stated that "helping learners to make personal meaning of learned material will help ensure their lifelong progressive learning" (p. 169). Assessment and evaluation practices should support learning transfer. Adult learners need to have personal agency and develop an understanding of the differences between learning contexts and the application context. In addition to a personal motivation to transfer knowledge, learners benefit from experiencing authentic learning experiences that promote learning transfer. Likewise, assessment and evaluation measures must be relevant to adult learners' goals. Assessment can support "problem solving and completion of tasks in context . . . to build learners' ability to effectively adapt to contextual changes in life (Su, 2015, p. 76).

Assessment and evaluation in adult education should be holistic, context driven, and extend past the learning encounter. Assessment should take into account learners' subjectivity and changes of identity in response to learning. Assessment and evaluation should be employed to assess not only learners' competence (knowing that and knowing how) but also their commitment (knowing why) involving affective learning and actions. As a part of the teaching and learning processes, assessment and evaluation can be employed to

> develop lifelong learners' needs to transcend their interest in knowledge acquisition and competence building and to additionally assess their personal commitment to finding connections of meaning in an uncertain world to anchor one's sense of belonging and provide certainty on an ongoing, sustainable basis. (Su, 2015, p. 87)

To unearth power and influence in society, assessment practices should recognize adult learners' diversity of knowledge, experience, and personhood. This allows those with little social and political power to have more influence and greater opportunities for self-advocacy.

All forms of assessment are socially constructed processes that have social consequences (Read, Francis, & Robson, 2005). Societally, we seem unable to rid ourselves of racial, ethnic, and gender stereotypes; poorly conceived or culturally inappropriate language; mismatch between learning content (knowledge and skill performance) and assessment and evaluation processes; and other forms of cultural insensitivity that might interfere with ratings of student performance that favor some candidates over others. Marbley, Bonner, and Berg (2008) said that

> instruments used to measure achievement and competence are being more urgently called for and more widely used than ever before whereas, on the other hand, tests [and other forms of assessment] are, at the same time, being more sharply criticized and strongly opposed. (p. 13)

Critiques of assessment are based on assessment practices, current and historical, that have been harmful to marginalized groups, especially people of color and women, exemplified in biased assessments that have sometimes been expressly intended to cause harm. More commonly, we hold unconscious biases that are reflected in our teaching and assessment methods. To combat these, designing learning assessments can be a mutual process between instructors and learners; however, this only addresses biases when learners feel able to speak their truths and when these truths are taken seriously and acted on.

Assessment, Evaluation, and Accountability in Adult Education

The metrics of program viability require adult educators to develop the ability to advocate for valuable programs using language that is most likely to be heard by those holding the purse strings and institutional power. Adult educators need to become proficient with assessment and evaluation processes while simultaneously resisting demands for conformity and couple these skills with a critical viewpoint so the ways that neoliberal values are influencing educational practice can be contested. Concerns about program effectiveness and quality of education are on the national agenda, and education is increasingly being equated with preparation for employment. Societal demands are said to be for capable, competent, and informed citizens to meet the challenges of the twenty-first-century workplace with its needs for higher order thinking skills and attendant soft skills of communication, teamwork, leadership, and critical thinking. Legislation and assessment polices require program administrators to demonstrate that they are making data-driven decisions linked to the values embedded in assessment and evaluation requirements imposed on many programs. As a field, adult education often spearheads educational innovation and service to marginalized populations. Because of differences in values, educational strategies, and goals, adult education programs are often questioned and subject to additional scrutiny. Additionally, expanding federal oversight may serve to curtail program innovation and threaten program survival.

It is not necessary for adult educators to acquire sophisticated statistical and analytical skills to conduct effective assessment and evaluation, but because national trends increasingly emphasize quantitative measures, it is useful to work in partnership with individuals who have those skills. Many adult educators tend to be more invested in qualitative research methods (Boeren, 2018); however, some assessment and evaluation practices require knowledge of quantitative methods and statistics. Quantitative measures can be standardized and efficient, but if not well designed and linked to learners' interests and goals, they can be shallow, irrelevant, or harmful. Inevitably, they only provide answers to the questions we thought to ask. Qualitative measures produce more in-depth information, may reveal reasons why people choose to participate or are motivated to learn, and may surprise us with the information they provide. In designing and administering adult education programs, it is important to plan for and use multiple data types and sources that can provide indications about desired outcomes. Ideally, qualitative and quantitative approaches can be combined to inform assessment and evaluation. However, this can be costly in terms of time investment, and scarce financial resources may limit the use of comprehensive assessments.

The use of quality assessment and program evaluation practices can provide information to answer concerns about accountability. However, adult educators should be cautious about assessment language related to continuous improvement in student learning outcomes. Critiques of higher education assessment revolve around the bureaucratization that occurs when measurements are conducted to document institutional outcomes for accreditation purposes rather than for improvement of learning and instruction. Lederman (2019) reported on a panel convened at a regional accreditation conference in which "experts on student learning" told attendees

> that most assessment activity [in higher education] to date has been a "hot mess" and that efforts to "measure" how much students learn should be used to help individual students and improve the quality of instruction, not to judge the performance of colleges and universities. (para. 2)

Although those of us in the field of adult education have much to learn from higher education's work in assessment, it is also important to prevent implementation of problematic assessment practices that have become prevalent.

Instead, we should strive to improve on instruction, or facilitation of learning, and our knowledge of assessment and evaluation practices. Given the scarcity of resources and skepticism about adult education that threaten our programs and practices, we cannot afford to make poor decisions or perpetuate ineffective practices out of habit, lack of time, or ease of use. Therefore, a culture of evidence and learning from that evidence should become an integral part of adult education practices. That kind of culture provides a platform to advocate for programmatic viability.

To successfully advocate for program value, it is important to use defensible assessment and evaluation practices. In chapter 10, Simone S.O. Conceição reminds us that robust program evaluation requires the use of a "systematic process for collecting, analyzing, and presenting information about an adult education program's activities, characteristics, and outcomes" (p. 164, this volume). Program purposes, goals, and objectives should be linked to assessment practices so that instruction is effective and assessments provide useful information about student learning. Strategic program processes can examine policies and procedures, alumni perceptions, and, when useful, employer perceptions. Caution must be taken in the selection of indicators of program quality to balance answering funders' economic concerns about return on investment and the resulting emphasis on education for employability with meeting adult learners' goals for learning. In other words, assessment and evaluation should not be conducted on adult learners without their consent and willing participation. Instead, assessment and evaluation can be a collaborative process "mutually constructed between learners and assessors" (Boud & Soler, 2016, p. 402).

Our perspectives about assessment and evaluation should be informed by our focus on social justice. Accountability requirements often impose inflexible and standardized metrics that can serve as challenges in meeting our social justice orientation, particularly in higher education settings. Nevertheless, it is imperative for us to continue our work with poor and marginalized communities and work alongside them to address conditions that threaten health, reduce viable employment opportunities, and compromise the environment. We need to continue our work with racial and ethnic minorities, immigrants, and the poor. We need to advocate for educationally disadvantaged adults and examine not only educational practices but the policies that inform our work. We need to use caution about who is using the information we produce and for what purposes. We should be thoughtful about ways to defend and advocate for adult education work.

Conclusions

Vella, Berardinelli, and Burrow (1998) asked, How do they know they know? In other words, How will adult learners know they have met their goals for learning? It is also useful to ask how adult educators serving as program developers, teachers, and administrators will know they know. Adult learners will learn that they know based on the provision of clearly articulated learning objectives, particularly if they have been involved in creating them, instruction that is closely aligned with those objectives, detailed and meaningful feedback, and opportunities to reflect on their own learning. Adults investing their limited time and attention deserve to participate in adult education programs designed to meet their needs. Adult educators serving as program developers, teachers, and administrators will know they know based on well-designed assessments they integrate into their instruction to produce meaningful information. Adult educators are able to critically examine the effectiveness of their work through the use of robust program evaluation practices. Finally, quality assessment and evaluation practices enable us to answer questions of accountability that often involve an accounting of whether program funding is being used effectively and if it should continue. For adult education itself to remain viable, we need to demonstrate that adult learning is meaningful, viable, and contributes to society.

References

Boeren, E. (2018). The methodological underdog: A review of quantitative research in the key adult education journals. *Adult Education Quarterly, 68*(1), 63–79.
Boud, D., & Associates. (2010). *Assessment 2020: Seven propositions for assessment reform in higher education.* Sydney, Australia: Australian Learning and Teaching

Council. Retrieved from https://www.uts.edu.au/sites/default/files/Assessment-2020_propositions_final.pdf

Boud, D., & Soler, R. (2016). Sustainable assessment revisited. *Assessment and Evaluation in Higher Education, 41*(3), 400–413.

Galbraith, M. W., & Jones, M. S. (2001). Assessment and evaluation. In C. E. Kasworm, A. D. Rose, & J. M. Ross-Gordon (Eds.), *Handbook of adult and continuing education* (pp. 167–175). Thousand Oaks, CA: Sage.

Lederman, D. (2019, April). Harsh take on assessment . . . from assessment pros. *Inside Higher Ed.* Retrieved from https://www.insidehighered.com/news/2019/04/17/advocates-student-learning-assessment-say-its-time-different-approach

Marbley, A. F., Bonner, F., & Berg, R. (2008). Measurement and assessment: Conversations with professional people in the field of education. *Multicultural Education, 16*(1), 12–20.

Read, B., Francis, B., & Robson, J. (2005). Gender, "bias," assessment, and feedback: Analyzing the written assessment of undergraduate history essays. *Assessment and Evaluation in Higher Education, 30*(3), 241–260.

Smith, L. T. (2013). *Decolonizing methodologies: Research and indigenous peoples.* New York, NY: Zed Books.

Su, Y. (2015). Targeting assessment for developing adult lifelong learners: Assessing the ability to commit. *Australian Journal of Adult Learning, 55*(1), 75–93.

Vella, J., Berardinelli, P., & Burrow, J. (1998). *How do they know they know? Evaluating adult learning.* San Francisco, CA: Jossey-Bass.

EDITOR AND CONTRIBUTORS

Editor

Lilian H. Hill is professor of adult and higher education at the University of Southern Mississippi. Her research interests are in adult health learning and health literacy, professional education, and assessment and evaluation. She has held executive-level positions for the Commission of Professors of Adult Education of the American Association of Adult and Continuing Education and served as coeditor of *Adult Learning* in 1994–2005 and 2020–2023. Hill served on the assessment committees of two universities, and her past administrative roles have involved assessment, evaluation, and accreditation responsibilities. She was recipient of the 2015 Okes Award for Outstanding Research in Adult Education; was inducted into the International Adult and Continuing Education in 2018; and was selected for the UGA Circle of 50, honoring 50 alumni for the 50th anniversary of the Adult Education Program in 2019.

Contributors

Mary V. Alfred is professor of adult education and human resource development in the College of Education and Human Development at Texas A&M University. Her research interests include international adult education; learning and development among women of the African diaspora; sociocultural contexts of migration, literacy, and women's development; and issues of diversity, equity, and inclusion in higher education and in the workplace. She received her PhD in adult education and human resource development leadership from the University of Texas at Austin.

Alisa Belzer is a professor at Rutgers University where she is director of the master's program in adult and continuing education. She is currently coeditor of the journal *Adult Literacy Education: The International Journal of Literacy, Language, and Numeracy.* Belzer's research focuses on adult literacy policy, professional development, and learner experiences.

Natalie Bolton is an associate professor at the University of Missouri–St. Louis. She earned her PhD in educational leadership from the University of Louisville. She has an MA in secondary education with an emphasis in social studies education and a BA in secondary education from the University of Kentucky. Bolton's work experiences include middle school teacher, middle school assistant principal, Kentucky Department of Education social studies consultant, director of the Office of Civic Education and Engagement, and assistant professor at the University of Louisville. Bolton conducts research on assessment, program evaluation, and social studies and civic education. She teaches courses related to education research, quantitative statistics, and program evaluation and serves as a research methodologist on doctoral committees. Additionally, she is an assessment and program evaluation consultant independently and with the Assessment Training Institute. She works with schools and education organizations in the United States and internationally on designing assessments, program evaluations, and assessment literacy.

Royce Ann Collins is associate professor in adult learning and leadership at Kansas State University. She is director of assessment for the master's and doctoral programs, chaired the Assessment Committee for the Graduate Council for eight years, and has researched assessment throughout her academic career. Collins has won national and regional awards for her teaching, research, and scholarship. Her recognition from Kansas State University includes the 2014 Michael C. Holen Excellence in Graduate Teaching Award and her inaugural appointment to the Kansas State University Academy of Fellows. She was recognized for her work in accelerated adult education by the Council for Accelerated Programs, which presented her with a Lifetime Achievement Award. In addition, she has provided services to her profession in a number of ways, including four years with the Association of Continuing Higher Education as editor of the *Journal of Continuing Higher Education*.

Simone C.O. Conceição, PhD, is professor and chair of the Department of Administrative Leadership at the University of Wisconsin–Milwaukee. She received her doctorate in adult and distance education from the University of Wisconsin–Madison. She serves on the editorial board of more than six journals in adult education and technology and is the coeditor in chief of *eLearn Magazine*. Her research interests include distance education, adult learning, impact of technology on teaching and learning, and assessment and evaluation in online environments. Conceição is the coeditor of *Mapping the Field of Adult and Continuing Education: An International Compendium* (Stylus Publishing, 2017) and editor of *Teaching Strategies in the Online Environment* (Jossey-Bass, 2007). She coauthored *Creating a Sense of Presence in Online*

Teaching: How to "Be There" for Distance Learners (Jossey-Bass, 2010), *Managing Online Instructor Workload: Strategies for Finding Balance and Success* (Jossey-Bass, 2011), and *Motivating and Retaining Online Students: Research-Based Strategies that Work* (Jossey-Bass, 2014).

Patrice B. French serves as manager for assessment and high-impact practices in the College of Education and Human Development at Texas A&M University. She oversees academic program assessment, enhances opportunities for high-impact learning experiences, and provides support to various evaluation and assessment processes in the college. She holds bachelor and master of social work degrees from Texas Christian University and University of Michigan and is currently pursuing her PhD in educational human resource development, adult education emphasis at Texas A&M University. Her research interests include social justice educator training and development, culturally relevant practices in workplace environments, multi- and transdisciplinary collaboration, and high-impact learning assessment.

Cyndi H. Gaudet is professor emerita of the University of Southern Mississippi–Gulf Coast Campus. Gaudet is a scholar practitioner whose passion is developing people through academic programs of excellence. She championed the development and implementation of the MS and PhD in human capital development at the University of Southern Mississippi, programs designed to prepare senior learning leaders who can strategically lead and manage talent in organizations. Her research agenda to help organizations implement a systematic approach for developing human capital has been disseminated through professional conference presentations, numerous publications, and earned national awards of research recognition. Her commitment to excellence and innovation resulted in awards such as the NASA Public Service Group Achievement Award, U.S. Department of Labor Recognition of Excellence—Educating America's 21st Century Workforce, Southern Growth Policies Board Innovator in Workforce Development, LSU School of Human Resource Education and Workforce Development Alumnus Award of Excellence, Gulf Coast Women of Achievement Woman of the Year Award, University Commencement Grand Marshal, College of Science and Technology Outstanding Research Award, Southern Miss Distinguished Professor of e-Learning, You Rock! Professor of the Year, and the Students' Choice Award. Gaudet's consulting services for organizational learning and development, leadership development, talent management, training, executive coaching, and strategic planning span public and private sector organizations. Gaudet holds ROI certification from the ROI Institute, a BS and MEd from Southern Miss, and a PhD in human resource education and workforce development from Louisiana State University.

Wendy M. Green specializes in the areas of adult learning and development, health professions education, organizational culture, and diversity. She is an assistant professor at Cleveland State University in the College of Education and Human Services and teaches in the health professions education and adult learning and development master's programs. Her research interests are focused on the development of people across contexts. She has investigated how social identity–based affinity groups facilitate individual learning and organizational change in higher education and for-profit contexts. She has worked in continuing medical education in East Africa on a global health fellowship designed for midcareer doctors and nurses. Her current research is situated in Kasese District, Uganda, and examines women's empowerment through educational and health perspectives. Green earned her PhD from the University of Pennsylvania.

Daphne Greenberg is a Distinguished University Professor of educational psychology at Georgia State University. Greenberg is the principal investigator of the Center of the Study of Adult Literacy, a national research center on adult literacy funded by the Institute of Education Sciences at the U.S. Department of Education. She is also the principal investigator on a newly funded award from the Institute of Education Sciences: Georgia Partnership for Adult Education and Research. She has served on numerous expert panels such as the Institute of Education Sciences, Writing, and Language Peer Review Panel and the National Center for Educations Sciences Focus Group on Adult Education and Training Data Collection. She is a founding member of the Georgia Adult Literacy Advocacy group and the Literacy Alliance of Metro Atlanta. She has tutored native and nonnative English-speaking adults and has helped communities organize and develop adult literacy programs.

E. Paulette Isaac-Savage is a professor of adult education at the University of Missouri–St. Louis. She serves as a consulting editor for *Adult Education Quarterly*, *Adult Learning*, *Education and Urban Society*, and *PAACE*. She has written on several topics including adult religious education, assessment, and African American adult learners. She was inducted into the International Adult and Continuing Education Hall of Fame in 2019.

Nima Khodakarami is a PhD candidate in the Department of Health Policy and Management at Texas A&M School of Public Health. Khodakarami was appointed in 2018 and 2019 as a research fellow at the American Economic Association Summer Program in Lansing, Michigan, and received an Outstanding Research Fellow certificate in 2019. His research interests lie in the area of health service research, insurance and coverage, quasi experimental design, insurance claims data analysis, and health economics and outcome research.

James B. Martin is the dean of academics at the U.S. Army's Command and General Staff College, one of the two graduate schools in the Army. He also serves as the chief academic officer for Army University. He has spent more than 20 years in the field of adult education in the civilian and military worlds, with an emphasis on accelerated adult education and training programs. In his role at the staff college, Martin was one of the original stakeholders during the creation of the Army Learning Concept, a radical shift in the U.S. Army's approach to professional military education and lifelong learning. Martin speaks regularly on adult learning in the military and civilian worlds and has recently become very active in working with international partners in professional military education.

Larry G. Martin is professor emeritus of adult and continuing education leadership at the University of Wisconsin–Milwaukee. As a faculty member for more than 36 years, he routinely taught graduate courses on program planning in adult education, administration of adult education programs, evaluation of adult education programs, and others. A 2015 inductee of the International Adult and Continuing Education Hall of Fame, he has published 8 edited books, and numerous articles and book chapters. His latest contribution is an international compendium titled *Mapping the Field of Adult and Continuing Education: An International Compendium* (Stylus Publishing, 2017). The purpose of this compendium is to produce and encourage the use of a major reference work based on mapping the knowledge base of the adult and continuing education field. He earned a PhD at University of Wisconsin–Madison.

Paul E. Mazmanian is a professor in the Department of Family Medicine and Population Health at Virginia Commonwealth University, where he serves as associate dean for assessment, evaluation, and scholarship in the School of Medicine. For 10 years, he served as editor of the *Journal of Continuing Education in the Health Professions*. Mazmanian has long-standing interests in assessment of change and learning in the health professions. His current projects include developing a longitudinal database and medical learner registry; examining competency at transitions from training to initial certification and from certification to recertification; investigating the use of portfolios for improved learning and performance in practice; exploring the roles, responsibilities, and credentialing of community health workers; and evaluating use of a lifelong learning and guided practice model to increase workforce capacity for providing specialty care and reducing health disparities.

Meagan W. Rawls is the program coordinator for the Office of Assessment, Evaluation, and Scholarship at Virginia Commonwealth University's School of Medicine. She holds an MS in sociology from Virginia Commonwealth University and is a doctoral student in the Virginia Commonwealth University's School of Education, with a concentration in research, assessment, and evaluation. Her current interests include diversity, inclusion, and well-being in medical professions.

Kevin Roessger is an assistant professor of adult and lifelong learning at the University of Arkansas. He received his BS in psychology, MS in administrative leadership, and PhD in adult and continuing education from the University of Wisconsin–Milwaukee. Roessger has served on the executive committee of the Commission of Professors of Adult Education for the American Association for Adult and Continuing Education and currently serves on the review boards of *Adult Education Quarterly*, *Adult Learning*, and the *Journal of Continuing Higher Education*. He has published numerous articles and book chapters in the field's most respected outlets and is currently overseeing a grant that examines the effect of correctional education programs on recidivism and postrelease employment. Roessger's research interests include reflective learning strategies and developing reflective skills in adult learners.

Jovita M. Ross-Gordon is professor emeritus of adult, professional, and community education at Texas State University. Ross-Gordon's research centers on teaching and learning of adults, focusing particularly on adult learners in higher education and on issues of diversity and equity in adult and higher education. Her publications include *Foundations of Adult and Continuing Education* (Jossey-Bass, 2017), with Amy Rose and Carol Kasworm, and the 10th edition of *SuperVision and Instructional Leadership: A Developmental Approach* (Pearson, 2017), with Carl Glickman and Stephen Gordon. She serves as coeditor in chief for *New Directions for Adult and Continuing Education* along with Joellen Coryell. Her recent honors include the International Adult and Continuing Education Hall of Fame, the Career Achievement Award of the Commission of Professors of Adult

Education, and the Distinguished Alumni Lifetime Achievement Award from the University of Georgia College of Education.

Elizabeth A. Roumell earned her PhD in education focusing on adult education and international and comparative education from the University of Wyoming in 2009. Currently, Roumell is an associate professor in the educational administration and human resource development department, in the program leader for and teaches courses in the adult education specialization at Texas A&M University. Roumell's research is focused primarily on three areas: adult and workforce education policy, distance and online learning, and adult identity development in intercultural contexts. Roumell also has more than 10 years of experience as a state evaluator for prevention and health education programming, focusing on capacity development, implementation, and culturally congruent evaluation practices.

Sharon E. Rouse is a nationally and internationally published author on computer and human interactions in teaching, leading, and the workplace, which includes 21st Century Teaching and Leadership Skills. She was honored as Southern Business Education's Association's Senior College 2016 Teacher of the Year and Mississippi Business Education Association 2012 Senior College-University Business Educator of the Year. She is an associate professor of Human Capital Development at the University of Southern Mississippi.

J.K. Stringer is a postdoctoral fellow with the Office of Assessment, Evaluation, and Scholarship at Virginia Commonwealth University School of Medicine. His research interests are student identity and motivation, adaptive learning, and well-being supports in curricula. Stringer's undergraduate degree is in psychology, and his doctorate in education with a focus on educational psychology was completed at Virginia Commonwealth University. His dissertation focused on the validation and development of motivation scales for use in the medical student population.

Corina Todoran, PhD, is a success coach and trainer who oversees retention efforts as the online student success coordinator at Loyola University New Orleans. Her research interests include sociocultural issues in adult education, international and comparative education, and adult education policy analysis.

COL Ryan Welch is the strategic plans director at the U.S. Army Aviation Center, Fort Rucker, Alabama. He has commanded at the company and battalion levels and deployed to multiple theaters of operations. He has a bachelor's degree in English literature from Norwich University, a master's degree in adult and continuing education from Kansas State University, and a master's degree in strategic studies from the U.S. Army War College.

AACU. *See* Association of American Colleges and Universities
AAR. *See* after action review
ABE assessment. *See* adult basic education assessment
Academy of Human Resource Development, 122
accountability
  ABE assessment for, 58–61
  defined, 5–6
  through direct measures, 3–4, 214
  indirect measures and, 191
  of online program evaluation approaches, 176
  Voluntary Framework of Accountability, 199
  Voluntary Systems of Accountability, 199
accountability, in adult education
  with assessment and evaluation, 233–36
  explanation of, 10–12
  higher education and, 191–94
  need for, 3–5
  requirements and graduate programs, 200–201
accreditation
  for CGSC, 75
  Council for Higher Education Accreditation, 202
  evaluations, 44
Accreditation Council for Continuing Medical Education, 91
Accreditation Council for Pharmacy Education, 91

Accreditation Council of Graduate Medical Education, 154–55
accrediting commissions, for online education, 178
accreditor, role of, 202
ACE. *See* American Council on Education
Ackroyd, S., 94
action, continuing professional education with, 92–93
active learner, sustainable assessment and, 23
Addae, D., 6–7, 18
ADDIE. *See* analyze, design, develop, implement, and evaluation
admission for graduate education, with assessment, 204–6
adult basic education (ABE) assessment
  for accountability, 58–61
  for credentialing, 63–64
  for diagnosis, 61–62
  discussion, 66–68
  funding for, 28
  for population studies, 64–66
  terminology complications, 57–58
adult diploma program, 64
adult distance education
  growth of, 164–65
  online program evaluation approaches, 172–77
  quality assurance in online, 177–79
  student learning assessment strategies and practices, 165–72
  unanticipated consequences program evaluation and, 176

Milliron, Mark, 73
Mission Essential Task List (METL),
    81, 83
Mitchell, N., 214
Mittman, B. S., 130
models of student work, 219
Mojave Desert, 81
Moore, D. E., 9, 94, 95–96
Moore, J. C., 177
morpheme, 61
Moseley, J. L., 117–18
Motyka, J. K., 27
Murrell, V. S., 173
Muth, B., 67
Muzio, D., 94

NALS. *See* National Adult Literacy
    Survey
Nastasi, B. K., 135
National Academies of Sciences,
    Engineering, and Medicine,
    98–99
National Adult Literacy Survey
    (NALS), 65
National Assessment of Adult
    Literacy, 65
National Assessment of Educational
    Progress, 65
National Association of State Boards
    of Accountancy, 91
National Council of Examiners for
    Engineering and Surveying, 98
National Education Association, 177
National Guard, 75
national policy, for online education,
    178–79
National Reporting System for Adult
    Education, 58, 59
National Training Center (NTC), 73,
    81–84
NCOES. *See* Noncommissioned
    Officer Education System
needs analysis, 111–12, 114

needs assessment
    faculty development, 225–26
    HRD, 111–14
    methods of, 25–26
    rapid, 112, 113–14
    role of, 172–73
New Zealand, 3
Noncommissioned Officer Education
    System (NCOES), 75, 79–80
nongraded assessment strategy,
    170–71
norm-referenced test, 28, 49
NTC. *See* National Training Center
nuclear reactor operator, 90

Office of Academic Affairs, 222
one-minute paper, 170
online education. *See also* adult
    distance education
    accrediting commissions for, 178
    benchmarks for, 177–78
    national, state, regional or
        institutional policies for, 178–79
    quality assurance in, 177–79
online journals, 170
online program evaluation approaches
    accountability, effectiveness and
        impact of, 176
    adult distance education and,
        172–77
    formative and summative, 172–73
    with organizational context and
        unanticipated consequences, 176
Open University of Great Britain,
    174
oral presentation, 25, 333
organization
    online program evaluation
        approaches in context of, 176
    program evaluation in adult
        education and, 43–44
Orzoff, J. H., 208
outcome

Adult Education books from Stylus Publishing

Authoring Your Life
Developing an INTERNAL VOICE to Navigate Life's Challenges
Marcia B. Baxter Magolda
Foreword by Sharon Daloz Parks
Illustrated by Matthew Henry Hall

Creating the Path to Success in the Classroom
Teaching to Close the Graduation Gap for Minority, First-Generation, and Academically Unprepared Students
Kathleen F. Gabriel
Foreword by Stephen Carroll

Improving Professional Learning
Twelve Strategies to Enhance Performance
Alan B. Knox
Foreword by Ronald M. Cervero

Mapping the Field of Adult and Continuing Education
An International Compendium
Four-Volume Set
Edited by Alan B. Knox, Simone C.O. Conceição, and
Larry G. Martin
Foreword by Steven B. Frye

Portfolio Development and the Assessment of Prior Learning
Edition 2
Perspectives, Models and Practices
Elana Michelson and Alan Mandell

Understanding the Working College Student
New Research and Its Implications for Policy and Practice
Edited by Laura W. Perna
Foreword by Glenn DuBois

Leading Assessment for Student Success
Ten Tenets That Change Culture and Practice in Student Affairs
Edited by Rosie Phillips Bingham, Daniel Bureau, and Amber Garrison Duncan
Foreword by Marilee J. Bresciani Ludvik

A Leader's Guide to Competency-Based Education
From Inception to Implementation
Deborah J. Bushway, Laurie Dodge, and Charla S. Long
Foreword by Amy Laitinen

Enhancing Assessment in Higher Education
Putting Psychometrics to Work
Edited by Tammie Cumming and M. David Miller
Foreword by Michael J. Kolen

Coming to Terms With Student Outcomes Assessment
Faculty and Administrators' Journeys to Integrating Assessment in Their Work and Institutional Culture
Edited by Peggy L. Maki

Assessing for Learning
Edition 2
Building a Sustainable Commitment Across the Institution
Peggy L. Maki

Assessing and Improving Student Organizations
A Guide for Students
Brent D. Ruben and Tricia Nolfi

Community College books from Stylus Publishing

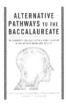

Alternative Pathways to the Baccalaureate
Do Community Colleges Offer a Viable Solution to the Nation's Knowledge Deficit?
Edited by Nancy Remington and Ronald Remington
Foreword by Carol D'Amico

Assessing Student Learning in the Community and Two-Year College
Successful Strategies and Tools Developed by Practitioners in Student and Academic Affairs
Edited by Megan Moore Gardner, Kimberly A. Kline, and Marilee J. Bresciani Ludvik

The Community College Baccalaureate
Emerging Trends and Policy Issues
Edited by Deborah L. Floyd, Michael L. Skolnik, and Kenneth P. Walker

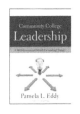

Community College Leadership
A Multidimensional Model for Leading Change
Pamela L. Eddy
Foreword by George R. Boggs

Community Colleges as Incubators of Innovation
Unleashing Entrepreneurial Opportunities for Communities and Students
Edited by Rebecca A. Corbin and Ron Thomas
Foreword by Andy Stoll, Afterword by J. Noah Brown

Developing Faculty Learning Communities at Two-Year Colleges
Collaborative Models to Improve Teaching and Learning
Edited by Susan Sipple and Robin Lightner
Foreword by Milton D. Cox

Faculty Development books from Stylus Publishing

Adjunct Faculty Voices
Cultivating Professional Development and Community at the Front Lines of Higher Education
Edited by Roy Fuller, Marie Kendall Brown and Kimberly Smith
Foreword by Adrianna Kezar

Advancing the Culture of Teaching on Campus
How a Teaching Center Can Make a Difference
Edited by Constance Cook and Matthew Kaplan
Foreword by Lester P. Monts

Faculty Development in the Age of Evidence
Current Practices, Future Imperatives
Andrea L. Beach, Mary Deane Sorcinelli, Ann E. Austin, and Jaclyn K. Rivard

Faculty Mentoring
A Practical Manual for Mentors, Mentees, Administrators, and Faculty Developers
Susan L. Phillips and Susan T. Dennison
Foreword by Milton D. Cox

The Prudent Professor
Planning and Saving for a Worry-Free Retirement From Academe
Edwin M. Bridges and Brian D. Bridges

Reconceptualizing Faculty Development in Service-Learning/Community Engagement
Exploring Intersections, Frameworks, and Models of Practice
Edited by Becca Berkey, Cara Meixner, Patrick M. Green, and Emily Eddins Rountree
Foreword by L. Dee Fink

Graduate and Doctoral Education books from Stylus Publishing

From Diplomas to Doctorates
The Success of Black Women in Higher Education and its Implications for Equal Educational Opportunities for All
Edited by V. Barbara Bush, Crystal Renee Chambers, and Mary Beth Walpole

The Latina/o Pathway to the Ph.D.
Abriendo Caminos
Edited by Jeanett Castellanos, Alberta M. Gloria, and Mark Kamimura
Foreword by Melba Vasquez and Hector Garza

On Becoming a Scholar
Socialization and Development in Doctoral Education
Jay Caulfield
Edited by Susan K. Gardner and Pilar Mendoza
Foreword by Ann E. Austin and Kevin Kruger

Developing Quality Dissertations in the Humanities
A Graduate Student's Guide to Achieving Excellence
Barbara E. Lovitts and Ellen L. Wert

Developing Quality Dissertations in the Sciences
A Graduate Student's Guide to Achieving Excellence
Barbara E. Lovitts and Ellen L. Wert

Developing Quality Dissertations in the Social Sciences
A Graduate Student's Guide to Achieving Excellence
Barbara E. Lovitts and Ellen L. Wert

Leadership & Administration books from Stylus Publishing

The Department Chair as Transformative Diversity Leader
Building Inclusive Learning Environments in Higher Education
Edna Chun and Alvin Evans
Foreword by Walter H. Gmelch

Community Colleges as Incubators of Innovation
Unleashing Entrepreneurial Opportunities for Communities and Students
Edited by Rebecca A. Corbin and Ron Thomas
Foreword by Andy Stoll, Afterword by J. Noah Brown

Contingent Academic Labor
Evaluating Conditions to Improve Student Outcomes
Daniel B. Davis
Foreword by Adrianna Kezar

Community College Leadership
A Multidimensional Model for Leading Change
Pamela L. Eddy
Foreword by George R. Boggs

College in the Crosshairs
An Administrative Perspective on Prevention of Gun Violence
Edited by Brandi Hephner LaBanc and Brian O. Hemphill
Foreword by Kevin Kruger and Cindi Love

Building the Field of Higher Education Engagement
Foundational Ideas and Future Directions
Edited by Lorilee R. Sandmann and Diann O. Jones

Online & Distance Learning books from Stylus Publishing

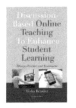

Discussion-Based Online Teaching To Enhance Student Learning Second Edition
Theory, Practice, and Assessment
Tisha Bender

Social Media for Active Learning
Engaging Students in Meaningful Networked Knowledge Activities
Vanessa Dennen

High-Impact Practices in Online Education
Research and Best Practices
Edited by Kathryn E. Linder and Chrysanthemum Mattison Hayes
Foreword by Kelvin Thompson

The Productive Online and Offline Professor
A Practical Guide
Bonni Stachowiak
Foreword by Robert Talbert

Jump-Start Your Online Classroom
Mastering Five Challenges in Five Days
David S. Stein and Constance E. Wanstreet

eService-Learning
Creating Experiential Learning and Civic Engagement Through Online and Hybrid Courses
Edited by Jean R. Strait and Katherine Nordyke
Foreword by Andrew Furco

Scholarship of Teaching and Learning books from Stylus Publishing

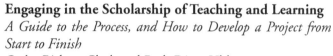

Engaging in the Scholarship of Teaching and Learning
A Guide to the Process, and How to Develop a Project from Start to Finish
Cathy Bishop-Clark and Beth Dietz-Uhler
Foreword by Craig E. Nelson

Engaging Student Voices in the Study of Teaching and Learning
Edited by Carmen Werder and Megan M. Otis
Foreword by Pat Hutchings and Mary Taylor Huber

Exploring Signature Pedagogies
Approaches to Teaching Disciplinary Habits of Mind
Edited by Regan A. R. Gurung, Nancy L. Chick, and Aeron Haynie
Foreword by Anthony A. Ciccone

A Guide to Building Education Partnerships
Navigating Diverse Cultural Contexts to Turn Challenge into Promise
Matthew T. Hora and Susan B. Millar
Foreword by Judith A. Ramaley

SoTL in Action
Illuminating Critical Moments of Practice
Edited by Nancy L. Chick
Foreword by James Rhem

Teachers As Mentors
Models for Promoting Achievement with Disadvantaged and Underrepresented Students by Creating Community
Aram Ayalon
Foreword by Deborah W. Meier

Student Affairs books from Stylus Publishing

Developing Effective Student Peer Mentoring Programs
A Practitioner's Guide to Program Design, Delivery, Evaluation, and Training
Peter J. Collier
Foreword by Nora Domínguez

The First Generation College Experience
Implications for Campus Practice, and Strategies for Improving Persistence and Success
Jeff Davis

Intersections of Identity and Sexual Violence on Campus
Centering Minoritized Students' Experiences
Edited by Jessica C. Harris and Chris Linder
Foreword by Wagatwe Wanjuki

A Guide to Becoming a Scholarly Practitioner in Student Affairs
Lisa J. Hatfield and Vicki L. Wise
Foreword by Kevin Kruger

Making Global Learning Universal
Promoting Inclusion and Success for All Students
Hilary Landorf, Stephanie Doscher, and Jaffus Hardrick
Foreword by Caryn McTighe Musil

Overcoming Educational Racism in the Community College
Creating Pathways to Success for Minority and Impoverished Student Populations
Edited by Angela Long
Foreword by Walter G. Bumphus

Study Abroad/International Education books from Stylus

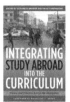

Integrating Study Abroad Into the Curriculum
Theory and Practice Across the Disciplines
Edited by Elizabeth Brewer and Kiran Cunningham
Foreword by Madeleine F. Greene

Integrating Worlds
How Off-Campus Study Can Transform Undergraduate Education
Scott D. Carpenter, Helena Kaufman, and Malene Torp
Foreword by Jane Edwards

Leading Internationalization
A Handbook for International Education Leaders
Edited by Darla K. Deardorff and Harvey Charles
Foreword by E. Gordon Gee
Afterword by Allen E. Goodman

Making Global Learning Universal
Promoting Inclusion and Success for All Students
Hillary Landorf, Stephanie Doscher, and Jaffus Hardrick
Foreword by Caryn McTighe Musil

Assessing Study Abroad
Theory, Tools, and Practice
Edited by Victor Savicki and Elizabeth Brewer
Foreword by Brian Whalen

Becoming World Wise
A Guide to Global Learning
Richard Slimbach

99 Tips for Creating Simple and Sustainable Educational Videos
A Guide for Online Teachers and Flipped Classes
Karen Costa

A Concise Guide to Improving Student Learning
Six Evidence-Based Principles and How to Apply Them
Diane Cummings Persellin and Mary Blythe Daniels
Foreword by Michael Reder

Connected Teaching
Relationship, Power, and Mattering in Higher Education
Harriet L. Schwartz
Foreword by Laurent A. Parks Daloz
Afterword by Judith V. Jordan

Facilitating Seven Ways of Learning
A Resource for More Purposeful, Effective, and Enjoyable College Teaching
James R. Davis and Bridget D. Arend
Foreword by L. Dee Fink

POGIL
An Introduction to Process Oriented Guided Inquiry Learning for Those Who Wish to Empower Learners
Edited by Shawn R. Simonson

Team-Based Learning
A Transformative Use of Small Groups in College Teaching
Edited by Larry K. Michaelsen, Arletta Bauman Knight, and L. Dee Fink